Psychotherapy
and Politics

Perspectives on Psychotherapy

editor: Colin Feltham
Sheffield Hallam University

Each book in this challenging and incisive series takes a particular
perspective on psychotherapy to place it in its intellectual and cultural
context. Disciplines which will be brought to bear in this series will include
sociology, anthropology, philosophy, psychology, science and feminism.

Books in the series:

Philosophy and Psychotherapy
Edward Erwin

Psychotherapy and Society
David Pilgrim

Feminism and Psychotherapy
edited by
I. Bruna Seu and M. Colleen Heenan

Therapy Across Culture
Inga-Britt Krause

Psychotherapy and Science
Robert Langs

Psychotherapy and Spirituality
William West

Psychotherapy and Politics
Nick Totton

Psychotherapy and Politics

NICK TOTTON

SAGE Publications
London • Thousand Oaks • New Delhi

SAGE Publications Ltd
6 Bonhill Street
London EC2A 4PU

SAGE Publications Inc
2455 Teller Road
Thousand Oaks, California 91320

SAGE Publications India Pvt Ltd
32, M-Block Market
Greater Kailash - I
New Delhi 110 048

British Library Cataloguing in Publication data

A catalogue record for this book is
available from the British Library

ISBN 0 7619 5849 5
ISBN 0 7619 5850 9 (pbk)

Library of Congress catalog card record available

Typeset by SIVA Math Setters, Chennai, India.
Printed and bound in Great Britain by
Athenaeum Press, Gateshead

Contents

Introduction

For the rough century of psychotherapy's existence,[1] it has found itself
constantly interacting with politics – with both a 'big P' and a 'small p'. It has
been used – by therapists and others – to question established political positions
and structures; and, more rarely, to shore them up. It has also found itself
to 'have' a politics: to have, that is, internal structures of power and contesta-
tion, in its institutions and also, more problematically, in its fundamental
operating system, the dyad of therapist and client. Different branches of psychotherapy have repeatedly been purged of their (explicit) politics; and have
repeatedly been criticized for their 'apolitical' posture. How are we to find a
shape in all this?

It is useful to begin with definitions. According to the *Shorter Oxford English
Dictionary*, 'politics' encompasses, among other things,

> Activities concerned with the acquisition or exercise of authority or status; manage-
> ment or control of private affairs and interests within an organization, family, etc. ...
> The ideas, principles, or commitments of an individual, organization, etc., in political
> life; the organizational process or principle according to which decisions are made
> affecting authority, status, etc.

We can supplement this with statements from psychotherapists who have written about these themes. The most succinct comes from the 'anti-psychiatrist'
David Cooper: 'politics', he says, 'has to do with the deployment of power in
or between social entities' (Cooper 1976, 4). Cooper, in other words, influenced by Michel Foucault,[2] stresses the *deployment* rather than the *acquisition* of
power – he assumes that power will always be present as a principle of interaction, but may be organized and utilized in a variety of ways.

Andrew Samuels, in his important book *The Political Psyche*, is more expansive,
and more precise about the connection between politics and psychotherapy:

> By 'politics' I mean the concerted arrangements and struggles ... for the organization
> and distribution of resources and power, especially economic power. ...On a more
> personal level, there is a second kind of politics [which] reflects struggles over ... the
> ability to choose freely whether to act and what action to take in a particular situation.
> ... But politics also refers to *a crucial interplay between these two dimensions* [which is
> where] there is a special role for depth psychology in relation to political change and
> transformation. (Samuels 1993, 3–4, my italics)

With typical thoroughness, Carl Rogers states that:

> Politics, in present-day psychological and social usage, has to do with *power and control*:
> with the extent to which persons desire, attempt to obtain, possess, share or surrender
> power and control over others and/or themselves. It has to do with *the maneuvers, the
> strategies and tactics, witting or unwitting*, by which such power ... is sought and
> gained – or shared or relinquished. It has to do with *the locus of decision-making power* ...
> [and] with *the effects of these decisions and these strategies* ... . (Rogers 1978, 4, original italics)

These passages reflect the sort of brief which I have derived from the phrase 'psychotherapy and politics': a focus on the relationship of psychotherapy to issues of power and control, and to the 'maneuvers, … strategies and tactics', the 'arrangements and struggles', which human beings engage in around these issues. Once we turn to 'psychotherapy'[3] itself, however, we find that defining the term is itself a political act, raising thoroughly political questions. What is the difference (of power, status, influence, remuneration) between psychotherapy and counselling, between psychotherapy and psychoanalysis, between all of these and psychiatry? Who is entitled to call themselves a psychotherapist? Who is eligible to receive psychotherapy, and what are its goals?

These questions have been hotly contested throughout the rough century of psychotherapy's existence. I shall try to show that the arguments have been, explicitly or implicitly, political ones – in a sense shared by all four definitions quoted above: arguments about the control and deployment of power and privilege. These arguments constitute the *internal* politics of the field; while its *external* politics is constituted by equally controversial questions, such as: What is 'human nature'? What sorts of individual and collective behaviour, therefore, can be seen as normal and expectable, and what sorts as abnormal and unacceptable? Is the relationship between the individual and the collective basically syntonic or dystonic – is our individuality, that is, *expressed* or *suppressed* through our existence in society and culture? And, of course: What is the meaning and purpose of human existence? Answers to such questions constitute, among other things, building blocks of our *political* position; and they are clearly questions on which psychotherapy can reasonably be expected to have some sort of informed view.

There is so much material on 'psycho-politics', once one starts looking, that this book cannot claim to be complete even as a survey. Instead, I am offering a series of examples, with commentary. In many cases what is discussed stands for several other cases which could not be included. The aim of the commentary is to build towards a perspective on psycho-politics; some of what emerges is worth previewing here.

A distinction central to what follows is that between two wings of the psychotherapy mansion: 'psychodynamic' (which encompasses all forms of work descended directly from Freud, including psychoanalysis, analytic and psychodynamic psychotherapy and counselling, and Jungian analytic psychology) and 'humanistic' (forms of therapy descended from the break with Freud made by Rogers, Berne, Maslow and Perls in the 1950s, and including person-centred or client-centred therapy and counselling, Transactional Analysis, Gestalt therapy, and a multitude of other approaches, some of which group themselves as 'growth work').

Historically and currently, these two great currents in psychotherapy and counselling are very different, in ways which we cannot explore here in depth.[4] The politics of their relationship is itself fascinating, veering between open conflict and attempts at theoretical and organizational rapprochement. We will find, though, that the two approaches are also politically distinguishable. Broadly, psychodynamic therapy has contributed a good deal to politics, but has drawn little from it; while humanistic therapy has drawn a great deal from politics, without contributing much to it.

Psychodynamic and psychoanalytic thinkers have always felt entitled to speak authoritatively about social and political matters. And because these therapies have tended to offer a whole worldview, a portrayal of human beings in culture, their contribution has often been welcomed and utilized as, in Jacqueline Rose's phrase, 'politics tries to open itself up to the ravages of the unconscious mind' (Rose 1986, 163). Psychoanalytic ideas have been important especially in twentieth-century attempts to account for the dark and brutal side of political reality – what Joseph Berke calls 'the tyranny of malice' (Berke 1989).

Psychoanalysis and its relations, however, have generally been uninterested in the possibility of *learning from* political thinking. Only very rarely have they criticized or altered their own practices in the light of political critiques of, for example, sexism, classism, or the general exclusion of economic and social life. As Kovel puts it:

> [t]he great illusion of psychoanalysis … has been to imagine itself free from society. … Psychoanalytic propositions rarely contain the proviso that the psyche whose innards are being laid out like a patient on an operating table is no physical body but a part of a given social setting at a given time. (Kovel 1995, 205)

Nor have they generally been willing to consider the power relations inherent in therapy and training. If political developments have influenced psycho-dynamic therapy, it has been through long, slow seepage. Those committed to a politicized therapy have mostly fallen away or been driven out.

An important current exception is Andrew Samuels, who in his book *The Political Psyche* (Samuels 1993) and a number of articles has argued for 'a psychological extension of the feminist insight that the personal realm reflects the political' (Samuels 1994, 27) and asked whether therapy can 'suggest a *strategy for the empowerment of citizens as therapists of the political world*' (ibid., 26, original italics). Samuels suggests that:

> Disempowered people … need validation from the profession that makes its living and derives its authority – its power – out of working with the feelings, fantasies, behaviours and embodiments that are banned and marginalised in life in the late modern world. There is a potential in everyone to be a therapist of the world. (Ibid., 28)

In looking for allies in this project, Samuels has (to a very unusual extent for an analyst) forged links with the humanistic world.

Humanistic therapy has tended to be less ambitious than its sister in terms of grand theoretical overviews. This is partly a legacy of its identification as a spokesperson for feeling rather than thinking, experience rather than abstraction, practice rather than theory. Thus humanistic work, by and large, has had less to offer in the way of an account of the relationship of the individual with culture, for example – apart from a burning conviction that human beings are innately creative and loving, and that if something goes amiss with this it is not our individual fault.

By the same coin, humanistic therapy has been more willing to learn from political ideas. It has taken in and digested a lot of liberation politics of all kinds, and a lot of counter-cultural critiques of capitalism and hierarchy. These

4678

ideas have not always been applied very deeply; but they have always been an important part of humanistic therapy's culture. This stems partly from its earlier role as the rebel force in relation to psychodynamic orthodoxy, creating a natural alliance with other rebel elements in – particularly American – culture. By the 1990s, of course, many humanistic therapies had hung up their leathers and bought pin-stripe suits; but the effect of history remains.

We shall map out in what follows the specific effects and vicissitudes of these differences. But one other point worth touching on here is the question of whether psychotherapy has any *innate* allegiance to a particular political belief. For example – and recognizing that these are not the only polarities to be found in politics – is psychotherapy innately 'left wing' or 'right wing'? I think what follows will force us to conclude that it is neither: that, as Barry Richards says of analysis, psychotherapy in general 'does not bear with it a stable set of political values, which act as a constant factor in combination with other intellectual elements' (Richards 1988, 6).

Therapy which does take an explicitly political stand, however, is overwhelmingly on the left of the political spectrum. But we must balance this against the 'silent majority' of officially 'apolitical', 'neutral' psychotherapy; reminding ourselves that conservatism generally tends to identify itself as neutral and central, and often succeeds in pushing the left into a 'fringe', 'extreme' position. Few therapists have identified publicly with the 'radical right'; not many have even come out as explicitly conservative; but very many have been and are implicitly conservative, believing in the private individual, the nuclear family, the need for convention and restraint in human affairs, and a minimum of state intervention.

At the same time, though, many therapists (and I include myself) feel a strong desire to argue that therapy is 'really', if understood 'properly', a politically radical activity (Totton 1997a), and that those who disagree misunderstand their own work. This is a common and effective political tactic: identifying an 'authentic', 'original' version which is – surprise! – what we ourselves believe. What may perhaps be true, though – and we shall return to this – is that more than one activity currently goes under the name of psychotherapy.

Enough of an introduction. It remains only to thank those who have helped with the writing of this book: Colin Feltham, who encouraged my original submission; colleagues in the Independent Practitioners Network, especially Sue Hatfield, Cal Cannon, Denis Postle, and the Aire and Travellers groups; Richard House, for conversations and references; fellow students on the MA Course in Psychoanalytic Studies at Leeds Metropolitan University, and Alison Hall, the course leader; Em Edmondson, and colleagues and trainees in Energy Stream and Selfheal, for endless debates and conversations, and much practical psycho-politics; Dany Nobus, for a manuscript of his paper 'The colours of Oedipus'; and Hélène Fletcher for her many contributions.

I also want to acknowledge how much, in researching this book, I have appreciated the contribution to our collective understanding, of Robert M. Young, Free Association Books, the journal *Free Associations*, and his various other initiatives, which have made so much material in this area available.

I have used 'she' and 'her' wherever necessary to represent the generic human being.

One aspect of writing the book which has been personally important has been revisiting in memory the 1970s, when many important psycho-political initiatives took shape. I want to dedicate the book, therefore, to the memory of my friend Jerry Cohen, with whom I would have loved to discuss it.

1

Psycho-politics: Entering the Twenty-first Century

A STRUCTURE FOR ENQUIRY

From the century of psychotherapy, many examples of psycho-politics are available. To present this mass of material in a manageable and coherent way, I use a matrix with four axes: psychotherapy *in* politics, psychotherapy *of* politics, politics *of* psychotherapy, and politics *in* psychotherapy. Although these categories are in some ways arbitrary, they are also practically useful, and to some extent at least represent real distinctions. Organizing the material like this means that some topics – feminism, for example – are scattered in pieces through the book in a way which is less than ideal. However, this would have been true for some topics whatever scheme I adopted; and my approach has the advantage of keeping a firm focus on the theme of psycho-politics itself.

PSYCHOTHERAPY IN POLITICS

This comprises a range of interventions by psychotherapists in the political process itself. Some of these are by therapists *acting as therapists* rather than as private individuals: saying, in one way or another, 'Through our clinical experience we have concluded that the following political programme is desirable...'. In other cases, the therapists are *acting as citizens*, and putting their therapeutic skills and understanding at the service of a political goal to which they give priority.

In many ways this section is a work of recovery, parallel to feminist or working-class history: a work which I believe has an intrinsic political value. Before embarking on the research, I had thought myself quite familiar with the field; but I was staggered by the wealth of material, and hence, by the amnesia which affects it – even quite recent projects based in my own country, let alone those further away in time and space. It seems to me a worthwhile achievement simply to establish that there is and has been such a thing as practical psycho-politics.

PSYCHOTHERAPY OF POLITICS

Overlapping with the above category, this covers a range of attempts to *understand* and to *evaluate* political life through the application of psychotherapeutic concepts. This is partly about creating explanations of why people act as they do politically. Also – and the task of explanation draws on this – it involves setting up models of 'human nature' and of 'the good life', with which to evaluate specific cultural and political phenomena.

It will be noticeable that most of the contributions here are from psychoanalysis and its cohorts, which are far more comfortable than most humanistic therapies in operating on this level of metapsychological abstraction.

POLITICS OF PSYCHOTHERAPY

Here I include two kinds of material: firstly, the power relations and power structures that operate within the profession of psychotherapy – and sometimes act to enforce a particular viewpoint on the appropriate relationship between psychotherapy and politics, as when several analysts were silenced in the 1930s because of their left-wing activism. We can see how the political systems operating in society as a whole affect the ways in which psychotherapy as an institution functions. Also included here are attempts to reform and reshape the institutions of psychotherapy – often, initiatives to apply therapy's clinical understanding *to its own organizational procedures.*

POLITICS IN PSYCHOTHERAPY

This refers to the various ways in which political concepts and viewpoints are used to criticize or to change the theory and practice of psychotherapy. Examples include: feminist psychotherapy; campaigns against homophobia and racism in psychotherapy; critiques of private practice and its inevitable elitism; and critiques of the therapeutic relationship from the point of view of inequalities of power. Many of these views are very much identified with humanistic psychotherapy. It also covers attempts to apply political theories to the technique of psychotherapy; and a very mixed bunch of projects for moving beyond the field of psychotherapy altogether, taking with us some of what we have discovered there.

PSYCHO-POLITICS AT THE NEW MILLENNIUM

The tremendous recent growth of psychotherapy in many Western countries is putting stress on practitioners' established habits of thought and behaviour; and bringing attention to, among other issues, the internal and external politics of psychotherapy. In order to situate our exploration of psycho-politics in relation to therapy's present situation, I will try to outline some of the key current issues.

PROFESSIONALIZATION

Top of the list of 'hot issues' comes the question of 'professionalization'. The received wisdom in first world countries, at least since the early 1980s, has been that psychotherapy needs to claim a higher status – one placing its practitioners alongside doctors, lawyers, architects and other elite groups. Theoretically there are at least two political interests represented in this debate: the 'consumers' – psychotherapy clients, with their perceived need for protection from unscrupulous practitioners; and the 'providers' – psychotherapists, with their need for proper recognition and recompense, and also protection from malicious and frivolous complaint. This second group subdivides into trainers and trainees, whose interests, as we shall see, are not identical. A further interest, perhaps, is that of the state – as umpire, but also as enforcer of society's consensus on what is acceptable behaviour.

Professionalization flags up a range of political questions along all the dimensions we have outlined. A profession must be 'self-regulating' – setting and enforcing its own standards of behaviour; this is, by general agreement, part of what makes it a profession. However, a profession is not a monolith, but a conglomeration of views, interests and power blocs, some of them seeking to regulate the whole; it is not a simple matter for consensus on standards to emerge. In fact, it is the *failure* of consensus among psychotherapists in the UK which successive governments have pointed to as a reason to avoid legislation (Mowbray 1995, 45; House and Totton 1997, 1–2).

A profession, though, also operates as a social institution – raising the question of psychotherapy in relation to society. According to specialists in the study of professions, they have two defining features: the possession of or claim to 'expert knowledge' (Giddens 1991; Stehr 1994), and the use of *political strategies* to establish an elite group which controls its own boundaries – strategies including 'social closure' (Parkin 1974), 'occupational imperialism' (Larkin 1983), state support and market control (Larson 1977). The classic example is the medical profession, which created itself ruthlessly out of an alliance of barbers, bone-setters, astrologers and patent medicine salesmen; a number of authors have described medicine's use of political strategies to establish a uniquely powerful role for itself (e.g. Cant and Sharma 1996; Griggs 1982; Stacey 1992).

Psychotherapy and counselling in Britain, certainly, have been embarking on a similar course, as powerful groups try to repeat the success of medicine – not without creating a good deal of disquiet and disaffection (Totton 1999). For example Ernesto Spinelli, Academic Dean of the School of Psychotherapy and Counselling at Regent's College, London, has questioned the introduction of new standards through a plethora of working parties, committees and guidelines.

> [A]ll of these things give an illusion of professional bodies. We say: 'Look, if we go to all of these meetings, if we have all these standards, if we have these codes of ethics, we must be professionals.' And we can hide our questions, about what we are professionals *of*, or *in*, or *about*, by having all these bodies to protect us. (Spinelli 1998, 182)

And Brian Thorne, Professor and Director of Counselling at the University of East Anglia and a leading figure in the creation of the British Association for Counselling, has written powerfully that 'I have felt for some years now like a man who is in danger because he has become imprisoned in the profession of therapy' (Thorne 1995, 141). The very different situation of psychotherapy in the United States is moving from an open to a closed environment in parallel ways, through the imposition of the 'managed care' insurance structure on the practice of therapy.

> Managed care spokespeople openly describe their revolution as the industrialization of health care and, with unconcealed enthusiasm and frequently contempt, declare that the days of 'therapy as a cottage industry' are over. What is happening to therapists in the 1990s is equated with what happened to butchers, bakers and candlestick-makers in the 1800s. (O'Hara 1997, 24)

This process is accompanied by a diminishing, or often an elimination, of any *explicitly* political aspect of psychotherapy. While in the 1970s most humanistic therapies, certainly, and some branches of psychoanalytic work, saw themselves as intrinsically part of a radical social movement, those same therapies now portray their activity as what David Smail calls 'a *technical* procedure of the cure and adjustment of emotional or psychological "disorder" in individual people' (Smail 1987, 3);[5] and present themselves as experts in technique whose political position is a private matter. This shift of therapeutic culture parallels a shift in the culture as a whole, from the upheavals and idealism of the 1970s to the bland pragmatism of the 1990s and beyond.

The debate about professionalization, although it appeals frequently to the interests of the client and potential client, has been conducted largely without the client group being heard from, except for a few examples of abused victims. This is unsurprising, given the inherent tendency of therapy clients towards isolation and disempowerment – itself an important political theme in what follows.

CREDIBILITY

Psychotherapy is also going through a crisis of credibility, clearly linked to the issue of expertise. Does it work? Who decides whether it works? Is it cost-effective – and who decides *that*?[6] Its major competitors in helping the unhappy or disturbed are neuroscience and behavioural therapy, and in many ways therapy (or rather, the majority group within therapy) has allowed the battle to be fought out on the ground of its opponents' choosing – it has allowed them to define 'working', in medical terms of 'cure' and 'outcome' which are perhaps neither appropriate nor relevant for the kind of activity that psychotherapy is (House 1997; Smail 1987, 79–81; Totton 1997b).

Psychotherapy has capitulated in this way because it wants to compete in the market-place: to gain access to the economic security represented in the USA by managed care, and in the UK by the NHS, both providers of therapy and counselling which, although the consumer ultimately pays, is free at the point of access. To succeed in this, therapy as a whole has to prove its worth in accountancy terms; while different forms of therapy also need to compete with each other as to which is the most 'effective'.

'Outcome research' on psychotherapy is extremely difficult to construct (Mair 1992; Seligman 1995), partly because of the questions outlined above. Defining criteria of success is complex, and in many ways ultimately political: does the client have the final say in whether their therapy has been helpful? Or does the therapist ('the operation succeeded, but the patient died')? Or perhaps the 'care provider' has the last word, on the cost-saving criterion of whether or not the patient stopped demanding care in general. It is an open question whether arguments for 'brief psychotherapy' are not largely a *post facto* justification of what seems to be the inevitable, which would be an example of the provider defining effectiveness.

In discussing these matters we are touching on what Andrew Samuels (personal communication) has called the 'economic shadow' of psychotherapy: its financial aspects, which many therapists are unwilling to discuss – the fact that they are getting *paid* for offering a deep and authentic emotional relationship. There is a perception, at least, of something incongruent in this, which perhaps creates a defensiveness leading to bizarre claims that unless the client pays money, the therapy will not be fully effective. It also makes it hard to discuss how the cost of psychotherapy training (which for some years now has been becoming longer and longer) skews the social make-up of the occupation towards the white male middle class.

The whole issue of training is of course also a political one. According to Katharine Mair's survey of research, 'The opinion of the United Kingdom Council for Psychotherapy seems to be that a recognised training is required in order for psychotherapists to be effective. There does not appear to be much evidence to support this opinion' (Mair 1992, 150). If 'effectiveness' is a matter of human qualities such as wisdom, empathy and kindness which cannot be 'trained in' (cf. Lomas 1997; Masson 1990, 41), then the whole position of a body like the United Kingdom Council for Psychotherapy (UKCP) is put in question. The UKCP is essentially an alliance of training organizations, which claim that this function entitles them to control the profession of psychotherapy and who has access to it. If it is not training, but *living*, which creates good psychotherapists, then this claim does not stand; and one starts to notice that running trainings is, for many people, what makes the occupation of psychotherapist financially viable.

WHO IS PSYCHOTHERAPY FOR?

The spread of psychotherapy and counselling to new countries and cultures, and to new client groups within the West, highlights important questions about its class and cultural bias. There is a widespread assumption that psychotherapy is of benefit to all people in all situations of crisis – only on this assumption can arguments be made about 'elitism' and the need for universal access. Thus Holmes and Lindley argue that psychotherapy offers 'something essential to decent human existence' (Holmes and Lindley 1991, 67), and therefore, like basic health care, should be available to all. This claim has been questioned by people like David Smail (1987) and James Hillman (Hillman and Ventura 1992), who argue that for many human crises psychotherapy is simply not the most useful resource, and may even be counter-productive.

The claim of universal benefit has also been criticized from a rather different angle in the context of the application of psychotherapy to the Third World. Bracken (1998) attacks the construction of Post Traumatic Stress Disorder (PTSD) as a diagnostic category, and its wholesale application to third world populations. He questions 'whether the assumptions about suffering and healing, incorporated into this discourse, are valid in the diverse situations in which they are applied' (1998, 40) and concludes that

> it makes sense only in the context of a particular cultural and moral framework. Its focus on the intrapsychic and its proposals for technical solutions are at least meaningful, even if disputed, within a Western context. However, when exported to non-Western societies the discourse becomes confusing and problematic. (Ibid., 55–6)

Bracken draws an explicit parallel with Christian missionaries, also well-intentioned people who saw themselves as exporting 'truth' from the West to less fortunate countries. He suggests that belief in the 'truth' of PTSD – not even justified by current knowledge in Western terms – entails reliance on experts from the West to run 'projects', and the dismissal of 'local concepts of suffering, misfortune and illness ... which may be extremely important in helping a community recover from the destruction of war' (ibid., 57).

These arguments can be applied in a different form to the situation of psychotherapy in Western countries. Certainly they are relevant to psychotherapy with members of minority cultures, who need to be understood on their own terms. But don't we *all* need to be understood on our own terms? From the client's point of view, the experience of psychotherapy will always combine feeling understood as *oneself*, and feeling understood as *other* – being assimilated into a foreign world-view, reflected in a strange mirror. This experience is shocking, difficult to bear, not always helpful; and should surely always be a matter of genuine and careful personal choice.

The wholesale use of therapy as a response to *every* situation of distress and crisis is at least questionable. We have grown used to the announcement that 'survivors of the disaster are receiving counselling', as if this were obviously and inevitably a good idea. But is it? Are people in shock and grief really able to decide properly whether they can be helped by the interpretation of strangers? To some degree a similar question can be asked about the incorporation of counselling into GP practices: do those patients who are offered counselling really feel that they have a free choice about whether to accept it or not? Are they not, at least, going to be influenced by the social consensus which says that counselling is good for you in the same sort of way that antibiotics are good for you? Even antibiotics are recognized to be bad for us in some circumstances.

These may seem strange arguments to be made by an enthusiastic practitioner of psychotherapy. But my own experience leads to me to understand therapy as a very different activity from the psycho-technology that is its most widespread self-presentation. I have argued elsewhere (Totton 1997a) that, in terms of other human cultural expressions, psychotherapy is best understood as a spiritual and political practice, aiming to release the client from imprisonment within a set of impossible and ultimately unreal demands. This would clearly impact on the professionalization debate: 'So far as I know, there is no powerful lobby for the registration of political activists, or the establishment of effective training standards for spiritual teachers' (1997a, 139). But it also impacts on the arguments about availability, about who psychotherapy is for. Psychotherapy conceived in this way is clearly a minority interest (however much one might wish it to be otherwise); it is certainly not something to be appropriately provided by the state.

There may be two different, even antipathetic, activities going on under the banner of 'psychotherapy and counselling': one of them, the provision of technically expert 'help' in better conforming to and coping with the exigencies of modern life; the other, the creation of a space within which immensely difficult and painful questions can be formulated about identity, responsibility, and desire. An extreme version of the first of these activities is argued for in several pieces by Tantam and van Deurzen, who are both leading proponents of the professionalization of psychotherapy in the UK and Europe. They suggest that therapy can and should become a prosthetic substitute for what they portray as women's traditional role of emotional support: 'As women are now absorbed into the workforce the function of holding individuals' well-being safe needs to be taken care of by professional structures' (Tantam and van Deurzen 1999, 232). This bizarre positioning, which van Deurzen describes, wholly without irony, as 'the professionalization of motherhood' (van Deurzen 1996, 17), leads on to the claim that expert psychotherapists can function as 'gatekeepers of the quality of life' (Tantam and van Deurzen 1999, 233). In an interesting paper, Sonu Shamdasani characterizes this sort of project as an attempt to 'establish a marriage of psychotherapy and the state' (Shamdasani 1999, 65), and traces antecedents throughout the history of therapy.

Exemplars of the second form of psychotherapy, which concerns itself more with posing questions and deconstructing certainties than with seizing social and cultural power, might include Peter Lomas (1994; 1997), Carl Rogers (1980), and indeed many other figures from almost every therapeutic school (see Totton 1997a). Unfortunately, though, these two activities, which we might call intervening and studying, cannot be neatly partitioned off – so that two different occupations could be defined. Probably all practitioners do at least some of each; though some do very little of one or the other. Even the most detached analyst at time finds herself simply trying to help in an emergency, however theoretically clear she is that this will muddy the unfolding of the transference; even the most briskly outcome-focused brief therapist occasionally finds herself simply sitting with the client in silent contemplation of the mystery of existence. Or so one hopes.

HISTORY

These, then, are some of the key issues which psychotherapy must face to construct its future in the 21st century. In a sense, this book aims to provide a set of source materials to help with this task: to remind therapy of its *history* – just as therapists so often seek to do with their clients. Reinserting therapy into its historical context implies re-embedding it in its *political* context, from which it has so carefully separated itself. As Marx famously said, if we do not understand history, we are doomed to repeat it. Someone else pointed out that history is written by the victors; all other versions tend to vanish into oblivion. Just as our clients (or we as clients) tend to find, remembering our history makes some things much more problematic; but it is also immeasurably enriching.

Part I
Psychotherapy in Politics

2

'Right' and 'Left' Therapists up to 1945

Although the line between 'right' and 'left' is, as I have suggested in the Introduction, not the only meaningful dimension of politics, several significant figures in psychotherapy have taken up positions on that axis. The more explicitly political the position, the more on the left it tends to be. Jung's activities in the 1930s are a partial exception to this ('partial' because he portrays himself as speaking from above the fray) – perhaps the only prominent therapist so far to become involved with the radical right.

Some psychotherapists are activists simply as citizens, who happen to be therapists by trade – like activist lawyers or plumbers (all of whom will offer their particular skills as resources for the political struggle). Others are politicized *as therapists*, through the experience and theoretical insights of therapy: they support a political programme because as therapists they believe it is good for people. Of those discussed in this chapter, Otto Fenichel is an example of the former position, Carl Jung of the latter; Wilhelm Reich combines elements of both, justifying politics and therapy each in terms of the other.

THE 'LEFT FREUDIANS'

Not because primitive instincts are still effective within us do we have wars, misery and neuroses; rather, because we have not yet learned to avoid wars and misery by a more reasonable and less contradictory regulation of social relations, our instincts are still kept in an unfavourable form. (Fenichel 1945, 589)

Psychoanalysis grew out of Viennese marginal groups – Jewish, intellectual, bohemian – at the turn of the twentieth century: social strata which naturally embraced socialism and communism. It was itself often seen as part of the left-ist scene; hence Ferenczi's short-lived university professorship of psycho-analysis under the revolutionary Hungarian regime – not because he was a communist (he wasn't), but because he was an analyst (Erös 1993).

As Jacoby (1986, 12) says: 'Today it is easy to forget how many early psychoanalysts identified themselves as socialists and Marxists. They may even have constituted a majority of the analysts.' This is probably an exaggeration, but certainly several older analysts (Federn, Nunberg, Simmel) and many younger ones in Vienna, Hungary and Berlin in the 1920s and 1930s were socialist or communist in orientation; a smaller number of the young were active militants, including, besides Edith Jacobson, Annie Reich, Erich Fromm, Marie Langer and others, two major figures: Wilhelm Reich and Otto Fenichel. There were also those like Geza Roheim – 'apolitical' but socioculturally radical: 'He was sublimely contemptuous of all ideologies and intellectual traditions which in any fashion served to justify the established cultural order' (Robinson 1970, 75–6).

Even Freud, often portrayed as personally conservative despite his theoretical radicalism, called for state-run free psychoanalytic care: 'Some day, the conscience of society will awaken and admonish it that the poor have just as much right to help for their minds as they already have to life-saving surgical help' (Freud 1918, 167). Freud lays out his 'fantastic dream': public institutions will employ psychoanalytically trained physicians to aid men who would otherwise be alcoholics, women who might break down under their burdens, children whose only choice seems to be delinquency or neurosis. 'These treatments will be free of charge.' He suggests that initially private philanthropy could provide such help, but 'some day it will have to come to' state funding (Gay 1995, 462).

In 1920, Freud's 'fantastic dream' became a partial reality when a free clinic opened at the Berlin Psychoanalytic Institute. Later, Eitingon complained of the decline of 'authentic proletarian elements' and the rise of bourgeois intellectuals among clinic patients (Jacoby 1986, 66); but for now, both here and in the Vienna Polyclinic, this was a genuine social initiative by psychoanalysis, creating access throughout the class structure, with individual practitioners donating their time. Through this initiative Wilhelm Reich, for example, analysed waiters and working-class mothers – work which helped shape his ideas (Sharaf 1984, 67).

At the Berlin Institute the first organized training programme for psychoanalysis was worked out (Gay 1995, 463); it has remained the basis of mainstream analytic training up to the present – and, as we shall see, has come under fire for its hierarchical and bureaucratic elements. Despite its liberal social values, the Berlin Institute's formal structure discouraged open political exchange; so Fenichel, who was on the teaching staff, organized and led an independent seminar for the younger analysts – the 'Children's Seminar' (Jacoby 1986, 66).

Fenichel's political position emerges in some sections of *The Psychoanalytic Theory of Neurosis* (Fenichel 1945) – an important psychoanalytic textbook also incorporating passages like this:

> Neuroses do not occur out of biological necessity, like aging. ...Neuroses are social diseases ... the outcome of unfavourable and socially determined educational measures, corresponding to a given and historically developed social milieu. ...They cannot be changed without corresponding changes in the milieu. (1945, 586)

For Fenichel, in other words, political change comes first: although 'wars, misery and neurosis' (ibid., 589) are not unchangeable, psychotherapy cannot shift them without changes in the organization of society. Therapy can help to point the way in which society needs to go.

Fenichel was leader of the group Jacoby calls 'political Freudians'. However, he led it, especially during World War II, in the direction of extreme quietism: while putting tremendous labour into sustaining the group across geographical barriers, he also insisted it should keep its head down and not rock the boat of psychoanalysis. 'Fenichel ... tried to lead the opposition in such a way that, as far as possible, no one should learn of its existence' (Reich 1953, 180). Jacoby's book demonstrates his considerable success: until it was published, Fenichel's group was almost wholly forgotten.

WILHELM REICH AND SEXUAL POLITICS

By contrast, Wilhelm Reich, although frequently misunderstood and misrepresented, has never been forgotten. During the 1920s and 1930s Reich was alone in offering a coherent programme for linking and cross-fertilizing psychoanalysis and Marxism – both theoretically in works such as *Dialectical Materialism and Psychoanalysis* and *What is Class Consciousness?* (both in Reich 1972c), and practically through the Sexpol movement.

> When I founded the Socialist Society for Sexual Advice and Study in Vienna in 1928, *the genital rights of children and young people* were forbidden. ...The very thought that young people should satisfy their need for love in natural embrace was horrifying. Anyone who so much as mentioned these rights was vilified. (Reich 1972b, xiii, original italics)

Reich was motivated partly by indignation and sympathy about the plight of young people and others; but equally by a realization that these issues could politicize the working class, who were turned off by the arid economic tracts of the left.

> Reich sought a perspective that would stimulate them to look at what was relevant to their own emotional needs. ...Reich began what he was to call the 'sex-pol' movement: a complex theoretical and practical effort – first, to help the masses with their sexual problems; and second, to render the sexual needs of normal love life relevant political issues within the framework of the larger revolutionary movement. (Sharaf 1984, 129–30)

In 1928 and 1929, Reich spent the spring and summer in a practical sexual-political project (ibid., 130–1). He, his friend and fellow-analyst Lia Lasky, a pediatrician and a gynaecologist would drive in a van to some park on the edge of Vienna and set up a sort of underground sexual-political roadshow, offering advice and information plus political lectures. The gynaecologist would also prescribe and fit contraceptive devices for those who asked. Before the evening political talk by Reich, the group performed agit-prop entertainment; for instance, singing Marlene Dietrich's *Falling in Love Again* with new lyrics.

In 1929 Reich and his associates opened sexual hygiene clinics around Vienna, with four analysts and three obstetricians, offering abortion on demand (which was illegal), contraception, and sexual counselling (Sharaf 1984, 133–4). According to Reich in 1930, several hundred cases were seen over 18 months; 30 per cent were successfully advised, and 70 per cent of problems were too severe for short-term counselling (ibid., 136). After he moved to Berlin in 1930, Reich carried on similar work there, together with a group of young analysts including Annie Reich, Fenichel, and Jacobson (ibid., 160–1).

Reich moved to Berlin both for his personal analysis, and because of the stronger position of the German Communist Party (ibid., 157); he joined the same Berlin CP cell as Arthur Koestler (Jacoby 1986, 79–80). Through the force of his personality and ideas, Reich dominated the Left Freudian group of analysts. He set up a united-front organization combining the many existing sex reform bodies and the Communist Party: the German Association for Proletarian Sexual Politics. This soon claimed 40,000 affiliated members (Sharaf 1984, 162–3). For a while, in line with its general 'popular front' policies, the CP backed Reich, distributing his sexual education pamphlets. In 1932, however, Reich attended a CP youth conference which, with his encouragement, 'endorsed adolescent sexuality within the framework of the revolutionary movement' (ibid., 169). Horrified Party bosses disowned Reich, declaring him a 'counter-revolutionary' who 'wishes to make fornication organizations out of our associations' (ibid., 170).

This coincided with Hitler's appointment as Chancellor, then the Nazi electoral victory, which ended Reich's work in Germany; he had to escape back to Austria and then to Scandinavia. During Reich's two months in Vienna, the government curtailed civil liberties, and Freud personally cancelled the contract of the Psychoanalytic Press to publish Reich's *Character Analysis*. 'Undoubtedly Freud's decision was not due simply to political caution … but to his distaste for Reich's sex-political activities' (ibid., 171).

The Left Freudians split in 1934, one group following Reich, the other – including most of the experienced analysts – Fenichel (Jacoby 1986, 80–2). 'Fenichel and the other political Freudians became convinced that Reich was suffering a psychic break, and this was the prime reason for the formation of a separate circle of analysts' (ibid., 82). The 'evidence' for this was that Reich's work began to move beyond the narrowly political *and* the narrowly analytic at the same time. Without dropping his political radicalism, Reich became interested in bioenergetic aspects of psychotherapy, work which would in time be enormously influential on the humanistic movement. This was simply not acceptable to his analytic colleagues; and, perhaps, offered the last straw which allowed the camel's back, already straining under the load of Reich's sexual radicalism, gratefully to break.

As Reich said,

> In the fight against the first efforts to ensure the love-life of children and young people, groups that were usually sworn enemies of each other banded together: churchgoers of all faiths, socialists, communists, psychologists, doctors, psychoanalysts, etc. (Reich 1972b, xiii, original italics)

He argued that:

> Sex education raises serious problems of much greater consequence than most sex reformers even dream of. …We are up against a powerful social apparatus which for the time being offers passive resistance but which will proceed to active resistance with the first serious practical endeavour on our part. (Ibid., 68)

Since he was forced out of the International Psychoanalytic Association (IPA) in 1934, Reich has been an unperson within psychoanalysis. I use the expression 'forced out' since the process was deeply manipulative (see Sharaf 1984, 186–91). Partly to appease the Nazis (Reich being a well-known communist), and partly because important analytic *apparatchiks* wanted rid of him, Reich was, without his knowledge, de-listed from the German Psychoanalytic Association 'because of the political situation'. When he found out, he was asked to agree, since he would be a member of the Norwegian Association as soon as it was accepted into the IPA (Reich was living as a refugee in Norway). However, the Norwegian Association was then told that it could not be accepted unless Reich was excluded! Despite Reich's demands, no public statement was ever made about his expulsion (Jacoby 1986, 91–3).

Looking at Reich's treatment during this period – excluded from both the Communist Party and the IPA; rejected by both the psychoanalytic establishment and the psychoanalytic opposition; persecuted in both Nazi Germany and liberal Norway ('collapse on all fronts' as he puts it: Reich 1967, 168) – it is clear that he was an exceptionally annoying individual. But to annoy so many different people, Reich must have been saying something both important and unpalatable. His core message at this period was a restatement and generalization of the original psychoanalytic theory that neurosis originates in sexual frustration, in the blocking of libidinal energy. For Reich, this idea represents the deepest truth about human life, not only on an individual level but also on a social one – sexual frustration creates a neurotic society – and leads directly to a simple goal, both therapeutic and political: creating the conditions for free sexual expression. We shall see in Part Two how Reich analyses Western society through this central concept.

THE REPRESSION OF RADICAL PSYCHOANALYSIS

Slowly but surely [psychoanalysis] was cleansed of all Freud's achievements. Bringing psychoanalysis into line with the world, which shortly before had threatened to annihilate it, took place inconspicuously at first. Analysts still spoke of sexuality, but they had something else in mind. ... Form eclipsed content; the organisation became more important than its task. (Reich 1983, 125)

During the early 1930s psychoanalysis went through tremendous internal changes. Sandor Ferenczi, a founding figure, was suppressed for clinical and theoretical heresy; Reich was expelled; and an ego psychology which privileged internal conflict over social factors took centre stage. The institutional compromise with fascism coincided with this – as in Reich's expulsion. Many analysts, often Jewish and urgently needing safe haven, emigrated to America, encountering a very different intellectual and social environment. By the end of World War II, the process of becoming respectable was more or less complete.

The realities of exile compounded by the conservatism of the psychoanalytic establishment forced the radicalism of Fenichel and an entire network of analysts underground. Within a generation the past was dislodged; few wanted to remember; even fewer knew about this tradition. (Jacoby 1986, 13)

Jacoby argues that the left Freudians co-operated in their own disappearance: in the USA 'a hostility to Marxism intimidated the immigrants; it forced radicals, especially radical refugees, to clean out their bookshelves and censor their pasts' (ibid.). One may question this *'forced'*: many radicals in equally inhospitable circumstances have stuck with their principles. What is it about *psychoanalysis* that made this particularly difficult? We will return to this question later.

Because of his own allegiances, Jacoby emphasizes the collapse of one 'left Freudian' movement, and downplays the importance of another one which simultaneously developed. The 'neo-Freudians' – Fromm, Horney and others – created a left-wing, humanistic version of psychoanalysis which criticized Freud for his exclusive focus on sexuality and on early infancy, his concept of the death instinct, and his denial of the meaningfulness of social and political reform (Robinson 1970, 148; cf. Fromm 1980, 6–11). Jacoby (1986, 142) accuses the neo-Freudians – whom he associates, as both 'cause and effect', with the 'Americanization' of psychoanalysis – of a revisionism which abandons some essential planks of the Freudian platform. While the neo-Freudians criticize orthodox psychoanalysis for its overemphasis on sexuality, Fenichel simultaneously says the exact opposite:

> Fenichel ... witnessed everywhere a flight from classical analysis. After reading a summary of a psychoanalytic congress, he observed that no one talked of sexuality, proof of the self-sublimation of analysis. 'How right Reich was once again!' Fenichel noted, alluding to Reich's belief that establishment psychoanalysis deemphasized sexuality. (Ibid., 125)

JUNG AND THE NAZIS

As the left Freudians actively opposed Nazism, and the analytic leadership tried to appease it, Carl Jung was taking a different and more sinister position. Jung's attitude to German fascism has long been a painful and controversial issue in Jungian circles. I will largely follow the analysis by Andrew Samuels (1993, 287–316), which I regard as the deepest and best documented treatment. Samuels' concern is not simply with the details of what Jung did or didn't do but with more fundamental questions:

> When Jung writes about the Jews and Jewish psychology, is there something in his whole attitude that brings him into the same frame as the Nazis, even if he were not shown to have been an active Nazi collaborator. Is there something to worry about? My brief answer, in distinction to that of many well-known Jungians, is 'yes'. (Samuels 1993, 290)

In 1933 Jung became president of the General Medical Council for Psychotherapy, based in Germany and therefore, like all public organizations, controlled by the Nazi party. Jung later claimed that he took this on 'expressly to defend the rights of Jewish psychotherapists' (Samuels 1993, 291); his reorganization of the society as an international one made Jewish membership still possible. Jung also became editor of the society's journal, which published not only explicitly pro-Nazi and anti-semitic papers (ibid., 296), but also articles *by*

Jung himself saying things like 'The "Aryan" unconscious has a higher potential than the Jewish', and 'the Jews have this peculiarity with women; being physically weaker, they have to aim at the chinks in the armour of their adversary' (ibid., 292–3).

Also in 1933, Freud's books were burned and he was 'banned'. Although Samuels does not make this point, the envious attack on Freud is clear in Jung's writings in the journal, and seems to be a factor leading him into anti-semitism:

> Freud did not understand the Germanic psyche any more than did his Germanic followers. Has the formidable phenomenon of National Socialism, on which the whole world gazes with astonishment, taught them better? Where was that unparalleled tension and energy while as yet no National Socialism existed? Deep in the Germanic psyche, in a pit which is anything but a garbage-bin of unrealizable infantile wishes and unresolved family resentments. (quoted in Samuels 1993, 292)

For Jung it is Freud's Jewish unconscious – the unconscious of his theory, but perhaps also his personal unconscious? – which is a 'garbage-bin': a classically anti-semitic piece of abuse.[7]

There is little ambiguity in the grandiose language Jung uses about Nazism. At least temporarily, he was close enough to the Nazi movement to borrow its canting jargon – 'unparalleled tension and energy'. Samuels (294–305) systematically rebuts several arguments defending Jung, for example that he was just a person of his time – several contemporary figures explicitly dissociated themselves from Nazism (ibid., 294–6); or, a familiar defence of charismatic figures, that he didn't know what was done in his name. 'Even if Jung played little or no editorial role on the *Zentralblatt*, surely he at least read it? He was sole editor from 1933 to 1936. ...If he didn't read it at all, did nobody ever tell him what was in it?' (ibid., 297). Having demolished the apologies, including those offered by Jung himself, Samuels regretfully concludes that 'something goes very wrong with Jung's thought when he goes beyond the boundaries of psychology into what has been termed *racial typology*' (ibid., 309). He argues that

> it was Jung's attempt to establish a culturally sensitive psychology of nations that brought him into the same frame as Nazi anti-semitic ideology. In addition, Jung was absorbed by the question of leadership. ...We must couple a less simplistic methodology and a more sensitive set of political values to Jung's intuitions about the centrality of a psychology of cultural difference. (Ibid., 336)

Samuels still holds back from acknowledging that Jung was in fact personally racist, and used his theories to support racism; how can we distinguish between theories used to support racism, and theories which *lend themselves* to a racist interpretation? Both Jung and Freud clearly deploy in their work a set of racist assumptions which were, it is fair to say, part of the shared currency of their milieu – so that, for example, both can use black people as an easily available *metaphor* for the unconscious, the archaic and the infantile all rolled up into one. (For Jung see Dalal 1988, *passim*; for Freud, see Totton 1998, 43–4.)

However, Jung clearly goes further than this in his work on other cultures: he gives these assumptions specific intellectual weight, *contributes to* this way of seeing as well as drawing on it.[8] (See the very thorough critique in Dalal 1988.) For example, he describes North Africans ('these people') as follows:

> These people live from their affects, are moved and have their being in emotions. Their consciousness takes care of their orientation in space. ... But it is not given to reflection; the ego has almost no autonomy. ... At any rate the European possesses a certain measure of will and directed intention. What we lack is intensity of life. (Jung 1963, 228)

Here psychological theory is used to dignify patronizing clichés about noble savages. Jung continues: 'Without wishing to fall under the spell of the primitive, I nevertheless had been psychically infected' (ibid.): a classically racist image of dangerous contamination which must be fought by violent methods. This violence emerges in the dream Jung then describes, where he wrestled with an 'Arab prince', pushed his head under water, and 'forced him, with a sort of paternal kindness and patience,' to read a book (ibid., 229). One of Jung's books, perhaps.

As well as theorizing racial prejudice, Jung gave intellectual weight to Nazism in passages such as the following, part of a 1935 lecture in London, where he wonders uncritically at the marvellous power of Nazism to dethrone reason.

> Would you have believed that a whole nation of highly intelligent and cultivated people could be seized by the fascinating power of an archetype? I saw it coming, and I can understand it because I know the power of the collective unconscious. ... [W]hen I am in Germany, I believe it myself, I understand it all, I know it has to be as it is. One cannot resist it. It gets you below the belt and not in your mind, your brain just counts for nothing. ... I know highly educated Germans who are just as reasonable as I think I am or as you think you are. But a wave went over them and just washed their reason away, and when you talk to them you have to admit that they could not do anything about it. ... You cannot say it is right or it is wrong. It has nothing to do with rational judgement, it is just history. (Jung 1986, 183–4)

Claiming to speak from above the fray, this is an active political intervention designed to convince the listener that Nazism cannot be fought. Several statements are closely similar to the Nazis' own rhetoric: the inevitability of history, the primacy of gut feeling over intellect, and the irrelevance of moral judgements. '*You cannot say it is right or it is wrong*', Jung proclaims; and he does so on the authority of his own psychotherapeutic system, the role given to the archetypes. But of course one can say if it is right or wrong; and of course many individuals, inside Germany as well as outside, were able to 'resist it'. Jung is seduced by his own arrogance, his wish to be able to claim that he 'saw it coming, and ... can understand it': seduced into lying down and rolling over in the face of evil.

After the war, Jung – plainly and genuinely horrified by what had happened in Germany – published several pieces offering his analysis of Nazism (assembled in the *Collected Works*, Vol. 10). Unfortunately, they combine a continuing grandiose claim of expert understanding with an effective rewriting of his own position. 'When Hitler seized power it became quite evident to me that a mass psychosis was boiling up in Germany. But I could not help telling myself that this was after all Germany, a civilized European nation' (Jung 1946, 236). The refrain is still 'I saw it coming' and 'I can understand it'; but with a note of condemnation that was not there in 1935. Jung even has the effrontery, as we may feel, to lecture the German nation about acknowledging its mistakes: 'we must ask: Has Germany openly admitted that she is conscious of her guilt...?' (Ibid., 241). If only Jung could have 'openly admitted' his own errors, and asked himself how they came about, something useful might have emerged from this sad tale.

3

Alternative Realities

Several political movements have drawn on the visionary, utopian side of psychotherapy: tracing out the *artificiality* of many aspects of social and cultural life, therapy suggests the possibility of changing them into something conforming more closely with desire (see Chapter 8). This connection was expressed particularly strongly in the revolutionary and counter-cultural ferment of the late 1960s and 1970s, beginning with the French political explosion of May 1968.

MAY 1968 AND AFTER

May 1968 created an unusual and powerful relationship between radical activism and sophisticated psychoanalytic theory, something clearly depending on the specific intellectualism of French culture and politics. The relationship is symbolized in the urban myth of the student leader Dany Cohn-Bendit being smuggled over the French – German border in the back of the psychoanalyst Jacques Lacan's Jaguar (Turkle 1979, 86).

We shall encounter Lacan several times in this book: besides radical innovations in analytic theory and practice, he also took an axe to its conventional institutional forms. Naturally enough his training school, the *École Freudienne de Paris* (EFP), was affected like all other schools by the mood of the Paris students. In April 1968 the leadership was challenged by the students in a series of debates, leading to a meeting, at the school's request, between its leaders and Cohn-Bendit and his comrades in the *Mouvement de 22 Mars*, a meeting which Lacan attended without speaking. 'In point of fact, the two groups had nothing to say to each other' (Roudinesco 1990, 455).

The next day, 15 May, Lacan stopped his public seminar (a notable feature of Paris intellectual life at the time) to observe a strike call.

> Paying homage to Cohn-Bendit, [Lacan] lashed out at his own disciples: 'I am in the process of killing myself telling you that psychoanalysis should expect something of the insurrection. There are some who reply, What should the insurrection expect of us? The insurrection answers them, What we expect from you is occasionally to lend us a hand throwing a few paving stones.' Then Lacan announced that paving stones and tear gas were fulfilling the role of *objet 'a'* [the specific objects which become the focus of desire according to Lacan's ideas]. Finally, he situated matters on a theoretical level and criticized the ideas of Wilhelm Reich. (Ibid.)

Clearly Lacan was caught up in the romantic excitement of the moment. But there is no evidence that he ever did throw any paving stones; and certainly he never involved himself in direct political activity – according to

Turkle (1979, 85), his personal views were not notably to the left. The reference to Reich is interesting, since he was the other psychotherapist apart from Lacan who became a significant figure in post-1968 French radicalism (as in other Western countries). Hence Reich is swingeingly attacked by the socially conservative analysts Chasseguet-Smirguel and Grunberger (1986); and praised as a resource for revolutionary theory by the situationist Jean-Pierre Voyer (1973, 8) – 'the works of Reich are the first since Marx that concretely shed light on alienation'. Several times in his work Lacan quietly mocks or attacks Reich (Totton 1998, 122–3).

Groups were formed within the EFP representing the general ferment, parallel to those being formed in all sorts of institutions and organizations. Many in the Lacanian camp entered different radical groupings (Maoist, Trotskyist, etc.); as with the early left Freudians, one effect was a new initiative to make analysis more widely available, the *Laboratoire de Psychanalyse* founded in 1969 for low-income patients – funded by a Lacanian analyst from reparations paid to her mother, as widow of a persecuted Jewish doctor in Germany (Roudinesco 1990, 456).

Lacan's work became part of the intellectual armoury of the Communist Party, a large and powerful organization with a real hope of achieving government via the electoral route. 'The French Communist Party's long awaited reconciliation with psychoanalysis was made through a rigorous, Lacanian inspired interpretation of Freud which stressed his kinship to Marx as an epistemologist and scientific pioneer' (Turkle 1979, 71). Turkle refers to the work of the distinguished Marxist intellectual Louis Althusser (1971), who both supported Lacan personally and attempted to use a partial understanding of his ideas to develop a new account of how ideology affects the individual subject. There were 'numerous appropriations of a Lacanian discourse on the French radical left, some by Maoists who focus on superstructure and the workings of the symbolic order, some by naturalists who look to the power and primitivism of the imaginary' (Turkle 1979, 71).

During the decade after May 1968, then, 'Lacanianism ... dominated the scene with a brilliance it would never know again' (Roudinesco 1990, 479). As Turkle sees it, 'Many people who had been caught up in the May acts turned to Lacan in the years after the events for help in theorizing many aspects of their aspiration to have made a revolution of speech and desire' (Turkle 1979, 67). Syntactic clumsiness leads Turkle to an accidentally interesting characterization of post-revolutionary politics: 'their aspiration *to have made...*' brings out a characteristic sense of forward-looking nostalgia. She is aware of the ironic opposition between Lacan's rigorous anti-humanism, and 'the voluntaristic, humanistic spirit of May' (ibid., 71). However, she suggests that 'to the student movement in the throes of challenging the hierarchy of the French university system, the Lacanians – who had attacked the Americans, broken rules, and attacked hierarchy in the psychoanalytic world – seemed the natural allies of such struggles' (ibid., 67).

For whatever reasons, Lacan and his followers emerged with a dominant role in the University of Paris VIII at Vincennes. As Roudinesco (1990, 550) says, 'it was the student rebellion which finally enabled [analysis] to take root in the universities as a teachable subject'. Certainly the Department of Psychoanalysis, Paris VIII, was for some years the place to be, the height of radical *chic*. At the same time, Vincennes as a whole represented the disempowerment of the student movement – an isolated greenfield site, without the high entrance requirements of normal universities, but equally without the full qualification at the other end. Turkle quotes one Vincennes student's view that the government had neutralized student radicalism by 'giving them a playground to fight over' (Turkle 1979, 175).

However, Lacanianism was only one – if the most powerful – of a number of academic analytic projects in Paris at the time. (For example, Jacques Laplanche and others were also running a centre at the University of Paris VII, where 'each week, over two hundred analysts come to teach' – Turkle 1979, 171.) An influential and specifically *anti*-analytic and anti-Lacanian initiative during the same period was the writing partnership of Gilles Deleuze and Felix Guattari, whose *Anti-Oedipe* was described by the radical psychiatrist David Cooper as 'a magnificent vision of madness as a revolutionary force' (Cooper 1980, 138). Deleuze, perhaps the more important of the two from a literary and theoretical aspect, was a philosopher; Guattari was a Lacanian analyst and psychiatrist,

> but was politically engaged from very early on. This engagement became increasingly articulated through and after the events of May 1968, in which he played a major behind-the-scenes role. But also through the 1960s he worked at La Borde psychiatric clinic south of Paris where he elaborated his idea of 'institutional analysis' as a methodological critique of the 'institutional psychotherapy' which had been the ideology of the clinic since its institution. ... Since its formation in 1975 he has been centrally active in the International Network Alternative to Psychiatry. (David Cooper, Introduction to Guattari 1984, 2)

For Guattari, May '68 was only the start of a much larger transformation of politics which was required in France.

> Memory can play funny tricks! May '68 may well have liberated all sorts of revolutionary attitudes, but people's minds were still full of the bad old ideas, and it took some time to open them up on problems like madness, homosexuality, drug addiction, delinquency, prostitution, women's liberation and so on. (Guattari 1984, 46)

Guattari attacks Lacan for specific aspects of his theory, for the 'despotic' power relations of Lacanian analysis and teaching (ibid., 49–50), and implicitly for his conservative attitudes towards some of the issues listed above. He puts forward an unflinchingly radical programme demonstrating the visionary side of therapeutic thinking, its capacity to draw together the 'personal' and the 'political': a programme which also critiques the traditional ways in which radical politics organized itself.

> The real breakthrough will only happen once there is a new approach to such problems as the bureaucratism of organizations, the repressive attitude of revolutionary men towards their wives and children and their failure to understand the significance of fatigue, neurosis and delusion (it is quite usual for someone who 'breaks down' to be dismissed as 'finished', as of no more use to the organization if not a positive danger to it) ... (ibid., 65–6)

NEW AGE PSYCHO-POLITICS

Out of the backwash of initial excitement of the human potential movement emerged the issue of individual versus group, inner revolution versus outer revolution, personal growth versus social action. The formulation in some of the more righteous exegeses is narcissism versus selflessness. (Schutz 1979, 170)

While the French left drew mainly on psychoanalytic ideas, in America this role was played by the humanistic 'growth movement' which had been developing since the 1950s – filling the equivalent ecological niche to Lacanian analysis in France, as radical alternative to the orthodox psychoanalytic mainstream. Many American radicals were deeply influenced and excited by therapy; many others were deeply suspicious of it – just as therapists were suspicious of radicalism.

From the activist's point of view, the primary problem was that encounter was an opiate of the people. If we helped people resolve their personal problems, their motivation for righting social injustice would wane. I felt that social action without self-awareness leads to terrorist-type self-destruction. ... (Ibid., 170–1)

Will Schutz's approach is typical of that of many in the growth movement: basically sympathetic to the radicals, but suspicious of political activism which is either self-denying or (as analysts might say) 'acting out'. 'Unfortunately many socially-conscious people use social events to work out their own problems. As a consequence, they are often indignant with those who are not socially active, and their own work is of limited value' (ibid., 175). He tells a story (ibid., 175–6) of driving many miles to 'help' black activists, and being rebuffed – asked 'what are you doing here?' Schutz essentially agrees with the blacks: he sees no value in politics which is based on guilt.

Schutz puts forward the widely held but deeply problematic position that we create our own reality, choose our own experience: 'If people let themselves be aware, they can run their lives the way they want to' (Schutz 1979, 179). This implies a voluntarist political position, which in practice allows him to sound off in curmudgeonly fashion about every aspect of political and social life, presumably on the basis that his therapeutic skills give him some special insight. Most of his criticisms have a right-of-centre tone to them: 'Taxes are far too complicated' (ibid., 179), workfare should replace welfare, and so on. Occasionally he encounters the paradoxes – creative or otherwise – implicit in his 'all for the best in the best of all possible worlds' line: 'It's good to be honest and aware, responsible and simple, and if I do not feel like being honest and aware, responsible and simple, it is all right' (ibid., 202). What distinction is here intended between 'good' and 'all right'?

Carl Rogers (1978, 5) asks himself 'what are the political effects ... of all that I, and my many colleagues throughout the world, have done and are doing?' He answers himself that

from the perspective of politics, power, and control, person-centered therapy is based on a premise which at first seemed risky and uncertain: a view of man as at core a trustworthy organism. ... There is in every organism, at whatever level, an underlying flow of movement towards constructive fulfilment of its inherent possibilities. (Ibid., 7)

'Hence,' Rogers argues, 'simply describing the fundamental premise of client-centered therapy is to make a challenging political statement' (ibid., 9). He is explicit throughout the book, though, that in this, client-centred work is reflecting its milieu – a time and place where, according to Rogers, many thousands of people are in effect independently discovering person-centred principles. For example: 'An individual who is attempting to live his life in a person-centred way brings about a politics of family relationships, and marriage or partner relationships, which is drastically different from the traditional model' (ibid., 29). In fact, Rogers' finds person-centred principles all over the place – regarding the US Constitution, especially the Bill of Rights, as 'decidedly person-centred' (ibid., 255). He does not envisage a specifically activist role for his therapy and its practitioners (except perhaps in encounter groups – see Chapter 6). This is in contrast to, for example, Danaan Parry, whose *Warriors of the Heart* (1989) can represent many New Age political texts which draw deeply on humanistic therapy. Its intention, translated into traditional political terms, is to recruit activists.

> This book is for every woman and man who is ready to accept responsibility for their part in the passionate, positive change process that is about to transform our planet. ...This is a book about you – the possible one, the one who has that somehow unexplainable feeling that you were meant for something more, that your life has a greater purpose. ... Our planet is crying out for men and women to own their power and to be positive agents of peaceful change. (Parry 1989, Introduction, unpaginated)

Parry describes how he used to be a project manager with the Atomic Energy Commission, eventually reaching a point where, like so many Americans at the time, he was intolerably aware of a split in his life between 'work' and the 'personal'. He went on an intensive T-Group,[9] whose participants did not leave the suite of rooms for seven days.

> In the final three days, we somehow were able to reach past the years of deadness and confront and comfort and heal one another. ...I had found that I could feel. ...I had found a model of a new way of using power, of leadership. It is a force that can heal the world. (Parry 1989, 10–11)

This is a Pauline conversion experience, and Parry explicitly combines the political and the spiritual in his approach; his favourite bridge between the two is psychotherapy. His approach is eclectic, using a Jungian model of the psyche, but New Ageified – 'Carl Jung says that our center is whole, clear love. It is the layer upon layer of accumulated sophistication that keeps us from remembering this truth' (ibid., 35). He also casts his Jungian model into a form derived from Wilhelm Reich: a set of concentric layers of persona, shadow, self, etc. (ibid., 37; cf. Reich 1983, 294). Elsewhere in the book he draws on Transactional Analysis for the idea of the Rescue Triangle (ibid., 89, 164; cf. Steiner 1976b).

Gestalt therapy shared the general 1970s view of the radical, counter-cultural function of psychotherapy. 'Our society is witnessing an ongoing struggle between the forces for humanism and the forces for alienation and dehumanization. Gestalt therapy [is] a significant force in this struggle...' (M.M. Berger, Introduction to Polster and Polster 1974, ix). The work of psychotherapy is seen as providing both a sort of liberated zone, and a seed point of general social transformation:

> Since no one can escape the psychological pollution of his [*sic*] surroundings until we, in our groups or therapy, germinate the psychologically necessary changes in our

communal climate, we live a two-world existence, straddling the atmosphere of the encounter group and the world in which we live our everyday lives.... New ways of communicating, new values, new priorities on changing over institutions such as marriage, schools and government, new vocational requirements, new reward systems – all are part of a necessary change in the spiritual atmosphere of our society. (Polster and Polster 1974, 24–5)

We should note here that the desired change is defined as *spiritual* rather than as *political* – reflecting the general reluctance of the American counter-culture to grasp the nettle of hard politics. And when we look at the same authors' examples of transformation, it all seems a bit flat.

The loosening up of poisonous taboos is happening all around us. Boys are wearing very long hair, young men and women live in the same dormitories, black people appear on TV commercials as consumers, not servants, peace-niks influence the conduct of a nation at war, nude people are seen on stage and in movies and clothes have become a riotous delight. Psychotherapy has had an important place in all of these creations. ... (Ibid., 26)

This hardly constitutes a social revolution; and reveals the confusion between appearance and reality which bedevilled American activism at the time.

But how true is it that psychotherapy helped create these startling if limited cultural shifts? Is it not more likely that, as Rogers indicates, psychotherapy only responds to social currents that originate in much deeper waters? If it was indeed the task of therapy to 'germinate the psychologically necessary changes in our communal climate' to create radical social change, then therapy signally failed: those changes did not occur. Polster and Polster also suggest a less ambitious role for psychotherapy as a mixture of R&R for activists, and an environment for developing skills with radical applications:

Though retreats from the toxicity of the general culture are useful ... integrity requires that what one practices in a therapy situation be practiced there *primarily* so as to make one more skilful in engaging generally, not merely marking time in everyday life until one may retreat and be 'real' again. (Ibid., 309–10, original italics)

The growth movement created one enormous shift in psycho-politics: the idea that 'therapy is too good to be limited to the sick' (ibid., 7) – that it is, in fact, something positively *good for people*, rather than primarily for repair or cure. However, the major schools of humanistic psychotherapy – Gestalt, TA and person-centred therapy – have become largely conservative or 'apolitical' in their approach, professionalized psycho-technicians. It is figures such as Parry, or Arnold Mindell, who sustain the radical vision of the growth movement.

Arnold Mindell's Process Oriented Psychology (POP) is perhaps the most politically radical form of psychotherapy currently being taught and practised – the heir of 1970s counter-culture therapy. POP supports oppressed minority groups worldwide, arguing that '[t]he minority position contains nothing less than the key to the future' (Mindell 1992, 97). As we shall see later, the aim is not simply to put therapy at the service of minorities, but to bring about a shift of consciousness on *all* sides of political struggles by supporting and listening to all people's experiences. This has involved direct activism – for instance, organizing town meetings across Oregon that brought together gays and conservatives to debate the proposed abolition of affirmative action.

'Radical Therapy' in the USA

In Berkeley California, January 1973, there appeared the first issue of a new magazine, *Issues in Radical Therapy* (*IRT*). The editorial lays out the position of the collective behind the magazine (mostly members of the Berkeley Radical Psychiatry Center):

> We want to expose and stop the oppressive misuse of psychiatry by the psychiatric establishment. We want to expose and stop the co-optation of the revolutionary movement by liberal psychiatrists and counterculture 'hip shrinks'. … We believe that radical therapy is, at its best, community organizing. We believe that people have to act against oppression in their heads and oppression in the world. … We must unite to build a mass-based anti-imperialist revolutionary movement. (*Issues in Radical Therapy* 1973a)

As is apparent, the 1970s USA Radical Therapy movement was deeply embedded in the revolutionary politics of its time; in fact, one key debate was over whether a separate category of radical *therapy*, as distinct from generic activism, was acceptable. In the same issue, the political stance of *IRT* is attacked from the left by Michael Glenn, originally an air force psychiatrist and previously a key figure in the East Coast magazine *Rough Times* (*RT*) which had recently changed its name for ideological reasons from *The Radical Therapist*. 'Therapists, as therapists, serve the ruling class. Therapy, as therapy, serves the ruling class. … Individualist notions of bourgeois therapy combat healthy collective efforts, try to undercut struggle and deny the righteous anger of the masses' (Glenn 1973, 26). Glenn criticizes *Rough Times* itself as 'opportunist', for example in its support of 'bourgeois feminism' (ibid., 28). 'Either you believe that the main contradiction in this society is between the proletariat (and their allies) and bourgeoisie or you do not. That is, either RT follows a Marxist – Leninist – Mao Tse-Tung Thought line or it does not' (ibid.). Like a number of other figures in US radical politics at the time (with equivalents in Europe), Glenn has temporarily swallowed the *Little Red Book* whole.

There are several layers of 'more radical than thou' on show here. *RT* attacks *IRT*, Glenn attacks both. *IRT* attacks *RT* for its name change, described as 'depressing, destructive, a rip-off and a cop-out' (Marcus 1976, 29[10]). In the same article, Marcus articulates the generally libertarian political position of *IRT*: 'While we support the liberation of all oppressed people I think it's incorrect, it's patronizing, to actively do the work of organizing classes of people about whom we know little or nothing, especially if we haven't been asked' (ibid., 30). The radical therapy movement was reproducing the conflicts of its wider political environment – the Maoist versus libertarian struggles which eventually ripped apart American revolutionary politics.

Various aspects of Radical Therapy's theoretical positions – their main sources, apart from Marxism, were Herbert Marcuse and Wilhelm Reich (Brown 1974; *Issues in Radical Therapy* 1973b), and Transactional Analysis (Steiner 1976a) – will be explored below. The political *praxis* of the movement took several different directions. One of these was to criticize and contest the orthodox mental health system.

> Wherever you look, therapy has failed. The only persons consistently helped are the therapists, whose lives are comfortable. … Most therapists are men; most

patients, women. ...Most therapists are white and middle-class. ...The therapist touts himself as a magician. ...he allies himself to the status quo – and bolsters it. He sells his skills like a vendor of fried chicken. (*Radical Therapist/Rough Times* Collective 1974, Introduction, 7)

Both East Coast and West Coast groups worked actively to expose abuses in the mental health system, to oppose practices such as experimental brain surgery on mental patients, and to offer alternative sources of help for those in distress – for example through the Berkeley Radical Psychiatry Center and the Changes group in the Chicago area. A feature of this work was a strong emphasis on group rather than individual therapy – both to help more people, and because collective work was seen as politically preferable (Wyckoff 1976). They also conducted an ongoing debate about the validity of the concept of therapeutic skills *per se*: is it intrinsically mystifying and oppressive for someone to set up as a therapist (e.g. Henley and Brown 1974), or does therapy encompass objective skills which can be used either positively or negatively (e.g. Cousens 1974)?

Many of the other important themes and issues concerned sexuality, which was becoming an important political arena: feminism and gay liberation, moving beyond monogamy, masturbation as empowerment, sexual and emotional freedom, all feature in the pages of *IRT*. *RT* makes more of an attempt to stay soberly political, approaching feminism and gay liberation from a coalition-building perspective; but in Berkeley there is a joyous intoxication with the new culture of sexual self-expression. Radical Therapy was also deeply interested in how psychotherapy insights could be used to facilitate political organizing in general (Steiner 1974). This led on to a general analysis of power and hierarchy, which I will discuss later.

4

Therapy for the People

Here I want to examine some attempts by therapists to give practical expression to their ideas about human beings – to make a difference. All four examples are the heirs of initiatives which I have already discussed: Marie Langer of the 'left Freudians', Social Therapy of the Radical Therapy movement, and the two London schemes in some ways of the Sexpol movement and in some ways a first world emulation of Langer's Nicaraguan work (though also reminiscent of the 1930s Peckham Experiment: Pearse and Crocker 1943). All four are explicitly socialist in orientation. In many ways, they represent a descent from the grand visions of their sources into the mud and grime of everyday reality.

Marie Langer and the Sandinistas

Marie Langer is a transitional figure, originally one of the 'left Freudians'. While training as an analyst in Vienna in 1934, she was at the same time a Communist Party activist.

> At times, I would look at my watch during a meeting and get up and go to some unavoidable appointment, a supposed class, etc. The comrades thought that I was giving classes in order to earn some money, but in reality I wasn't leaving to go to a class but to a session. (Langer 1989, 78)

Langer had to keep each part of her life secret from the other; especially when, to avoid confrontation, the Vienna Psychoanalytic Institute forbade analysts to be active in any clandestine party or to treat activists as patients. At this point most parties were banned, so virtually any political activity was clandestine. Langer continued in the CP, was found out and threatened with expulsion from the Institute – even more alarming since 'in all the meetings, as in the meetings of all clubs, schools, etc. at the time, there were police present. The fact that whether my political activity was legal or not was going to be discussed in front of the police seemed to me a complete aberration' (ibid., 79). Langer avoided expulsion, but soon went to Spain as a medical volunteer in the Civil War. After many adventures, she and her lover left Europe for Uruguay, and then for Argentina, as part of the exodus of both analysts and leftists in the face of Nazism. In Argentina, she completed her training and came in on the ground floor, as it were, of psychoanalysis in Latin America. Langer left political activity behind her for many years after World War II:

> I was very afraid when Peron came to power ...; I thought that it was fascism. ... We stayed, but I had children and I didn't have relatives there to confide in; I was very

afraid of committing myself to any political activity whatsoever. ... [F]or a couple of decades I effectively substituted for my political militancy an institutional-analytic 'militancy' – in terms of dedication and loyalty – without ever completely breaking the tie with the Left. (Ibid., 96)

However, despite her avoidance of explicit activism, in 1951 she published *Motherhood and Sexuality*, a radical text for its time which argues that 'woman's conflictual relationship to sexuality and motherhood would only be resolved through the successful challenge to the legal, social and economic institutions which confined her to the home' (Hollander 1988, 93).

In the early 1960s, from a position of great seniority within Argentinian analysis, Langer began to take a highly critical view of analytic institutions which we will discuss below in Chapter 15. This led her into an organizational split from the Argentinian Psychoanalytic Association, and her co-founding of the *Plataforma* group of analysts. She began to work therapeutically with shanty-town dwellers through the Avellaneda Hospital:

Apart from bringing about symptomatic improvements, our aim was to help our patients lose ... their sexual and social prejudices and to liberate themselves relatively speaking from the ideology of the dominant classes. ... We tried to help them be able to discriminate between their responsibility for their personal history and that of their family's and society's. We tried to enable them to reach consciousness, ...to understand how they had been conditioned to occupy the place that society had allocated them and to make decisions which would offer them a way out of their situation. (Ibid., 177)

It is notable that here Langer uses the term 'consciousness' in a Marxist rather than a Freudian sense. (In her seventies, she commented that she had finally found the common denominator of Marxism, psychoanalysis and feminism – 'the consciousness to be able to achieve change': Hollander 1988, 107.) One of our recurring themes will be the overlap between the personal unconscious and the social unconscious – between what is repressed on an individual level and on a political level.

Langer was regarded as a dangerous radical by the Junta, and finally left Argentina under threat from the death squads in 1974. In Mexico, she continued the project of 'putting the discoveries and therapeutic possibilities Freud offers us within the reach of the non-wealthy classes' (Langer 1989, 133). This led her to visit Nicaragua at the invitation of the victorious Sandinistas. In 1981, she became co-ordinator of a group of 12 psychiatrists and psychologists who travelled monthly from Mexico to Nicaragua to train health and education professionals. 'For the last six years of her life Marie became passionately involved with the social experiment initiated by the Sandinista Revolution ... through her central role in the development of Nicaragua's first national mental health care system' (ibid., Introduction, 5).

In their work there, largely based on group therapy, Langer and her colleagues came up against the limitations of a purely political approach to therapy. She describes discussing with a young Nicaraguan psychologist how he would work with his first group:

I asked him what theoretical approach he had selected. He answered as though it was taken for granted, 'The Marxist approach, of course, because we know how relations of production are reflected in the psyche and how...' At that point it became clear to us that we had to start teaching seriously the basic elements of psychoanalysis and group therapy. (Ibid. 214–15)

Langer and her colleagues developed a synthetic approach in which 'assessment of the relationship between the individual and the family is based on psychoanalytic theory, the analysis of relationships within the family follows the systemic approach, and the role of the family in society is defined in terms of the Marxist approach' (ibid., 216). However the 'analytic approach' is itself heavily influenced by Marxist and socialist ideas and ideals, as the 'ten commandments' used in teaching psychoanalysis demonstrate:

1) We must be able to listen, to question, and to assimilate the meaning of catharsis.
2) The unconscious exists. … Everything which appears illogical in us has a meaning.
3) Hence our attitudes and actions are over-determined. Our ideology is in part unconscious.
    …
5) We are a sum of contradictions. Even the mother who loves her baby hates it at the same time.
    …
10) We are all wonderful, but also mad; we are heroes but also cowards (how to cope with fear?); we are loving but at the same time perverse. Feelings of guilt have to be diminished, as they don't help but paralyse. (Ibid., 215)

Kleinian thinking about ambivalence is apparent here (see Chapter 11), but in an unusual context. Its appeal to these workers seems to be that it encourages the acceptance of human imperfection, and hence the dissolution of guilt feelings. Guilt is an important motivator for political activism, but in Langer's view ultimately a destructive one.

Langer sees a progressive sequence whereby group therapy, itself a replacement for individual work, merges into a socio-political process of mutual aid and education. 'We have almost reached the point where group therapy will be phased out and replaced by community psychiatry' (ibid., 217). She makes clear that her experiences of practical activism have strengthened and extended her pragmatic attitude to *both* psychotherapy *and* politics. Her break with psychoanalytic institutions was about privileging Marxism over psychotherapy. Her work in Nicaragua led her to privilege 'usefulness' over both sets of theoretical concepts.

When we left [the APA] we left as defined Marxists, Freudo-Marxists. I believe none of us now are fixed on that; we are much more pragmatic. For example, we ask about Nicaragua, 'How can one be useful to Nicaragua, with certain psychoanalytic concepts?' We don't ask, 'Let us see if Nicaragua is Marxist and how we connect theoretically as Marxist psychoanalysts?'; we are not interested in that kind of question, which has lost much of its appeal. (Ibid., 229)

'SOCIAL THERAPY'

1970s Radical Therapy is a direct forebear of the Institute for Social Therapy – 'a controversial group therapy service and cluster of related organizations based at the edge of Greenwich Village in New York City' (Parker 1995, 1). The most unusual thing about the Institute is that, besides offering therapy, it also includes a fully functioning political party, the New Alliance Party (NAP), which has put up a (black, female) candidate for the Presidency of the United States.

Through the work of its leading figure Fred Newman, Social Therapy (ST) claims to have successfully drawn together political and personal change in a new form of Marxist therapy which empowers its participants equally as subjects and as activists. ST is an aggressively expansionist movement, setting up new centres across the United States and aiming to establish presence around the world. It identifies its own origins in the Black psychology movement of the 1960s; the work of the Russian psychologist Lev Vygotsky (Newman and Holzman, 1993); systems theory and developments in the philosophy of science; and radical psychiatry (Parker 1995, 2).

It emerges clearly from Parker's description of his visit to the organization in New York that it uses classic Trotskyist methods: a hidden core group, with its own revolutionary agenda, which spawns issue-based front organizations by the yard, so to speak (some of the many such organizations are named by Parker: 1995, 14n.). These fronts around various issues are used in order to recruit cadres, but the issues involved are seen as important primarily for general political education. ST is perhaps the only case so far of therapy being used as a 'mobilizing issue' – just as the issues of gender, race and sexual orientation have long been popular trawling-grounds for the ultra-left.

This Trotskyite agenda explains why it is so hard to grasp the goals and methods of Social Therapy;[11] and also why it seems to discard some of the basic boundaries – for example, sexual ones – which have been regarded as crucial for other forms of psychotherapy (Parker 1995, 16–18). ST claims to be based on 'new scientific breakthroughs', and 'a scientific advance in the field of psychotherapy' which 'cures psychopathology'. What it seems to be in reality is a well-organized and effective radical political group which uses group psychotherapy methods (a) to recruit and (b) to train its members.

According to Holzman (1995, 23) ST is an '"anti-institution" … self-consciously attempting to not replicate the traditional institution of psychotherapy'; the statement that for ST 'boundaries are not an issue' can only be made sense of 'in its *historical textuality*' (ibid., 24, original italics). It is not easy to see what this might mean; but reading on, Holzman seems to be arguing that ST is using the methods of therapy selectively for its own ends, rather than practising therapy *per se*: 'if … we are dealing … with the explicit, self-conscious, participatory activity of creating an environment in which such boundaries, categories, definitions, rules, and regulations are not necessarily built in, then applying such a criterion is methodologically impositional' (ibid.). Those familiar with the jargon of ultra-leftism will perhaps have a sense of familiar ground here.

Leonora Fulani, NAP presidential candidate, asserts that the Social Therapy Community Clinics (which she directs) 'work with the political/therapeutic perspective (a theory and practice) that therapy can only be curative, especially in communities of color, if it is a therapy of *empowerment*' (Fulani 1988, xiii). She criticizes 'traditional psychology and psychiatry in American society' for its role of 'adapting people to society as it is' (ibid.), and argues that the Radical

Therapy movement has not gone far enough towards 'commitment to the empowerment of an entire community through the practice of an empowerment therapy' (ibid., xvi).

There is still some difficulty in discerning what ST actually *does*; not particularly helped by the ensuing claim that 'there *is* something we can do other than adapting people to society. We can help people adapt to *history* ... by facilitating the collective experience of building new social environments that meet their emotional needs' (ibid., xvi).

Nor do we get a much clearer picture from Holzman's description:

> Social therapy is not an interpretative therapy; it is not a problem-solving therapy; it does not adhere to a particular method. ...It is the *practice of method* – a continuously transforming methodology, simultaneously the creating of an environment for the transformation of mundane life activities and the transformation of these activities into a qualitatively new way of life. (Holzman 1995, 25)

This is the opaque style in which ST *chooses to present and justify itself*. Something very exciting and creative may well be happening in ST groups. But unfortunately it is impossible to discern from their own theoretical statements quite what this might be.

'Around These Parts, It's What You Produce That Matters, What You Give' (Randhawa 1990) is an article in the form of journal entries by a participant in ST groups, printed in the organization's magazine *Practice*. From it, one gets a clear sense of excitement and personal fulfilment, together with a hearty dose of insider jargon and hero-worship.

> Well, the colloquium can only really be described as far out. We built an environment whereby it was possible for Fred [Newman] to show us some exercises in RE-SOCIALIZATION. I loved the idea of giving up my private emotional state to somebody else, but it really did seem a very difficult thing to do. ... So this exercise of actually asking somebody else to give expression to your emotional state was enormously, hugely, incredibly helpful. Fred broke the rules by bringing Warren close to him physically and the feeling of intimacy that was created as a result of this and the open showing of affection was really something to be seen to be believed. Then Baylah asked for her unworthiness to be expressed and said she wanted to be up there but was conflicted. Barbara said a similar thing. Warren then expressed his conflictedness around this. It was really wild, such amazing intimacy amongst a group of 30 or so people. (Randhawa 1990, 43)

I certainly don't want to mock the honest expression of experience in Randhawa's article; but its naïve jargonizing is the other side of the coin from the impenetrable mystification in ST's more official statements. Here, ST emerges more as a cult than a cadre organization. Perhaps Newman's achievement is to have found a style which combines features of both – Kim Il Sung and the Reverend Moon in one package. But just what is the difference between cult and cadre? We distinguish them chiefly in terms of their goals and analysis; and a group organized around politicized therapy, or therapeutic politics, seems precisely to interface between the two categories. We can perhaps expect before too long an explosive split or break-up in ST, from which some members will emerge deeply hurt, others strengthened and empowered.

In the very different context of the UK, social applications of psychotherapy have generally been attempted within the state system of the National Health Service and social work. This means an unstable balance between the political goals and aspirations of those involved, and the need to present a justifiable programme for the use of public funds. Not surprisingly, such projects have generally had a fairly short lifespan, ending with the inevitable collapse of funding.

In the current political and economic climate it is probably impossible to do much of this sort of work; but I want to present two examples from London in the 1970s and 1980s. The first is the Battersea Action and Counselling Centre (BACC) (Hoggett and Lousada 1985), created with the intention of intervening in what its initiators saw as 'an ongoing process of injury' created by contemporary capitalism, 'the progressive fragmentation and destruction of what we shall call ... "human relationship and the individual psyche"' (ibid., 126).

Although Hoggett and Lousada specifically chose to 'locat[e] ourselves organizationally outside the state' (ibid.), their funding nonetheless came from the state, and with the election of 'a politically hostile local government' the project collapsed. It is doubtful how far there can be anywhere 'outside the state' in advanced capitalist societies; certainly not somewhere dependent on state finance (ibid., 149–50). But this is not to deny that the paradoxical tension of working *within* the system, *against* the system, can be temporarily creative. Such work points up 'the ambivalent attitude of the state towards the provision of welfare' (ibid., 130), the role of the welfare state in policing and controlling society, and often in breaking up what are actually forces for healing and solidarity (ibid., 129). It also often demonstrates just how much space there is within even advanced capitalism for contestatory activity to flourish.

BACC established itself in shop-front premises on a busy Battersea street, with two 'community psychologists' and three day nursery staff. The initial goal was 'to prevent "mental breakdown" among local working-class people by providing a skilled psychotherapy service along with other more material forms of aid and action' (ibid., 126), including a food co-op, a day-care centre, and an advice and information service. '[A]s the project developed, so our aims widened and we became concerned not just with the prevention of unmanageable stress but with a variety of interventions designed to combat the progressive fragmentation of everyday life...' (ibid.). In other words, the organizers, having pulled a number of people out of the water, were now interested in looking further upstream to stop them falling (or being pushed) in. Developing the range of social and political facilities on offer at the centre, though, they found that psychotherapy itself was fading out – especially since many local people were ashamed and embarrassed to come for therapy. Accordingly BACC 'began to attempt to change the way in which the local community conceived and related to the question of the quality of human relationship and ... human distress' (ibid., 136). They offered a range of courses, workshops, and so on, aimed at connecting the personal and political spheres, the realms of psychotherapy and community activism. For example, in the later Lambeth project they ran 'counselling skills courses' for groups including mothers, tenants association organizers, voluntary or part-time youth and old people workers, and 'a sprinkling of people from the enormous range of voluntary and community groups' in London's inner city (ibid., 147).

The parallel with Langer's work in Nicaragua is striking, especially considering the tremendous difference of the two situations; like Langer, Hoggett and Lousada were aiming to move towards what she calls 'community psychiatry', a situation where 'such communities can contain and work creatively with their own distress' without drawing on outside experts (ibid.).

> Some groups, perhaps the more nurturant ones, tend to [become 'group therapy']; some groups seem to be much more about sharing of experience and knowledge; some groups pursue a more practical course. ... Most groups, in our experience, tend to have a bit of each of these elements within them, which means that we in turn have to know when to stop being 'therapist' and when to start being 'agitator', when to stop imparting information and when to start facilitating an embryonic sharing interaction, and so on. Needless to say we find this kind of work very hard. (Ibid., 149)

Like Langer, Hoggett and Lousada used a psychoanalytic framework (with a strong Kleinian flavour) for their interventions:

> one of the important 'subversive' aspects of psychoanalysis ... resides in the way in which it refuses to make artificial separations or contradistinctions when construing human experience. ... [I]t sees us all as made up of greater or lesser proportions of irrationality, wholeness, phobic and obsessional tendencies, melancholia, etc. (Ibid., 146)

They saw this feature as helping them to break down the barriers set up by their clients between 'normal' and 'abnormal', 'sane' and 'crazy' – or, one imagines, politically conformist or deviant.

In the early 1980s, Sue Holland developed a project in the White City area of London, funded by the Department of the Environment, and aimed at preventing the development of mental health problems among local women (Holland 1992). Holland had lived in the neighbourhood for ten years, and worked as a clinical psychologist and 'community mental health "innovator"' (Holland 1992, 147). As well as providing psychotherapy and counselling, she sought to set up a mutual self-help network of 'ex-clients'. After three years, her project was seen as successful enough to become part of the general local social services system. In the mid-1980s, thanks to left-wing dominance of the Greater London Council (before it was abolished by the Thatcher government), the ex-clients' group was itself able to get funding as Women's Action for Mental Health (WAMH), a neighbourhood counselling and advocacy service.

In Holland's project, individual therapy and counselling was seen as a (relatively) short-term measure; 'usually, towards the end of this one-to-one work the woman is expressing a greater social interest in the world around her' (ibid., 148). Referral to WAMH often followed: 'By way of this networking with other women helpers on the estate, each woman can discover that she is not uniquely mad, bad or alone in her private symptoms, but shares common suffering and collective strengths with other women' (ibid., 149). Like Reich, Langer, Social Therapy and Hoggett and Lousada – each in their different ways – Holland sees a natural development from individual distress towards social activism. 'Finding this more social sense of herself reveals that demands cannot be met without confronting the social system and structures which both meet and limit people's needs and choices' (ibid.). This Holland describes as 'the most difficult stage in any programme of neighbourhood mental health': as several other writers have indicated, this is the point at which one begins to realize that, in effect, society as currently constituted is psycho-toxic. A difficult stage indeed.

Holland argues that 'it is not so much the patient who is chronic but the [orthodox] psychiatric treatment' (ibid., 150). She maps out a series of stages – from 'psychic' to 'social' to 'political' – through which women involved in the project can 'astonish us all with their radical change'; and accurately highlights the distance between her work and ordinary psychotherapy by reporting that 'some of my clients are now among my closest colleagues, a fact which other colleagues ... find unorthodox or even unethical' (ibid., 151).

5

Deconstructing Mental Illness

The historical relationship between psychotherapy and psychiatry – psychological treatment by doctors – has been complex. Although psychotherapy often supports orthodox psychiatric views of 'mental illness', it can also question the whole concept, and the dehumanizing ways in which mental patients have often been treated. Much of the radical politics of mental health has been *survivor-led* – that is, organized and theorized by those defined as mentally ill, rather than by 'experts' of any sort (see Parker et al. 1995, 112ff.). In this chapter, I am looking only at the contribution of *therapists* to the critique of mental health work. We will see how two kinds of politics coexist here: a very practical empowerment politics, and arising out of that, a much broader critique of the social order.

LAING, COOPER AND ANTI-PSYCHIATRY

'There are no personal problems, only political problems' (Cooper 1980, 120)

Perhaps the most famous critique of 'mental illness' and its 'treatment' is that made by R.D. Laing, David Cooper and others from the 1960s onwards. Although the label has become widely used, 'anti-psychiatry' is not a unified, coherent body of theory and practice; it represents a loose, often conflictual alliance between several different initiatives – and is itself only a part of a much larger international movement, or ensemble of movements (Cooper 1980, 130–40).

The two initial components of the UK 'anti-psychiatry' movement were a theory of schizophrenia which placed its origin in dysfunctional families (Bateson et al. 1956, Laing and Esterson 1964); and an 'existential' critique of orthodox psychiatric diagnosis and treatment as objectifying and dehumanizing (Laing 1965). These strands came together in a redefinition of schizophrenia, not as a disease entity, but as a *political event*:

> Schizophrenia is a micro-social crisis situation in which the acts and experience of a certain person are invalidated by others for certain intelligible cultural and micro-cultural (usually familial) reasons, to the point where he [*sic*] is elected and identified as being 'mentally ill' in a certain way, and is then confirmed ... in the identity 'schizophrenic patient' by medical or quasi-medical agents. (Cooper 1970, 16)

The so-called schizophrenic is subjected to a process of 'social invalidation' (ibid., 10) through being fitted into the passive role of patient, and through having 'almost every act, statement, and experience … systematically ruled invalid … to produce the vitally-needed invalid-patient' (ibid.).

These ideas had major implications for *practice*, which were tested out in several initiatives; one of the best known being 'Villa 21', the mental hospital ward for which David Cooper was responsible between 1962 and 1966, where the boundaries between staff and patients and the power of one group over the other were steadily dissolved (Cooper 1970, 96–116). For example, according to Cooper,

> One of the commonest staff fantasies in mental hospitals is that if patients are not coerced verbally or physically into getting out of bed at a certain hour in the morning they will stay in bed until they rot away. … The patient is that frightening aspect of themselves that sometimes does not want to get out of bed in the morning and come to work. … [I]t was found that if the usual vigorous rousing procedures were abandoned and patients left to get up themselves, they invariably did rise, even if in some cases they would spend most of the day in bed for some weeks. (Ibid., 101–2)

The gradual 'breakdown of role boundaries' (ibid., 104) in Villa 21 led to a crisis of identity for the staff. 'If the staff rejected prescribed ideas about their function, … why do anything?' (ibid., 105). The staff group eventually cut down their function to controlling the drug cupboard, and administrative dealings with other hospital departments on the phone. The ward came under huge pressure from the hospital to operate conventionally; and this was combined with internal difficulties about the authority of the doctor – Cooper – who both authorized the unconventional style of the ward, and at the same time was trying to give away the authority on which everything depended. In Cooper's view, 'the advance made by the staff group was frankly to recognize their anxiety as intolerable and … to re-impose some staff controls' – over eating and cleaning, meeting attendance, and leave of absence for patients.

The central issues in Villa 21 seem to have developed from the treatment of mental illness to general group-political issues such as 'distinguishing between authentic and inauthentic authority' (ibid., 108). Certainly, it was more or less impossible for a project like this to continue indefinitely in a conventional mental hospital – roughly equivalent to 'socialism in one country'. The experiment came to an end, and Cooper moved out of the mental health system. The ideas of anti-psychiatry were perhaps more effectively practised in independent settings, such as Kingsley Hall (Barnes and Berke 1982; Laing 1971, 59–61), and other households set up by the Philadelphia Trust and the Arbors Association (Cooper 1980, 129–30).

Both Laing and Cooper were politicized by their attempts to change psychiatry; but in different directions, paralleling the two main tendencies in radical politics of the period: individual or lifestyle politics on the one hand, and varieties of Marxism on the other. Laing represents the first tendency, for instance in his visionary work *The Politics of Experience and the Bird of Paradise*, with its famous conclusion: 'If I could turn you on, if I could drive you out of your wretched mind, if I could tell you I would let you know' (Laing 1967, 156). From his experience with his patients (and his use of psychedelic drugs) Laing portrays the schizophrenic voyage as an initiation, a rite of passage. 'The process may be one that all of us need, in one form or another. This process could have a central function in a truly sane society' (ibid., 106–7). Ordinary society is 'egoic'; ego-loss is a necessary step forward, the sort of transcendental experience widely discussed by mystics (ibid., 112–19).

Laing argues that 'the condition of alienation, of being asleep, of being unconscious, of being out of one's mind, is the condition of the normal man' (ibid., 24), and contrasts this with the free perception of the 'insane'. He gives a very specific role to psychotherapy:

> Psychotherapy consists in the paring away of all that stands between us, the props, masks, roles, lies, defences, anxieties, projections and introjections, in short, all the carry-overs from the past, transference and counter-transference, that we use by habit and collusion, wittingly or unwittingly, as our currency for relationships. (Ibid., 39)

Thus he emphasizes 'the *non*-transference elements in psychotherapy' (ibid., 40); and asserts that '[p]sychotherapy must remain *an obstinate attempt of two people to recover the wholeness of being human through the relationship between them*' (ibid., 41, original italics). Alongside Laing's visionary rhetoric goes a sustained attempt to use reasoning in a liberating way to undo the 'knots' (Laing 1970) that damage the 'wholeness' of interpersonal and intrapersonal relationships: therapy as *communion*. At some points this becomes a systematic, mathematical treatment of the family origins of schizophrenia in the 'double-bind' and more complex operations, drawing on systemic approaches (see e.g. Laing 1971, Part II).

Laing extensively critiques the closed systems of psychiatry and psychotherapy with their self-fulfilling diagnoses. Looking at a case history by the psychoanalyst Wilfred Bion, for example, he argues that

> [i]t is difficult to imagine anything the patient could say that could tell Bion anything he does not think he knows. … It is difficult to imagine anything anyone could say which could possibly reveal to Bion that his constructions could be wrong. (Laing 1982, 52)

And speaking generally about psychiatry:

> A psychiatrist has been trained to believe that, if he were to think that he thought and felt much the same as those people he diagnoses as psychotic, this would not mean that they would not be psychotic, it would mean that he was psychotic. There is, in a sense, a bigger difference between a psychiatrist of this persuasion and a schizophrenic than there is between a normal human being and a normal rat. (Laing 1982, 38)

Starting with *The Divided Self* (1965), Laing consistently tries to understand those defined as 'mentally ill' both in and on their own terms. This insistence on the patient's right to their own reality, so to speak, feeds into his later apocalyptic condemnation of the social order: by defining society as mad, he can validate the reality of those which *it* defines as mad.

Cooper for a while seemed to share the idealization of madness in an insane world:

> There is … something remarkably healthy about the chronic schizophrenic, preoccupied with his inner world, spending the day hunched over the central heating fitting in a decrepit back ward. If he does not have the solution to the riddle of life, at least he has fewer illusions. (Cooper 1970, 103)

Over the next decade, though, Cooper developed a more conventionally 'political' theory within which to situate madness. Losing faith in therapy, he advocates that all psycho-techniques including chemical and bodily manipulations – including all the commercialized versions of this in the capitalist world ('alternative therapies') – be abandoned. These must be replaced by political recuperation (*by* the people *from* the repressive system) of disorder. By the rediscovery of orgasm and madness (including the 'madness' of artists) as radical needs for the transformation of persons. (Ibid., 13–14)

'The politicization of madness', for Cooper, 'is indispensable if we would create a future' (ibid., 18).

In a search for effective methods of creating this future, Cooper at times is influenced by Felix Guattari's espousal of '[a]n anti-psychoanalysis, concerned with the *defamilialization of discourse* moving out of the family model of experience ... towards the political analysis of actual current relationships' (ibid., 22). At other points, he moves from anti-psychiatry to 'non-psychiatry':

> Non-psychiatry means that profoundly disturbing, incomprehensible, 'mad' behaviour is to be contained, incorporated in and diffused through the whole society as a subversive source of creativity, spontaneity, not 'disease'. Under the conditions of capitalism, this is clearly 'impossible'. What we have to do is to accept this impossibility as the challenge. (Ibid., 117)

The British anti-psychiatry movement was paralleled by struggles in a number of other countries: apart from the USA, which we shall consider below, there were important groups in Italy, Germany, France, Belgium, Switzerland, Portugal and other countries, which in 1977 came together in the International Network (Cooper 1980, 164–71). The different national groups had very different experiences, ranging between the German 'Socialist Patients Collective' (Cooper 1980, 140; Guattari 1984, 67n.), which encountered heavy police persecution and ended up merged into the armed ultra-left, and the Italian 'Democratic Psychiatry' movement which had a major influence on social policy (Basaglia 1987; Cooper 1980, 142–6; Mebane-Francescato and Jones, 1974).

RADICAL THERAPY

Radical Therapy in the USA grew out of a Radical Psychiatry movement; an important part of its platform was always a critique of and alternatives to orthodox treatment of 'mental illness'. At the centre of both of these was the assertion that psychological distress is political in its origins.

> [I]n the absence of oppression, human beings will ... live in harmony with nature and each other. Oppression is the coercion of human beings by force or threats of force, and is the source of all human alienation. ...The condition of the human soul which makes soul healing necessary is alienation. Alienation is a feeling within a person that he is not part of the human species, that she is dead or that everyone is dead, that he does not deserve to live, or that someone wishes her to die. ... *Alienation is the essence of all psychiatric conditions. ... all alienation is the result of oppression about which the oppressed has been mystified or deceived.* (Steiner 1974, 16)

The argument here is tight and coherent. If we know we are oppressed, then we fight back at or evade our oppression. If we are unaware of oppression, then we become alienated, which is interpreted as mental illness. The radical approach to mental illness, therefore, is to help individuals become aware of their oppression. There follows from this an emphasis on treating the designated 'mentally ill' as *ordinary people* – 'heavy strangers and friends' (Glaser 1974, title). Alongside publicizing and supporting survivor-led struggles against the mental health system and its abuses (e.g. New York Mental Patient's Liberation Front, 1974), Radical Therapy created a number of self-help networks like 'Changes' in Chicago (Glaser 1974), and many self-help leaflets on topics such as 'Handling Psychiatric Emergencies': 'You and your friends can handle many psychiatric emergencies. The crucial elements are *trying* (instead of drawing back), and trusting your own intuition' (Glenn 1974, 251).

The leaflet goes on to advise its readers, when faced with someone in an extreme state, to listen; stay calm; offer support and accurate information; let the individual decide what they need; and 'remember that the roles of therapist and patient are interchangeable. You may be helping someone today, and be helped tomorrow. That's the way it should be' (ibid., 254).

THE HEARING VOICES NETWORK

There are currently a large number of mental health 'user organizations' – often very loose support networks, and often with little or no involvement on the part of psychotherapists or other mental health professionals. Some examples are Survivors Speak Out, ECT Anonymous, and Support Coalition International.[12] While their work is admirable, it is not part of the subject of this book. But it does seem relevant to discuss one such grouping, the Hearing Voices Network (HVN), which has its origin in *the 'conversion' of a therapist by a client*.

HVN is an international movement of 'voice hearers and their allies': one 'not easily characterized as anti-psychiatry, anti-psychology or anti-drugs, although … predicated on challenging illness models and the resistance to talking about, or to, *voices*' (McLaughlin 1996, 239). McLaughlin also describes HVN as 'a network of shifting alliances between voice hearers, therapists of all hues and indeed beyond such disciplines, those who do not conflate voices and distress' (ibid). Parker et al. call it 'a radical movement distinguished by its continuity with the tradition of Democratic Psychiatry and a critique of the medical model' (Parker et al. 1995, 123). It developed from the meeting of Marius Romme, professor of social psychiatry and his patient, Patsy Hage in Maastricht, Netherlands (see Romme and Escher 1993): Romme was able to recognize that Hage had a stable relationship with her voices based on an explanatory model (in her case taken from Jaynes 1976) which allowed her to integrate them into her life.

From a survey and a conference of voice hearers, Romme and Escher discovered that tactics of ignoring or distracting oneself from the voices are generally ineffective; what works is acceptance of the voices as part of the self, together with some sort of explanatory model – exactly what this is seems not to matter (Thomas 1997, 188–9). Romme and Escher helped set up HVN, now based in Manchester, with 'over 30 groups, led by voice hearers for voice hearers' (ibid., 190). From initial stupefaction – 'Initially I found it hard to follow these conversations [between voice hearers]: to my ears, the contents were bizarre and extraordinary, and yet all this was freely discussed as though it constituted a real world of and unto itself' (Romme and Escher 1993, 11) – Romme has moved to a position where he regards hearing voices as 'part of a pattern of personal growth and ... a facet of human experience such as left-handedness or homosexuality' (Parker et al. 1995, 123). Interesting analogies, since both were until recently regarded as flawed and/or (literally in the first case) sinister.

Hearing Voices has formed creative alliances with researchers and theorists. In 1995 the Discourse Unit at Manchester Metropolitan University organized a conference of voice hearers and professionals – more of the former than the latter (McLaughlin 1996, 242–3). Thomas (1997), drawing on work with HVN members, uses the theoretical work of Mead, Vygotsky and Bakhtin to argue that 'hallucinatory voices are a form of inner speech shaped by the dialogical organization of human experience' (Thomas 1997, 198). Suitably enough, considering the organization of HVN as a support group network, Thomas argues for a move from theories of schizophrenia which focus on individual process to approaches based in the social and interpersonal realm.

6

Conflict and Community

Psychotherapy offers enormous resources for the political project of confronting conflict, through its work on and in groups. (A good general source on group work approaches is Shaffer and Galinsky 1974.) We will look at the more theoretical side of this in Chapter 11. However, many psychotherapy schools, in particular the analytic and psychodynamic ones, have been extremely reticent about trying to apply their knowledge of groups in a practical political context. Andrew Samuels has run workshops in this area (Samuels 1993, 27), although he does not describe them at all specifically in his published work on psychotherapy and politics. Another exception is Gordon Lawrence's work on 'social dreaming' (Lawrence 1998), emerging from the Tavistock tradition.

Encounter groups were developed by Carl Rogers and his associates in the USA in the late 1940s. The essence of the encounter group is that it is *unstructured*. (On a different theoretical basis, exactly the same is true of the classic analytic group.)

> Often there is consternation, anxiety, and irritation at first – particularly because of the lack of structure. Only gradually does it become evident that the major aim of nearly every member is to find ways of relating to other members of the group and to himself [*sic*]. ... Only cautiously do the real feelings and real persons emerge. The contrast between the outer shell and the inner person becomes more and more apparent. ... [A] sense of trust slowly begins to build. ... Participants feel a closeness and intimacy ... because they have revealed themselves here more deeply and fully than to those in their own family circle. (Rogers 1973, 15–16)

This is Rogers' conception of the encounter group in a nutshell; and the experience has been powerful and effective for thousands of people. (The model has influenced or been appropriated by a number of other approaches, and the name has become almost generic for many sorts of group therapy – including some where the leader plays a more active role.) Originally, encounter groups responded to a perceived 'hunger for relationships which are close and real' (ibid., 18); arguably, they directly influenced the enormous cultural shift of the 1960s and 1970s, with its central values of 'reality' and 'genuineness'. Once successful, they began to be applied experimentally to specific conflict situations, on the theory that 'open and honest communication, of feelings as well as thoughts' could only be helpful. Encounter groups have been used in industry and business, in educational institutions, in churches, in government departments, in situations of racial conflict (ibid., 138–50).

Rogers' approach to conflict has been sharply criticized by Marxists such as Jacoby for its lack of social awareness: 'as if "the Person" existed in a no-man's-land of free-floating interpersonal relations, and not in a society that threatens to reify the last spontaneous movements' (Jacoby 1977, 64). Certainly one can question the political credibility of a style of work which claims to be equally applicable to transnational business executives and ghetto kids, to senior police officers and to single-parent families, without distinguishing explicitly between their different social positions and access to power. This is in a sense the ultimate liberal posture, that we are all really just the same, and that what oppressive institutions need is more 'real relationships' – as Jacoby puts it, 'not the dissolution of dehumanization but its humanization' (ibid.).

However, Rogers is at least aware of this problem, and stresses that encounter 'is not simply a means of damping down tensions so that the situation is quieter' but a way of bringing out underlying tensions so that the whole community can face and address them (Rogers 1973, 142). He emphasizes that encounter groups can be deeply stressful for institutions, and

> can definitely bring about highly constructive change, but may also create sharp division between members of the establishment; may be upsetting to members of the community; may be deeply upsetting to those who are bound by tradition, and may thus raise the question whether constructive change or disaster has occurred. (Ibid., 88)

Thus, at any rate for Rogers himself, encounter groups do not simply maintain the status quo, but render some positions within institutions less tenable.

'WORLD WARRIORS': MINDELL AND PARRY

An ambitious and intensely practical approach to working with conflict is that developed by Arnold Mindell, the founder of Process Oriented Psychology, under the name of 'Worldwork'. Worldwork is in theory applicable to any group conflict situation; like Mindell's work in general, it is based upon a specific conceptualization of 'dreaming', defined as a fundamental process operating not only in literal dreams but also in bodily symptoms, relationship conflicts, and many other contexts.

> [G]lobal processes are organized by a dream-like field, a troubled sea of projections, feelings and ecological confusion, floating between both individuals and groups, confusing communication and creating war. When properly recycled, this 'information float' creates the harmony and wholeness we are looking for. ... When unused, it becomes ... an explosive dump responsible for nightmarish planetary problems. (Mindell 1989, 11)

Mindell treats human interaction as patterned by *fields*:[13]

> natural phenomena that include everyone, are omnipresent, and exert forces upon things in their midst. ... We think we manage or organize our lives and groups, but actually fields create and organize us as much as we organize them. Fields organize people into groups ... they can be as pushy and as troublesome as an impossible spirit. (Mindell 1992, 15)

Mindell was originally a Jungian analyst, and here we can see the influence of Jungian ideas of the 'collective unconscious'. For Mindell, conflict indicates unprocessed dream-like material – generally, some minority experience or viewpoint which is not being adequately represented in the group situation. He emphasizes the need for 'deep democracy', which is 'the realization that everyone is needed to represent reality' (Mindell 1992, 155), or 'the inherent importance of all parts of ourselves and all viewpoints in the world around us' (ibid., 5): worldwork is thus a practical experiment in deep democracy, bringing unrepresented aspects of the group experience into awareness. '[T]he tools of worldwork can only succeed with the attitude of deep democracy. ... Deep democracy is our sense that the world is here to help us become our entire selves, and that we are here to help the world become whole' (ibid., 96).

There are deep similarities between the approach of Mindell and his co-workers, and that of Danaan Parry, who parallels deep democracy with the assertion that 'if *anyone* loses, everyone loses' (Parry 1989, 79). Both authors take an approach of welcoming conflict as its own best path to resolution: 'engaging in heated conflict instead of running away from it is one of the best ways to resolve the divisiveness that prevails on every level of society' (Mindell 1995, 12); or '*you can't have* conflict *resolution without* conflict' (Parry 1989, 55, original italics). Thus, worldwork demands considerable nerve to facilitate: 'in worldwork, conflict and moments of chaos are valued within group process because these can quickly create a sense of community and a lasting organization' (Mindell 1995, 17).

In the practice of worldwork, large groups of people meet together, representing as wide a range as possible of global positions and experiences. This range can be within a specific environment – for example a neighbourhood or city, or a political struggle; or seminars can draw several hundred participants from all round the world, from many ethnic groups, classes, genders and sexual orientations (great effort is expended to make it financially possible for participants to attend from economically disadvantaged groups). At first, everyone expresses the attitude they came with – and perhaps feel stuck in. Conflicts emerge which operate in the world and also in the group – often including those between women and men, black and white, third world and first world, gay and straight. Frequently much anger, grief, terror and despair is expressed. As each experience is attended to, acknowledged, accepted, fought against and worked with, hopefully new roles come into being. In theory at least, silent roles are every bit as important as noisy ones – those who feel helpless, who listen and feel, who create the space within which other people can be more visibly active.

In my own experience at least, this work is terribly difficult: experimental, stirring, demanding every ounce of flexibility and awareness from all the participants as they endeavour to 'sit in the fire of conflict and not be burned' (Mindell 1995, 18) – but also tremendously hopeful. Its most striking subjective aspect, despite its difficulty, is its lack of *effort*: this is a yielding approach, working with the detail and grain of what *is*, affirming how people are acting and feeling – however painful and unpleasant this may be – in the belief that we are all bound to be doing the best possible thing at the time. However, we are not always doing it consciously, carrying it through to the point of completion; and this extra element of awareness often makes an astonishing difference. (For a participant's account of a worldwork seminar, see Heizer 1993.)

A corollary of the concept of 'deep democracy' is a reframing of the concept of leadership.

> If we understand the leader as just another role, we see that the power projected upon our leaders is apparent, not absolute, since real leadership comes from those who are aware of the process trying to happen in their community. The apparent leaders are representations of field roles, which are parts each of us can and sometimes must fill. (Mindell 1989, 88)

According to Mindell,

> our ability to facilitate global processes peacefully depends upon … one person in a hundred who (a) realizes that every role in a field is important, (b) realizes that every living person is needed to fill those roles and (c) can help people to realize their potential in doing this. (Ibid., 73)

Without any actual revision in the approach, the emphasis in worldwork has shifted more than once, reflecting shifts in Mindell's own interests and experience, and in the overwhelmingly complex dynamics produced by processing pain and anger on the sort of scale this work involves. For a few years it became intensely confrontational, influenced by the radical activism of some of its workshop participants, especially people of colour, women and gays. At times there was even a flavour of coercive 'political correctness', with WASP workshop participants bathing in guilt about their own racism, sexism, anything-ism.

Though worldwork has never compromised its support for minorities oppressed for their gender, colour, sexual orientation or economic position, it has perhaps recovered the ability to make connections *between* all of these in a coherent analysis, which also criticizes some of the assumptions of psychotherapy:

> It is devastating to assume, as some Western therapies do, that certain races and myths are more primitive than others. And most therapists assume that the only conscious human beings are ones who think about themselves all the time. Such apparently 'harmless' assumptions are so full of naive prejudices that it is not surprising that our Western therapies and group and organizational practices are not solving city and international problems. (Mindell 1992, 4–5)

There has also been a growing awareness that social conflicts cannot be solved by parachuting in experts: 'People in conflict do not want to need help from outside to show them the way. Outside help has no grassroots effects. People living in conflict areas need love and encouragement first and education second' (ibid., 59).[14] In a striking demonstration of its own principles, worldwork first of all unreservedly took on the standpoint and experience of oppressed minorities; and then, out of this, found the space to recognize that the 'mainstream' experience also had to be recognized and validated if deep democracy was to mean anything.

> [T]hose of us who want to facilitate should not fall into one-sided support of minority positions. … That makes the majority feel marginalized. The facilitator's task is not to do away with the use of rank and power, but to notice them and make their dynamics explicit for the whole group to see. (Mindell 1995, 37)

Worldwork is a so far unique attempt to apply psychotherapy in the sphere of political conflict *without privileging the therapeutic over the political* – without falling into the error, for which Jacoby criticizes Rogers, of treating conflict as something which occurs and can be resolved simply on the level of individual human beings, rather than on the level of social structure. Its main tool for this, which derives from its therapeutic genealogy, is deep democracy. Mindell explicitly recognizes a major problem here in combining real political analysis with support for all parts of the situation:

> The paradox of group process is this: to be useful, it must address everyone's social and rank issues. It's got to deal with the issue of who has the money. At the same time, a community dies if it focuses on only what is right or wrong about each side. (Ibid., 181)

So far worldwork has not resolved this problem – perhaps it cannot be resolved, but only held in continual tension. Mindell's own trajectory has been further and further into a Taoist spirituality which may or may not turn out to be capable of practical political application: 'Value trouble. Accept nature. Make peace with war' (ibid., 241).

COMMUNITY-BUILDING

A third approach to conflict is the well-known 'community building' work of M. Scott Peck (1987), whose background is as a US army psychiatrist and psychotherapist. Peck limits the term 'community' to 'a group of individuals who have learnt how to communicate honestly with each other, whose relationships go deeper than their masks of composure, and who have developed some significant commitment to "rejoice together, mourn together"' (Peck 1987, 59) Clearly this is very close to Rogers' account of the encounter group. Peck is equally close to Mindell's concerns when he speaks of the need to 'go beyond democracy' and 'transcend differences in such a way as to include a minority' (ibid., 63). How, then, does he try to facilitate community?

For Peck, human beings have an innate capacity to enter community – 'a natural yearning and thrust towards health and wholeness and holiness' (ibid., 68). What this capacity requires to express itself is above all *safety*. 'When we are safe, there is a natural tendency for us to heal and convert ourselves' (ibid.). Safety, however, does not imply the absence of conflict, but rather 'a place where conflict can be resolved without physical or emotional bloodshed and with wisdom instead of grace' (ibid., 71). Again, Peck parallels Mindell, in telling the story of a Sufi master asked by his students during a rebellion 'which side should we help?' 'Both,' the Master replies: '"we need to help the authorities listen to the aspirations of the people, ... and we need to help the rebels learn how not to compulsively reject authority"' (ibid.).

Peck believes that 'the process by which a group of human beings becomes a community is a lawful process' (ibid., 83) – that is, the 'how' can be specified. He defines four stages of community-building (ibid., 86–106): 'Pseudo community', when a group basically fakes agreement and avoids conflict; 'Chaos', when conflict insists on emerging; 'Emptiness', when in desperation or despair the group members drop their prejudices and assumptions, their need to solve and control; and 'Community', when the group is reborn out of a subjective experience which can feel like 'group death'. In their facilitation, Peck and his associates try to avoid giving rules and pointers, such as instructing the group to 'refrain from generalizations, to speak personally, to be vulnerable, to avoid attempting to heal or convert'; he likens the effect of such instructions to 'being lifted to a mountaintop by helicopter. The glory can hardly be appreciated as it is when one has to wade through the swamps and scramble over the boulders to get there' (ibid., 128). In other words, as is generally the case with psychotherapy, the crucial learning is *experiential*: a group finds out for itself how to reach community, with only a little help from the designated facilitators. Peck (himself coming from a Christian background and orientation) believes that community building lets us move beyond our particular set of cultural values, to 'reach toward the notion of world community and the possibility of either transcending culture or ... belonging to a planetary culture' (ibid., 202). He gently but strongly criticizes the US governmental system as 'oblivious to the rules of community', and stuck in the fight model and the avoidance of communication wherever possible; and envisions a future collective 'community presidency' to replace the current presidential system.

7

Pressing for Policy Changes

So far we have focused largely on psycho-political initiatives aimed at deep
structural change in society – political or cultural transformation. Now we will
consider initiatives with a more tightly focused goal, where therapists and counsellors seek to influence governmental and/or social policy in particular ways.
Even here, there is a characteristic tendency to look deeper, to ask – just as therapy asks with individual clients – what the fundamental conditions are which
have created the existing policies.

'EMOTIONAL LITERACY'

Psychotherapists and Counsellors for Social Responsibility (PCSR) was set up
in the UK in 1995 as 'a forum for psychotherapists, counsellors and members
of other professions who wish to influence and broaden the political process'
(PCSR, n.d.); among its founders was the Jungian analyst Andrew Samuels,
who has long argued for the importance of psycho-politics. One of the main
ways in which PCSR seeks to fulfil its aims is through 'incorporating emotional
and psychological perspectives into current debates on social, cultural, environmental and political issues' (ibid.). It also seeks to campaign and lobby around
specific issues on which it feels that psychotherapists and counsellors should
have a voice.

This idea of a singular voice for therapists is of course a problematic one, in
at least two ways. To begin with, there is the question we have already raised of
whether therapists are justified in speaking on issues of public policy *as therapists*, rather than as citizens. A recurring question throughout this book concerns what subjects, if any, therapists are justified in speaking about as experts.
What do we, as therapists, actually *know* about?

The discourse employed within PCSR and parallel initiatives (some of
PCSR's founders are also involved in Antidote, 'a think tank which ... uses the
perspectives and ideas of psychotherapy to engage with key social issues':
Samuels 1996, 28) frequently centres on the concept of 'emotional intelligence'
or 'emotional literacy', derived in a general sort of way from Daniel Goleman's
book *Emotional Intelligence* (Goleman 1996). Goleman argues for a new notion
of emotional competence, rather dubiously grounded in psychological and
neuroscience research; by this he basically means not so much the ability to be
aware of and to *express* emotions, as the ability to *manage* them, to subordinate
them to rational judgement.

These ideas were employed in quite a confused way by Susie Orbach, another founder of PCSR and Antidote, in her column in the *Guardian* newspaper:

> A mob ... lacks political nous or political sophistication and is always dominated and motivated by emotional considerations. That is what distinguishes it from a political protest or political expression. ... It is not that emotions have no place in political and public life. ... But at present they are there in a way that degrades the political process.... The reason why some politicians have supported Antidote ... is not because they want more raw emotions in public life ... but because they recognise only too well how many of our presumed political decisions are played as emotional decisions ... and how many of our emotional decisions (such as racism) require political and economic responses. They want to change this. (Orbach 1998, 7)

It is hard to say quite what Orbach is getting at here, and reading the entire text does not help much. Her point seems to be that feelings are feelings and politics are politics, and that the two should be clearly demarcated – 'joining issues where they need to be joined and separating political and emotional issues where they have become fused' (ibid.). This is a rather alarming sort of psychosurgery, but Orbach wants to stake a claim for therapists as experts at this particular operation. She also suggests that 'a political system that is adversarial is not the most enlightened way to move thinking, or society, forward' (ibid.) – again alarming, in its implication of the sort of 'government of all the experts' which in so many parts of the world is a cloak for semi-fascism. It seems that now the therapists will be added to the ranks of technocrats in the cabinet – since they know so much better than 'the mob' how to combine and separate emotions and politics!

Andrew Samuels (1999) offers a rather clearer and more palatable account of 'the politics of feeling':

> It is ... about doing something in a disciplined way so as to understand [feelings], to see how one feeling cultivates another, how some feelings are defensive and some self-expressive. ... Cool, dessicated [sic] ideology is just as damaging as out-of-control passion (Samuels 1999, 99–100).

Samuels is arguing that therapists are experts on emotion and its relationship with rationality. However, it is by no means clear that a broad group of therapists could agree on these issues – analysts would tend to privilege rationality over feeling, for example, while humanists would tend to do the opposite.

Orbach also exemplifies this second problem with the idea of a campaigning voice for therapists: therapists do not all think the same thing. In her contribution to the interesting collection *Living Together* (Kennard and Small 1997), which seeks to create 'a practical agenda for social change' by asking a range of therapists for their opinions,[15] Orbach proposes a spot of social engineering to eradicate 'the emotional illiteracy which bedevils our culture' (Orbach 1997, 30). Since she believes firmly, like most but not all therapists and counsellors, that psychological problems are caused by childhood difficulties, this is her chosen arena for intervention.

> We need to extend the useful information parents get about changing nappies or preparing for labour with an emotional primer about parenting. If we were to create a policy document about preparation for parenting, we could make extensive recommendations for what kinds of practices area health authorities should institute ranging from emotional preparation for the baby, what the baby's emotional needs are. ... (Ibid., 31)

Two questions immediately arise: who are 'we'? and what *are* a baby's 'emotional needs'? The vision of a committee of psychotherapists from even the smallest range of approaches trying to agree on an answer to this second question is terrifying. If therapists have an expertise, it is not of this sort.

PCSR functions very energetically and usefully as a forum for therapists and counsellors to *discuss* social and political issues. (There seems so far to be a lot less energy for the other main aim of the organization, to look at the politics of the profession.) But when it has tried to position itself as a political voice for psychotherapists as a group, the result has been largely bathetic – as when it wrote offering its support for the Northern Ireland Peace Process. As Calvin Coolidge said, we are all against sin; but beyond that, what evidence is there that therapists have a united view of any political issue at all?

THERAPISTS AND ANALYSTS AGAINST THE BOMB

One issue which might be a candidate for such a united view is the Bomb. Campaigning against nuclear war has always tended to occupy a unique place in psycho-politics. Therapists who would not usually consider political participation, because of the effect on their clients of knowing about their analyst's views (Greenacre 1954, 682–3), have made an exception for anti-nuclear work. In 1980 the International Psychoanalytic Association itself passed a 'Resolution Against Nuclear War' which had already been adopted by American and global psychiatric organizations. Of those present 60 voted in favour, 6 against, with 18 abstentions (Laufer 1982, 111; this does of course show that at least six analysts were *not* united with the majority in their views on deterrence).

The association rejected the idea of a resolution against war in general, proposed on the grounds that 'analysts are pacifists, aligned on the side of reason and against death, against all wounds, not only narcissistic wounds, and we must be prepared to take these principles outside of the confines of our analytic practice' (ibid., 110); but agreed to add a somewhat bland clause arguing that 'as psychoanalysts we have something special to contribute: a statement that we all have a tendency to deny painful realities' (ibid.). Wallerstein summed up the mood of the meeting:

> if there is ever a nuclear war, there would no longer exist the possibility for psycho-analysis to be practised again; ... it was essential to give this the highest priority, to join with other scientific organizations in expressing our feelings on this issue. It has an humanitarian objective that has an overriding importance. (Ibid.)

Of course, passing a resolution is one thing; taking action is another. However, a number of analysts and other therapists have acted directly on the nuclear issue, at least to the extent of holding meetings and circulating petitions. Over 130 out of 400 members of the British Psychoanalytical Society formed a group called Psychoanalysts for the Prevention of Nuclear War (Temperley 1989, 259). According to Jane Temperley, 'One of the few things that [this] has actually achieved is that those of us who have undertaken to give papers have actually bothered to inform ourselves of some of the facts' (ibid., 265).

In 1988 a collection of papers was published in America under the title *Psychoanalysis and the Nuclear Threat: Clinical and Theoretical Studies* (Levine et al. 1988);

its editors suggested that while ordinarily analysts might treat politics as irrelevant to the analytic space,

> we raise the possibility here that the potential of nuclear weapons for destroying the world intrudes into the safety of that space. ... Thus, the construction of a socially, culturally, and politically neutral analytic setting may be a fantasy, one that embodies the wish that the outside can be ignored, denied, or wished away. (quoted in Samuels 1993, 52)

It is not obvious why nuclear war should be the single exception to the rule of analytic neutrality. Even granted that it may be the largest single threat to existence which we face (and there are other candidates), why does scale make the difference? In Chapter 12 below we shall look at Janine Puget's powerful portrayal of the destruction of the 'neutral' analytic space under the Argentinian junta. As Samuels suggests – and many of the therapists who responded to an international survey which he organized agree – there are many political issues which can appropriately be allowed into the consulting room (Samuels 1993, 209–66).

DESPAIR AND EMPOWERMENT

Although therapists have organized against nuclear war, they have not gone very far in trying to understand the causes of the threat, speaking in general terms of the 'death instinct' and the 'paranoid-schizoid position' (e.g. Temperley 1989, 261–4). Nor has much been said about the psychological factors that inhibit people from taking action in the face of nuclear and ecological threats; it has fallen largely to non-therapists to try to think about this. Out of such thinking has grown one of the most remarkable examples of psycho-politics, the Despair and Empowerment movement. Its *locus classicus* is Joanna Macey's book *Despair and Personal Power in the Nuclear Age*, where she speaks of 'the psychological and spiritual work of dealing with our knowledge and feelings about the present planetary crisis in ways that release energy and vision for creative response' (Macey 1983, xiii).

The theory of despair and empowerment work is that the 'natural, normal and widespread feelings of distress' created by nuclear and ecological threats are largely suppressed through 'fear of pain' and 'social taboos against expressions of despair'.

> This repression tends to paralyze; it builds a sense of isolation and powerlessness. Furthermore, it fosters resistance to painful, but essential information. ... Information by itself can increase resistance, deepening the sense of apathy and powerlessness. We need to help each other process this information on an affective level. (Ibid.)

Most of the book, therefore, consists of exercises and guided meditations to assist this emotional processing, facilitating the descent into despair, followed by a rising sense of capacity to affect the situation positively, which Macey sees as a natural trajectory of empowerment – an 'alchemy' (ibid., 18) which has reliably been experienced by thousands of participants in workshops since 1979.

She emphasizes that the work is not simply about catharsis, about 'walk[ing] away purged of pain for our world' (ibid., 23). According to her, 'catharsis occurs – and something more than catharsis. That is because this distress reflects concerns that extend beyond our separate selves.... It is a testimony to our interconnectedness' (ibid.). This reflects the Buddhism which is an important source of Macey's work, and of the work of the Interhelp organization which offers despair and empowerment workshops around the world. Another source, though, is psychotherapy; in fact, several Interhelp activists (Carol Wolman, Hogie Wyckoff) were part of Radical Therapy in the 1970s. Macey's book includes a section on despair and empowerment work for counsellors and therapists, which looks at the reasons why practitioners may be unwilling to focus on these issues. She quotes psychotherapist Linda Monko:

> our professional training and theoretical foundations often do not prepare us for, nor support our interest in, dealing with global issues with clients. ... the ability to remain at a distance, to separate our clients' issues from our own, is a well recognized standard for therapeutic practice. However, the world is not just our clients' environment, but ours, also. (Ibid., 60–1)

Macey suggests that practitioners can appropriately respond to these concerns in their clients, and offers ideas about how to do so: validate distress about the world; encourage clients to talk about it (they may expect us to treat it as 'irrelevant'); 'counter fatalism' and do not support clients in using fear for the future as an excuse for self-destructive behaviour; and encourage an assertive response to these issues (ibid., 62–4). She also suggests that working in this area involves a re-evaluation of both the practitioner role and the client role:

> Far from being typecast as the fixer who 'makes everything all right', or as the oracle who 'has all the answers', the counselor emerges as a guide who accompanies. ...[T]he client also appears in a new perspective. Instead of a case to be solved or a person to be mended, he or she emerges as a fellow-journeyer.... (Ibid., 64)

ECOPSYCHOLOGY

Despair and empowerment work, then, goes beyond simply enlisting the prestige of psychotherapy in anti-nuclear and ecological campaigns: it is a psychologically informed method for liberating energy for such action. 'Ecopsychology' has tried to go one step further: to produce *new* psychological conceptualizations which might help us specifically to understand and to counter what Ralph Metzner calls 'the ecologically disastrous split – the pathological alienation – between human consciousness and the rest of the biosphere' (Metzner 1995, 55). In doing so, the ecopsychology movement (or 'psychoecology', 'eco-therapy', 'global therapy', etc: Roszak et al. 1995, 4) is taking up the project to which Freud referred in *Civilisation and Its Discontents*:

> May we not be justified in reaching the diagnosis that ... some civilisations, or some epochs of civilisation – possibly the whole of mankind – have become 'neurotic'? An analytic dissection of such neuroses might lead to therapeutic recommendations which could lay claim to great practical interest. (Freud 1930, 338)

Or as Metzner puts it,

> the purpose of such diagnostic speculations is ... to discern the nature of the psychological disturbance that has *Homo sapiens* in its grip, so that we can apply psychotherapeutic techniques and treatments to the amelioration of the present eco-catastrophe. (Metzner 1995, 56)

As Metzner recognizes, these 'diagnostic speculations' can only be 'psychopathological metaphors' (ibid.); and several different therapeutic diagnoses have been applied to the human destruction of nature, ranging from 'autism' (Berry 1988) and 'narcissism' (Kanner and Gomes 1995) through 'techno-addiction' (LaChapelle 1988, Glendinning 1995) and 're-traumatization' (Glendinning 1994, 1995) to 'dissociative disorder' (Metzner 1995). It will be apparent that these diagnoses are a pot-pourri of the most fashionable clinical entities of the late 20th century! – which does not make them any the less useful or relevant. Certainly the concept of traumatic dissociation seems highly relevant to our capacity for ignoring the environmental degradation all around us. There is a strong argument that much of the world's population must *always* have suffered from what is currently identified as 'post-traumatic stress disorder', and that this must necessarily have impacted on culture.

However, these remain diagnostic *metaphors*, pulled off the clinical peg and applied to a drastically different milieu. Shepard (1995) offers an original and much more deeply worked out diagnosis of what we might call 'eco-pathology': he suggests that we suffer from an 'ontogenetic crippling' which originated in the Neolithic adoption of agriculture. The civilizations which developed from this point no longer fitted what Shepard portrays as biologically programmed human adulthood, a 'normal ontogeny' suited to the slow, constant rhythms of hunter-gatherer culture, and embedded in the natural world; it was replaced by a sort of neoteny, a premature 'adulthood' which fixates us in infantile and adolescent patterns of feeling and behaviour.

In post-agricultural societies, Shepard argues,

> the persistence of certain infantile qualities might help the individual adapt better: fear of separation, fantasies of omnipotence, oral preoccupation, tremors of helplessness, and bodily incompetence and dependence. Biological evolution ... works much too slowly to make adjustments in our species. ... Programmed for slow development towards a special kind of sagacity, we live in a world where that humility and tender sense of human limitation is no longer rewarded. (Shepard 1995, 31)

These various diagnoses necessarily imply goals of ecologically healthy psychological states; and much ecopsychology writing consists of statements about what this health might look like, feel like – and, to some extent, how we might get there. Unsurprisingly, this is the least developed element, since – as with all psycho-politics – it is far and away the hardest. However, some therapists are placing their work with individuals in a wider global context, believing that this is affecting the client's personal experience even if they are unaware of it. Sometimes this happens in a challenging way: 'I have even, upon occasion, interrupted a client's obsessive, self-absorbed soliloquy with, 'Are you aware that the planet is dying?' I might interrupt a professional debate on the best therapeutic modality with the same question' (O'Connor 1995, 154). Sometimes it is more clearly supportive in intent:

> when a client ... began to have flashbacks of sexual abuse, I worked at accompanying her in individual sessions into the depth of her pain, while at the same time ... enlarging the context in which she experienced it. The larger context includes the amount of sexual abuse that is being addressed in the culture at present. ... I also include abuse that occurs in a still-larger context ... between men and women, between adults and

children, between humans and animals, and between humans and the Earth. (Conn 1995, 168)

This approach is equivalent to the way in which feminist therapy places individual women's experience in the context of sexism and patriarchy. However – again like feminist therapy – it is open to criticisms of imposing a world-view on vulnerable clients. Beyond that, it incorporates what Andrew Samuels has identified as an 'authoritarianism and depression' within the environmental movement as a whole (Samuels 1993, 103). It is not clear that the ecopsychology movement has seriously investigated the issues of transference, countertransference and projection and how they can contaminate work that includes this aspect of social reality.

Beyond the level of individual work, some ecopsychologists run workshops and seminars, each within their own modality and field of interest, aimed at strengthening the will and self-awareness of human beings seeking to protect the natural world. One striking form of work is 'wilderness therapy', where clients are taken out of the consulting room altogether into a direct confrontation with the natural world (Harper 1995). At best, there is a creative, multidimensional relationship between the capacity of nature to heal the person, and that of the person to heal nature.

Conclusions to Part I

An individual can be said to suffer from repression of political potential if he or she cannot engage with a political theme that, consciously or unconsciously, is exercising that individual. *My clinical experience is that people are already much more engaged politically than they think they are.* (Samuels 1993, 59, original italics)

I want to draw out three themes from the material presented so far. First, to reiterate what has already been said, the fact that a large majority of explicitly political therapists are on the left is partly the reflection of a general cultural truth: conservatism usually presents itself as normal, natural and central. One feature of radicalism is that it 'politicizes' reality, while conservatism depoliticizes it: one disagreement between the two positions is precisely over how much of our world is political.

Phyllis Greenacre states very clearly the traditional psychoanalytic view on therapists' involvement in politics.

The need to avoid violation of the transference field by the establishment of other avenues of relationship with the patient demands a high degree of restraint and sacrifice on the part of the analyst. It demands, among other things, the sacrifice on the part of the analyst of conspicuous public participation even in very worthy social and political 'causes' to which he may lend his name or his activities. (Greenacre 1954, 681–2)

This view depends, though, on the idea that the 'political' and the 'personal' can be safely demarcated. It embodies a sense of what politics is, and of the private individual as in some sense insulated from it, which is deeply conservative.

The many therapists who remain silent about politics in their work and in their theory can therefore reasonably be characterized as taking a conservative political stance. It remains true, however, that few psychotherapists align themselves publicly with the radical right, with fascism or other such movements. Jung was a temporary exception, who later changed his mind; Radovan Karadjic, the psychiatrist leader of the Bosnian Serbs, is a permanent one. A few more minor figures will be mentioned at various points in this book.

Interestingly – and this is my second point – psychotherapy itself has contributed to the redefinition of the 'personal' as 'political', and the deconstruction of 'normality'. These political concepts arose out of a complex interaction in the 1960s and 1970s between feminism, the counter-culture, and psychotherapy, where it would be hard to specify the precise source of any particular idea. We shall see in Part Two how some of the central theories of psychotherapy were fertile ground for 'the personal as political'; just as we have seen in Part One how this equation has been expressed in practice.

The third theme I want to identify is the repeated importance for psychopolitics of *group* therapy. Many of the leftist therapists discussed here are concerned with how to make therapy available on a mass level. From a socialist or communist point of view, psychotherapy, whatever its integral value, is deeply compromised by its *mode of production and distribution*: historically, and frequently still in the present, psychotherapy is available mainly on a private basis, at a price which puts it out of the reach of many people. Partly for this reason, and partly to counter what is seen as a more fundamentally 'individualist', asocial tendency in therapy – to bring in the social factor directly – many left therapists have focused on group therapy in their work.

In the next section, we move on from the practical *political* involvement of many therapists to look at the *theoretical* involvement of psychotherapy in trying to shed light on traditionally political issues such as oppression, aggression, prejudice and exploitation.

Part II
Psychotherapy of Politics

8

Culture on the Couch

From Freud onwards, psychotherapy has frequently seen it as part of its job to diagnose the ills of culture at large. Conversely, some forms of therapy have offered either explicit or implicit *support* to conventional values – and hence have diagnosed new rebellious trends as pathological in nature. As we shall see, there is no fixed aspect to psychotherapy's view of society; except, perhaps, its belief in its own expertise on the topic.

CIVILIZATION AND REPRESSION

Freud was a widely educated man, who originally wanted to be a philosopher (Gay 1995, 118–19); he always related his psychological studies to a broad view of human nature and human culture. As psychoanalysis became more established Freud spoke publicly from the position of expert on the nature of civilization. His essentially unaltering view was that civilization depends upon the renunciation and repression of the sexual drive, and the institution of sexual guilt. His sense of the painfulness this entails is acute.

> [T]he choice of an object is restricted to the opposite sex, and most extra-genital satisfactions are forbidden as perversions. The requirement ... that there shall be a single kind of sexual life for everyone ... cuts off a fair number of them from sexual enjoyment, and so becomes the source of serious injustice. ... [H]eterosexual genital love, which has remained exempt from outlawry, is itself restricted by further limitations, in the shape of insistence upon legitimacy and monogamy. Present-day civilization makes it plain that ... it does not like sexuality as a source of pleasure in its own right, and is only prepared to tolerate it because there is so far no substitute for it as a means of propagating the human race. (Freud 1930, 294)[16]

Freud's intention is 'to show that the price we pay for our advance in civilization is a loss of happiness through the heightening of the sense of guilt' (ibid., 327). '[T]he sense of guilt is an expression ... of the eternal struggle between Eros and the instinct of destruction or death. This conflict is set going as soon as men are faced with the task of living together' (ibid., 325). The *form* of this guilt, though – its relation to sexuality – in Freud's view depends on social arrangements. 'So long as the community assumes no other form than that of the family, the conflict is bound to express itself in the Oedipus complex, to establish the conscience and to create the first sense of guilt' (ibid.). In some ways this is a technical point, since Freud does not really envisage the possibility of any other form of community. However, *Civilisation and its Discontents* is based on a serious desire and hope to modify, though not to erase, the negative effects of civilization upon human beings.

> This struggle between the individual and society is ... a dispute within the economics of the libido ... and it does admit of an eventual accommodation in the individual, as, it may be hoped, it will also do in the future of civilization, however much that civilization may oppress the life of the individual today. (Ibid., 335)

Civilizations, in other words, vary in the extent of the damage they do to individual happiness. Civilizations themselves can become damaged, and in need of healing.

> May we not be justified in reaching the diagnosis that ... some civilizations, or some epochs of civilization – possibly the whole of mankind – have become 'neurotic'? An analytic dissection of such neuroses might lead to therapeutic recommendations which could lay claim to great practical interest. ... But we should have to be very cautious. ... [W]hat would be the use of the most correct analysis of social neuroses, since no one possesses authority to impose such a therapy upon the group? (Ibid., 338)

As an example of cultural neurosis, Freud suggests religion, 'the universal obsessional neurosis of humanity', which 'like the obsessional neurosis of childhood ... arose out of the Oedipus complex, out of the relation to the father' (Freud 1927, 226). He also suggests that ethics is a form of 'culture therapy' aimed at controlling aggression. 'Ethics is thus to be regarded as a therapeutic attempt – as an endeavour to achieve, by means of a command of the super-ego, something which has so far not been achieved by means of any other cultural activities' (Freud 1930, 336).

Freud sets up some of the thorniest problems for psycho-politics. Are human beings innately aggressive – and if so, can anything be done about it? Is civilization intrinsically oppressive, drawing its motive energy from the suppression of pleasure and sexuality; and if so, can the *degree* of this oppression vary (so that there is something worth fighting for)? And is there any sense in talking about mass therapy, or are we restricted to what can be achieved with individuals, perhaps within a very negative environment? We shall see that other theorists sometimes give answers very different from Freud's.

THE RETURN OF THE REPRESSED

The position outlined above – an incisive description of the misery caused by sexual repression, together with some mild hopes for its amelioration – is as far as Freud was prepared to go along the path of social activism. Others, however, have taken a practical stance, and argued that some or all sexual repression is *not* necessary to civilization, and should in fact be removed. The most important of these is Wilhelm Reich, who – partly because of this – was expelled from and ceased to identify with psychoanalysis; we shall look at Reich's work in the next section. Apart from Reich, the radical aspect of Freud's sexual thinking was mainly taken up by theoreticians who were not themselves therapists: Norman O. Brown, and Herbert Marcuse. Although this book is focused on *practitioners*, we need to look at their influential work (which nonetheless had strikingly little influence on practitioners).

In *Life Against Death*, written in the late 1950s, Norman O. Brown explicitly positions himself as continuing and developing Freud's own theories.

> Freud never faced fully the existential and theoretical consequences of taking what I call the general neurosis of mankind ... as the central problem. Nor could he see any way of defining the conditions under which mankind would be cured of its general neurosis... (Brown 1968, 12–13)

However Brown himself spends most of his energies on describing this 'central problem', and his perception that '[t]he whole world may be against it, but still man [*sic*] holds fast to the deep-rooted, passionate striving for a positive fulfilment of happiness' (ibid., 20). Freud would certainly agree with this picture of things; however, he did not believe that there was any way in which human 'polymorphous perversity' – the desire to engage sexually with a whole range of organs, orifices and partners – could be satisfied within civilization. Brown refuses to accept this limitation.

Only in the last (and easily the shortest) part of the book, though, entitled 'The Way Out' (ibid., 267–81), does Brown try to move from diagnosis to treatment. However, he finds little with which to bridge the gulf between the current state of affairs and his vision of an 'abolition of repression' which

> would abolish the unnatural concentrations of libido in certain particular bodily organs – concentrations engineered by the morbidity of the negative death instinct, and constituting the bodily base of the neurotic character disorders in the human ego. ... The human body would become polymorphously perverse, delighting in that full life of the body which it now fears. (Ibid., 270)

Yes, Dr Brown, but *how*? Brown has few suggestions for praxis which in any way measure up to the scope of the task – merely some remarks about the role of the dialectical method in contemporary theory! However, he does not try to conceal the utopian nature of his vision; pointing out, quite reasonably, that 'today even the survival of humanity is a utopian hope' (ibid., 267).

Brown accurately describes Herbert Marcuse's *Eros and Civilisation* (1955) as 'the first book, after Wilhelm Reich's ill-fated adventures, to reopen the possibility of the abolition of repression' (ibid., 14). Marcuse, who wants to bring together Marxist and Freudian ideas into a single critical theory of culture, underpins his position with a concrete conception of how repression can *vary* between civilizations. 'The return of the repressed makes up the tabooed and subterranean history of civilization' (Marcuse 1955, 16). As Freud says, repression results from the victory of the 'reality principle' over the 'pleasure principle'; but Marcuse argues that there is no single, universal reality principle – different cultures recognize different 'realities'.

Therefore, although all civilizations have some repression, the kind and amount of it vary according to which reality principle is recognized. In advanced capitalism, this is the 'performance principle', a system of domination according to economic performance, which generates *surplus repression* (over and above the 'basic repression' present in all societies), and hence *alienation*. Sexuality itself is organized according to the performance principle and its hierarchical centralization – leading to the concentration of all libido into genitality, and of all partial objects into a single object, so that penetrative intercourse appears as the prime sexual activity.

This account clearly opens up at least the theoretical possibility of revolutionary change, in that it identifies an oppressed element which may be motivated to rebel. And this is Marcuse's primary interest in Freudian theory – as a way of moving beyond the impasse of Marxism in advanced capitalism, where the supposedly 'revolutionary' industrial working class shows little interest in the role assigned to it. Why is there no revolution, and where could we look for it? Marcuse answers both questions with his concept of 'repressive desublimation' – the substitution of alienated, performative sex for real sexual satisfaction. The one aspect of human existence left untouched by alienation is 'phantasy', which sustains our allegiance to a free, polymorphous sexuality outside the reality principle. In a magnificent expropriation, Marcuse plunders clinical psychoanalytic theory for concepts which he applies to revolutionary critical thought.

From the side of psychotherapy, both Marcuse and Brown can be criticized for adopting technical terms which they lack the clinical experience to understand, and treating them as if they were philosophical concepts. From the side of politics, too, they can both be seen as abstract dreamers, putting forward a vision of universal carnival without recognizing the recalcitrance of concrete social relations (cf. Frosh, 1987, 160). Perhaps the reality is that both are actually *anarchists*, rather than socialists: from the anarchist perspective it is entirely appropriate to maintain that, in the absence of repression, human beings will act wisely and cooperatively, and to trust them to solve their own problems. However, this does leave an enormous gap in any programme for social transformation – one that can only be plugged with splendid rhetoric which boils down to 'it will be all right on the night'.

SOCIETY AND EMOTIONAL STRUCTURE

In the 1930s, Wilhelm Reich also attempted to create the theoretical basis for a 'Freudian-Marxist' analysis of social formations. One of his basic tools was his theory of character: a view of human development which dialectically unites the two great opposite poles of analytic thinking – the biologically based drives or 'instincts',[17] and human object relations together with their social context. Different schools of analysis have placed different emphases on these two poles, and this has a direct effect on political perspectives – if the drives, which are innate and 'hardwired', are the dominant force determining human behaviour, then little can be changed, much must be accepted.

From the 'drive' point of view, repression is viewed as primarily an *internal* struggle between our desire for pleasure represented by the id, and the 'reality principle' as represented by ego and super-ego. For some, like Anna Freud, there are even more fundamental repressive forces at work:

There is in human nature a disposition to repudiate certain instincts, in particular the sexual instincts, indiscriminately and independently of individual experience. This disposition appears to be ... a kind of deposit accumulated from acts of repression practised by many generations.... (A. Freud 1946, 171)

Reich places himself firmly in the opposite camp, asserting that

[t]he psychic process reveals itself as the result of the conflict between drive demand and the external frustration of this demand. Only secondarily does an inner conflict between desire and self-denial result from this initial opposition. ... The question of why society demands the suppression and repression of drives can no longer be answered psychologically. There are social, more correctly, economic interests that cause such suppressions and repressions in certain eras. (Reich 1972a, 287)

Reich's concept of character is that it embodies – quite literally – the ways in which the unfolding of libidinal drive during child development encounters and is shaped or misshaped by the specific demands of culture (Totton 1998, 184–7). Reich concludes that '*the character structure is the congealed sociological process of a given epoch*' (1972a, xxvi, original italics) – in other words, it expresses the end effect of social forces on individual development, the ways in which society forms human beings through its interventions in our attempts to satisfy our 'instincts'.

For Reich, 'every social organization produces those character structures which it needs to exist' (ibid., xxii); and in works such as *The Mass Psychology of Fascism* (Reich 1975a) he tries to show how the needs of the dominant class are mediated through the family to create a pliable and obedient individual character structure – and one which is confined within familial limits.

Authoritarian society's fight against the sexuality of children and adolescents, and the consequent struggle in one's own ego, takes place within the framework of the authoritarian family, which has thus far proven to be the best institution to carry out this fight successfully. Sexual desires naturally urge a person to enter into all kinds of relations with the world, to enter into close contact with it in a vast variety of forms. ... Sexual inhibition is the basis of the familial encapsulation of the individual, as well as the basis of individual self-consciousness. (Reich 1975a, 90)

The repression of sexuality is universal in our culture because it is the only way in which people can be made weak enough and manageable enough for the needs of capitalism.

Reich argues that while 'normal' authoritarian culture depends upon the family instilling a rigid, inhibited and repressed character structure, fascism itself appeals to the impulses which are held *below* that tight armour of musculature and character attitudes, and which curdle into hate and destruction.

The surface layer of social co-operation is not in contact with the deep biological core of one's selfhood; it is borne by a second, an intermediate character layer, which consists exclusively of cruel, sadistic, lascivious, rapacious and envious impulses. ... If one penetrates through this second layer ... one always discovers the third, deepest layer. ... In this core, under favourable conditions, man is an essentially honest, industrious, cooperative, loving, and, if motivated, rationally hating animal.... (Reich 1975a, 13–14)

This is one of Reich's deepest disagreements with orthodox Freudian analysis: his insistence that human beings are 'naturally' loving, decent and rational (although for Reich stripping away the civilized facade will initially reveal not 'natural sociality' but 'the perverse, sadistic character layer': ibid.). Unlike the fundamentally pessimistic Freud, Reich believes that there is a realistic hope both for individual happiness, and for social arrangements which are not fundamentally oppressive. Like Brown and Marcuse, he bases this position on the project of dissolving neurotic character structure (and unlike them he has very clear and radical *clinical* ideas about how to do this). However his goal is not a regressive liberation of 'polymorphous perversity', but its exact opposite: the attainment of what psychoanalysis understands as the culmination of 'normal' child development, and what becomes for Reich the Holy Grail: 'genitality'.

We shall look again at Reich's Freudo-Marxism in the next chapter; but now I want to outline Reich's social views in the later period of his life – contemporary with Brown and Marcuse – when he had rejected both Marxism and psychoanalysis. Reich maintains his basic vision of the human character structure as a compromise created between the individual's innate drive for pleasure and satisfaction, and society's requirement that we be willing to alienate our labour. He continues to see a fundamental conflict between human nature and its current social context: 'The living, in its social and human interrelationships, is naïvely kindly and thus, under prevailing conditions, endangered' (Reich 1975b, 8).

What increasingly dominates Reich's thinking, however, is a bitter frustration at the apparent impossibility of changing anything, since he believes character structure prevents people from accepting or creating such change.

> Wherever we turn we find man [*sic*] running around in circles as if trapped. ... *It IS possible to get out of the trap.* However, in order to break out of prison, one must first confess to *being in a prison. The trap is man's emotional structure, his character structure.* (Reich 1975b, 3, original italics)

In this later period Reich moves away from critical thought, or even political argument, into visionary rhetoric. In often beautiful passages, he asserts over and over again the difference between what is and what could be, and repeats his own creed:

> The bio-energetic core of life and its cosmic meaning is the orgasm function, i.e., the involuntary convulsion of the total living organism during the embrace of male and female at the discharge of the bio-energy into each other. (Ibid., 25)

Reich is still maintaining the central idea which he found in psychoanalysis nearly 40 years earlier: that sex is pure and good, and that the obstruction of sexual energy is what prevents human beings from maintaining their natural goodness.

What stultifies Reich's thinking, though, is precisely his unqualified assertion of human natural goodness and decency. If we are *simply* good, what has gone wrong? How can it be that we find ourselves in such an oppressive society? Reich is excellent at describing the *means* whereby, generation by generation, the undamaged child is turned into the damaged and damaging adult. But he has nothing to say about the *motor* of this process – which must, presumably, be external to the psyche.

SPLITTING AND REPARATION

Melanie Klein herself had little concern with politics, but she created some theoretical tools which are well-adapted to political analysis. Many later writers have used concepts such as projection, introjection, projective identification, splitting and reparation, to describe and criticize how our society functions.

Klein stands at the opposite end of the psychoanalytic spectrum from Reich, emphasizing not our innate goodness, but our innate destructiveness and envy.

> Ironically, it can be argued that this theory's focus on inborn negativity and what appears to be its neglect of the 'real' environment ... enables it to proffer some new insights into the penetration of individuality by social construction processes. (Frosh 1987, 114)

This happens through the Kleinian concept of 'objects': the elements which populate the infant's internal world of 'phantasy', and which we each struggle over time to bring into some relationship with the beings 'out there' in the external world. Initially, the objects of our love and our hate respectively are experienced as wholly distinct: in other words, the mother's breast, for example, is split in our phantasy into a 'good breast' which we love and a 'bad breast' which we hate. Much of growing up is the work of recognizing and overcoming this kind of split, and undertaking 'reparation' for our destructive impulses (Klein 1975, 33).

Klein thus speaks of an 'innate conflict' between love and hate (1975, 180) – her version of Freud's late concept of a struggle between libido and the death drive (Freud 1920), which many analysts opposed or ignored. However, she seems also to perceive an innate tendency towards integration and reparation. Kleinian theory

> begins with the concept of a contradictory being, split in its essence as well as in all its relationships, and traces the manner in which integrity can be achieved. As such, it directs interest towards the specific kinds of social relationship that may be organized for full reparation to take place. (Frosh 1987, 128)

Klein's own interest did not move in this direction, staying with the actual therapeutic task; but many writers influenced by Klein have considered these socio-political possibilities. Some of these we either will meet or have already met elsewhere in this book. We shall also meet the 'psychohistorical' work of Lloyd deMause, which uses core Kleinian concepts to construct a theory of society and historical social change centred on child-rearing practice.

SOCIAL ADAPTATION

At different points in its development psychoanalysis has appeared – and has in fact been - mainly radical, liberal, or conservative in its political implications. I suggest that it responds to two factors: the overall political atmosphere of society, and the degree of acceptability and power of psychoanalysis in society. One of the most conservative periods for analytic theory and practice was in the United States in the 1940s, 1950s and early 1960s, when psychoanalysis occupied a central position within a highly conservative social framework. The theoretical approach which developed in this climate was known as 'ego psychology'.

Heinz Hartmann, the leading figure in ego psychology, places *adaptation* at the centre of his picture of normal and desirable human development (Hartmann 1939a). Following Anna Freud, Hartmann 'forced psychoanalysis to move away from an overweening interest in the unconscious and in neurosis' (Levitt and Rubenstein 1974, 328), and re-centred it on the previously de-centred ego, as mediator between desire (the id) and reality (the external world - but also, for Hartmann, the super-ego). The 'well-adapted' ego accepts reality for what it is, and submits to its requirements – not only practical ones, but also moral ones: as Hartmann puts it, the healthy ego 'must be able to must', to force itself to obey society's demands (Hartmann 1939a, 93).

It is not surprising, then, that Hartmann is 'sceptical of the importance of knowledge' (Levitt and Rubenstein 1974, 328), and has a 'lack of concern with happiness as a social value' (ibid., 332). Happiness is deeply bound up with pleasure and the satisfaction of desire, as Freud would be the first to agree; while knowledge of social reality (Marx comes to mind here) does tend to interfere with its unquestioning acceptance. Thus ego psychology does not primarily offer tools for social analysis: it represents a social class at peace with itself, which largely identifies 'the way things are' with 'the way things should be', and locates problems in the dissatisfied rather than in the object of their dissatisfaction.

Hartmann develops Freud's ideas in precisely the opposite direction from Marcuse and Brown. He describes as normal and appropriate 'a modification ... or perhaps ... a partial domestication of the pleasure principle', whereby it 'comes partly under the control' of the ego and the superego (Hartmann 1956, 37). While the philosopher Marcuse and the classicist Brown develop Freud's radical implications, American clinicians take Freud back to the centre – which, in this time and place, is a centre very much to the right.

Ego psychology had an enormous influence on American cultural values in the time of its ascendancy; or rather, perhaps, it became a primary way in which traditional American values were expressed. 'Maladjusted' as a common description of nonconformity is a well-known example. Just *how* conservative ego psychology is in practice varies depending on who uses it: the concept of adaptation is based on a yardstick of 'average expectable' environmental situations to which one should be able to adapt. Hartmann accepted that 'the processes of adaptation are always appropriate only to a limited range of environmental conditions', and that 'the nature of the environment may be such that a pathological development of the psyche offers a more satisfactory solution than would a normal one' – for instance in Nazi Germany (Hartmann 1939b, 319). But who decides which societies are sufficiently 'averagely expectable' – or more simply, 'normal' – for adjustment to them to be seen as healthy?

One directly political application of Hartmann's thinking is Levitt and Rubinstein 1974, where the authors pose the question, 'is the behaviour of the counter-culture an adaptive or a maladaptive expression, i.e. is it at the service of growth or is it regressive?' 'We will leave for another time', they say in a footnote, 'the political argument that a society beset by violence, population metastases, pollution and political oppression is in itself a maladaptive one, and adjustment, therefore, is an act of poor adaptation' (1974, 326). Although they acknowledge the importance of this argument, they still feel that their question can be answered without reference to it. This is because, although the goals of the counter-culture 'are often the very ones to which many of us are similarly dedicated' (ibid., 334), they are, according to the authors, being approached in an unrealistic way.

> Goals have to be partial goals in a broader complex; hence ultimate ends and absolute goals cannot be considered rational. Most counter-culture aims are ultimate goals; for example, the elimination of technocracy, private property, money and formal institutions of learning. ... [T]he counter-culture view which equates any means with valid ends must be finally seen as irrational. (Ibid., 334–5)

This is clearly a respectable political or philosophical argument, whether or not one agrees with it; but is it a valid *psychotherapeutic* position? Is it not extraordinarily similar to the 'totalitarian', 'politicized' psychiatry of the Soviet Union, which also defined political protest as 'irrational'? (see Chapter 12 below.) Although Levitt and Rubinstein identify as one historical cause of the counter-culture 'a destructive technocracy and an impersonal governmental model which have created a deep-seated social crisis' (ibid., 336), they still diagnose the counter-culture as suffering from a range of psychological problems including its 'superego which is slanted towards a narcissistic ego ideal', the fact that it 'views ... feelings as central and values them over intellect', its 'emphasis upon oral and anal rather than genital achievements',[18] and the way that it 'often operates upon the pleasure principle'. In consequence, 'it must be concluded that counter-culture behaviour is maladaptive' (ibid.).

This view is possible because of Hartmann's biologistic presentation of adaptation: that human beings are *innately programmed* to adjust to the social environment (Frosh 1987, 91–2). If this is so, then a failure – or refusal – to do so can be seen as a failure of *health*. Kovel (1988, xcii) identifies this as the remedicalization of psychoanalysis, 'binding Freud into the ways of mainstream academic and medical discourse'. Oddly, at the same time that the political sphere is being biologized, all psychic activity beyond the ego is identified as 'subcortical, "animal" instinct' (ibid., xcv). Kovel characterizes ego psychology as representing the 're-Cartesianizing' of psychoanalysis (ibid., xciv): the rational ego of Descartes' 'cogito ergo sum', de-centred by Freud's discovery of the unconscious, comes back to centre stage. Frosh, using a Copernican rather than a Cartesian metaphor, describes how Hartmann's thinking lets the reality principle 'infiltrate the pleasure dome at the centre of the traditional psychoanalytic universe' (Frosh 1987, 91).

It is worth noting that Levitt and Rubinstein are not simply asking in their paper whether individual hippies are well-adapted to our society – they more or less take it for granted that they are not. More ambitiously, they are measuring the adaptiveness *of hippie culture itself* – how well it conforms with 'reality'. In other words, they are trying to forge from Hartmannian theory tools for critical social analysis! There is considerable slippage in the paper between two 'realities': that defined by mainstream society – so that the hippies' demand for the abolition of money, for example, can be termed 'unrealistic', since the mainstream will not accept it; and reality as some sort of transcultural absolute to which the authors have privileged access, and to which mainstream culture itself may be maladopted. As Marcuse argues, there is more than one 'reality principle', and which one is employed depends on political factors.

In his book *Carl Rogers' on Personal Power: Inner Strength and its Revolutionary Impact* (1978), Rogers explains that, having for years denied that person-centred therapy had any political implications, he realized – rather like Molière's invalid – that he had been doing politics all the time. Instead of introducing new material, therefore, in this book he runs through the familiar tenets of person-centred work (see Chapter 17) drawing out their political implications. He begins with a fundamental axiom of humanistic therapy in general:

> From the perspective of politics, power, and control, person-centered therapy is based on a perspective which at first seems risky and uncertain: a view of man [*sic*] as at core a trustworthy organism ... [with] an underlying flow of movement towards constructive fulfilment of its inherent possibilities. (Rogers 1978, 7)

Rogers rightly points out that this is in itself 'a challenging political statement' (ibid., 9). Much politics, both right and left, is based on the assumption that human beings are *not* 'trustworthy organisms', and therefore need surveillance and control. Rogers believes he recognizes, in the counter-cultural upheavals of the 1960s and 1970s, 'new persons' who consciously or unconsciously embody the fundamental values of his therapy. Among other characteristics, they are antipathetic towards 'all highly structured, inflexible, bureaucratic institutions' (ibid., 267). 'New persons' are building a 'new culture', which will have 'a more even distribution of material goods ... minimal structure ... leadership as a temporary, shifting function, based on competence for meeting a specific social need' (ibid., 282).

One can draw out an implicit position on some of the issues we have been considering. For Rogers, clearly, culture is not intrinsically oppressive – but our current one is, in ways suggested by the changes he looks forward to: 'An individual who is attempting to live ... in a person-centered way brings about a politics of family relationships, and marriage or partner relationships, which is drastically different from the traditional model' (ibid., 29). The aspects of society which Rogers' identifies as oppressive (and alterable), then, are family relationships; authoritarian and bureaucratic systems; and uneven distribution of wealth. This leaves open the depth of oppression which Rogers' sees in our culture, and the extent of the changes he envisages – reform or revolution? In a classically American tactic, he appeals to the US Constitution and Bill of Rights as 'decidedly person-centered'.

Gestalt Therapy (Perls et al. 1973) makes an angrier and more robust attack on American society – one of its three authors, Paul Goodman, was an anarchist theoretician. However, the book was first published in the US in 1951, in a very different climate from Rogers in 1978, and with the intention of making Gestalt respectable – so it is not until fairly late in the book that we find this:

> [In America today] there is little physical survival frustration but little satisfaction, and there are signs of acute anxiety. ... It used to be felt that science, technology, and the

new mores would bring on an age of happiness. This hope has been disappointed. Everywhere people are disappointed. ... Even on the surface, then, there is reason to smash things up, to destroy ... the whole system *en bloc*, for it has no further promise.... (Perls et al. 1973, 400–1).

Gestalt thus agrees with Freud, Reich, Marcuse and others that our civilization is basically neurotic. Again like Reich, whom they acknowledge, Perls et al. argue that the frustrations civilization creates lead to 'primary masochism' – the need for release of tension; 'the desire for final satisfaction, for orgasm, is interpreted as the wish for total self-destruction' (ibid., 402). This is projected on to 'the Enemy', and encourages preparation for war, the demonization of Russia which was already apparent. 'People observe the *debâcle* approach. They listen to rational warnings and make all kinds of sensible policies. But the energy to flee or resist is paralysed, or the danger is fascinating' (ibid., 403).

In terms strongly taken up later by the counter-culture, Perls et al. contradict the conventional valuation of 'adult' attitudes as superior to 'childish' ones, criticizing the description of

a 'childish attitude' as something to be transcended, and a 'mature attitude' as a contrasting goal to be achieved. ...[A] neurotic society ... considers many of the most beautiful and useful powers of adulthood, manifested in the most creative persons, to be merely childish. ...[H]abitual deliberateness, factuality, non-commitment, and excessive responsibility, traits of most adults, are neurotic; whereas spontaneity, imagination, earnestness and playfulness, and direct expression of feeling, traits of children, are healthy. (Ibid., 356)

Later Gestalt works (Polster and Polster 1974; Stevens, ed. 1977) continue to see Gestalt as intrinsically political in that it contests social convention:

One way of looking at the human condition is that we are all hypnotized. ... There is the hypnosis of parents, society, authorities, friends, spouses, etc. telling you how you should be. ... Much of gestalt work can be seen as revealing the hypnosis and uncovering the reality beneath the words. (Stevens, ed. 1977, 258)

This resembles the approach of Eric Berne, founder of Transactional Analysis (TA): 'Parents, deliberately or unaware, teach their children from birth how to behave, think, feel and perceive. Liberation from these influences is no easy matter...' (Berne 1967, 161). More recently, however, like many other humanistic approaches, both TA and Gestalt have quietly dropped their heritage of radical social analysis and concentrated on a technical, professional identity. The same is true of Rogerian work: for example, *Person-Centered Therapy: A Revolutionary Paradigm* (Bozarth 1998) restricts its use of 'revolutionary' entirely to the world of psychotherapy. When he finally comes briefly to consider the 'societal impact' of Rogerian therapy (ibid., 187), Bozarth can find *not one single other reference* to offer besides Rogers' 1978 work cited above.

It seems fair to say that the above passages demonstrate humanistic analysis of culture to work at less depth than that of Freud, Jung and Reich. Humanistic therapists have largely been content to describe the oppressive nature of much of Western culture without thinking too deeply about the 'why' and the 'how'. Those humanistic or growth practitioners who have looked for a political theory have been generally content to find it in the work of political theorists, rather than to create it themselves.

9

Psychohistory and the Family

Erik Erikson reminds us that

> students of history continue to ignore the simple facts that all individuals are borne by mothers; that everybody was once a child; that people and peoples begin in their nurseries; and that society consists of individuals in the process of developing from children into parents. (Erikson 1980, 17)

Several theorists have attempted different versions of 'psychohistory' – accounts of social, political and economic events giving a leading role to psychodynamic and psychological factors. Generally, these have centred on exactly the factor which Erikson picks out: the role of the family. As we shall see, however, very similar analyses can be given precisely opposite political 'spins'.

REICH'S MASS PSYCHOLOGY

We have already described Wilhelm Reich's view that 'every social organization produces those character structures which it needs to exist' (Reich 1972a, xxii). This is developed in *The Mass Psychology of Fascism* (Reich 1975a), where Reich tries to show, anticipating the French Marxist theoretician Althusser (1971), how the requirements of the dominant class are mediated through the family to create individual character structure. This leads him to a radical position on basic psychoanalytic categories, regarding *every* element as socio-economically created.

> [T]he family – which is saturated with the ideologies of society, and which, indeed, is the ideological nucleus of society – is … the representative of society as a whole … the Oedipus complex, like everything else, depends ultimately on the economic structure of society. More, the fact itself that an Oedipus complex occurs at all must be ascribed to the socially determined structures of the family. (Reich 1972c, 26)

The function of character for authoritarian societies, according to Reich, is to enable the control of the individual, by repressing the sexual energy which is the source of *all* energy. Repressed, neurotic characters are more biddable, less rebellious, less aspiring: Reich reports that when he began analysing working people, he quickly noticed that the more effective the analysis, the more likely they were to leave unsatisfying jobs or relationships (Reich 1983, 176–7).

The 'anal' character is the quintessentially *armoured* and *repressed* character, hence the first character type to be identified and described: anality, organized around sphincter tension, is the hallmark of the 'spastic ego' (Totton and Edmondson 1988, 17), the binding of energy into defence and alienation from one's own impulses and needs – the model, in a sense, for all character structures. 'The muscular pushing back and holding back of faeces', Reich says, is 'the prototype for repression in general' (1972a, 342). And from the beginning (Freud 1908b), analytic theory has aligned anality with capitalism: a theory developed to its furthest extent by Norman O. Brown, as we shall see below. As with other character structures, the anal character is clearly the product of *family life*, specifically of harsh and premature toilet training (paralleled by similar treatment in other spheres) which fixates the individual in a psychological style of self-restraint and mental and bodily rigidity. Qualities which are often strong in anal characters include neatness, reliability, orderliness, responsibility, predictability, obedience – all valuable traits for the workforce of capitalism. Thus the family transmits desirable qualities – desirable for the dominant social order – in the form of neurotic repression.

However, the concept of the family as the mechanism whereby society's values are installed in us is not *inherently* a radical/critical one. The analyst Thomas Lidz, for example, uses the same notions in a deeply conservative way, calling the family 'the most pervasive and consistent influence that establishes patterns that later forces can modify but never alter completely' (Lidz 1964, 20), and saying that society depends on the family to transmit its values to the child (ibid., 19–21) – but heartily approving of this process, and arguing only that it should operate more effectively to help the child learn 'about hierarchical systems of authority ... the role of father and mother, husband and wife, man and woman, boy and girl' (ibid., 43). By contrast, Poster makes the identical point: 'the family is thus the place where psychic structure is formed and where experience is characterised in the first instance by emotional patterns ... it generates and embodies hierarchies of age and sex' (Poster 1978, 144) – yet treats this as a *critical* view of the family.

Poster also argues that Reich failed in his project of uniting psychoanalysis and Marxism, since he could not successfully derive socio-economic reality from child-rearing patterns. 'Reich was not able to explain class difference in psychological terms because he did not properly define the structural categories of the family' (Poster 1978, 52). Reich can also be accused of an over-simplified, purely negative view of the family, underestimating its role as a locus of support, a sanctuary from capitalism: as Jacoby says in criticism of the 1970s Radical Therapy movement, the family 'is accepted as the *cause* of social oppression and not also its *victim*' (Jacoby 1977, 133, my italics).

THE NIGHTMARES OF CIVILIZATION

Life Against Death (Brown 1968) is subtitled 'The Psychoanalytic Meaning of History'. Brown introduces himself as

> concerned with reshaping psychoanalysis into a wider general theory of human nature, culture, and history, to be appropriated by the consciousness of mankind as a whole as a new stage in the historical process of man's [*sic*] coming to know himself. (1970, 12).

In other words, Brown's project (like Reich's) is about *making* history, not just writing it; even though, as we shall see, he has virtually nothing to offer by way of a political programme.

Brown echoes Freud in seeing 'the central problem confronting both psychoanalysis and history' as that of defining cultural health (ibid., 25). If culture and neurosis have a clear relationship, as Freud says in *Civilisation and its Discontents*, then can there be such a thing as a non-neurotic culture? Freud doubts it; but for Brown, 'psychoanalysis offers ... a way out of the human neurosis, a way out of history'. His book, although completely reliant on Freud's theories, is also a sustained argument with Freud's pessimism, claiming that what Freud describes as inevitable is in fact contingent.

To argue this, Brown has to describe how universal cultural neurosis has come to exist – demonstrating that there are other possible cultures. The one he finds most interesting is a culture that avoids the repression of infantile 'polymorphous perverse sexuality', an eroticism not limited to genitality. As Brown points out, 'Freud's definition of sexuality entails the proposition that infants have a richer sexual life than adults' (ibid., 34) – taking pleasure not only in genital contact, but from all the erogenous membranes of the body; and Brown wants to investigate the recovery of that richer sexuality, not only for greater pleasure, but because it offers access to the full human potential for creativity and productivity which repression closes off – a society based on play rather than on work (ibid., 41–3); a society unafraid of death.

> If we can imagine an unrepressed man [*sic*] – a man strong enough to live and therefore strong enough to die ... such a man would have a body freed from all the sexual organizations – a body freed from unconscious oral, anal, and genital fantasies.... Such a man would be rid of the nightmares which Freud showed to be haunting civilization. (Ibid., 255)

Specifically, Brown sets himself the task of demonstrating that the developmental stages of infancy as defined by psychoanalysis are not biologically determined; he needs to do this because it is these stages – 'oral', 'anal', etc. – which convey each of us gradually from polymorphous eroticism to a more or less neurotic genitality (Freud 1905). Like Reich, and indeed like Freud himself, Brown focuses on the family as the motor of neurosis, emphasizing how the long dependency period of the human infant – the years during which we need adults to survive – 'creates in the child a passive, dependent need to be beloved, [as well as] his dream of narcissistic omnipotence. Thus the institution of the family shapes human desire in two contradictory directions, and [this] produces what Freud calls the conflict of ambivalence' (Brown 1968, 105–6). Brown believes he can show that ambivalence, hence anxiety, hence neurosis, derive from specific social conditions – namely, the institution of the family; and thus that an alternative to universal cultural neurosis is, at least in theory, possible. His critique of Reich is extremely clear-sighted: Reich realized, he says,

> that the outcome of therapy could only be a more erotic mode of behaviour in the real world. But for Reich the problem was simplified and distorted by his assumption that the sexuality which culture represses is normal adult genital sexuality. ... [F]or him the abolition of repression would not threaten culture as such, but only patriarchal domination. (Ibid., 129)

Brown points out the implications of Freudian theory: that 'the abolition of patriarchal domination, or even the abolition of restrictions on genital sexuality, will not solve the problem' of repressed infantile perverse polymorphous sexuality. He shows in detail (ibid., Part V), using the example of anality and capitalism and dialoguing with Marxist theory, how cultures are formed and structured by repressed polymorphous impulses. Brown insists that 'sublimation' – Freud's term for the transformation of such impulses into culturally acceptable forms – is no sort of solution: he sees sublimation as an expression of the death instinct, having a deathly effect on humanity. He argues that the appearance of rationality presented by modern economic and scientific life is the merest illusion, covering a network of mainly anal phantasies.

> Excrement is the dead life of the body, and so long as humanity prefers a dead life to living, so long is humanity committed to treating as excrement not only its own body but the surrounding world of objects, reducing all to dead matter and inorganic magnitudes. (Ibid., 258)

MARCUSE, FROMM AND ERIKSON

These three are not a harmonious group – far from it – but leading representatives of competing approaches to 'cultural Freudianism'; they occupy three distinct *political* positions – Marcuse a revolutionary Marxist; Fromm, an ex-Marxist democratic socialist; Erikson an old-fashioned American liberal trying to apply ego psychology in 1950s Washington. Each appeals to history in support of his position.

For Herbert Marcuse, 'the return of the repressed makes up the tabooed and subterranean history of civilization' (Marcuse 1966, 16). He offers a taxonomy of civilizations based on the *kind* and *extent* of repression on which each depends; and distinguishes the basic, universal repression of libido which enables human beings to defer gratification and thus build for the future, from 'surplus repression' (modelled on Marx's 'surplus value'), the *additional* blocking of human desire which facilitates domination. This sophisticated development of Reich's model, as Frosh says, 'makes repression a specifically historical notion' (Frosh 1987, 153) by letting us plot variations of surplus repression over time and space.

The more technologically advanced a society, the more repression will be 'surplus', since the potential for freedom is greater (Marcuse 1966, 87–8). The degree of surplus repression relates to the specific 'reality principle' adopted by the hegemonic class – Marcuse contends that several different reality principles are possible. In our society, it is the 'performance principle' which structures our sense of reality, and determines what must be repressed: the performance principle engenders *alienation*, both economically – the worker does not own the product of her labour – and psychologically – human beings do not experience themselves as sharing in society.

Marcuse's vision of potential liberation is modelled on Marx's: as contradictions intensify between increasingly extreme surplus repression, which is increasingly practically unnecessary, and the return of the repressed libidinal impulses, so space opens up for revolutionary change – revolution based on the power of phantasy and the overturning of genitality, substituting, as with Norman O. Brown, a polymorphously perverse sexuality of play and carnival.

Marcuse wrote in 1950s America, where the dominant psychoanalytic tradition was that of ego psychology – a conservative politics masquerading as apolitical. Another strand of radical Freudian thought also survived: the 'humanistic psychoanalysis' of Eric Fromm, Karen Horney, and others. Fromm, however, 'humanizes' psychoanalysis so far that it is questionable whether anything really psychoanalytic remains – treating Freud's emphasis on sexuality as something which can be neatly snipped away, leaving the rest intact. He tries to substitute for libido, a generalized Eros (Fromm 1973, 59–60); arguing that Freud's emphasis on sexual repression applies only to overtly repressive societies like Freud's own, and that 'in present-day society it is *other* impulses that are repressed: to be fully alive, to be free, and to love' (ibid., 41).

This position sidesteps the whole interconnection between sexual freedom and characterological flexibility – the ability to be 'alive, free and loving' – which is made by Freud and even more by Reich. It also ignores, as Fromm generally does, the *unconscious* levels of experience. Fromm claims that 'the sexual liberation which Reich proposed ... is in full swing today' (ibid., 32); ignoring, again, the strong distinction which Reich made between promiscuity and sexual freedom. Thus although Fromm's whole analysis of cultural change is based on Reich's theory of character (Fromm 1960, *passim*) – and although Fromm follows Reich in believing human beings to be innately loving and creative – he leaves out what Reich sees as the motor of character formation: libidinal repression. Marcuse rightly criticizes him for 'cut[ting] off the roots of society in the instincts and instead tak[ing] society at the level at which it confronts the individual as his ready-made "environment"' (Marcuse 1966, 6).

Fromm sides with Reich against Marcuse over genitality versus polymorphous perversion (Fromm 1973, 31–3); but only because genitality is more humane and decent than polymorphy! Fromm tries to take a third position between the social conformism of ego psychology ('a drastic revision of Freud's system' – ibid., 41) and the 'metapsychological speculations' of Marcuse (ibid., 33–4): a third position, in the tradition of the 'left analysts', which proposes a 'creative renewal of psychoanalysis ... possible only if it overcomes its positivistic conformism and becomes again a critical and challenging theory in the spirit of radical humanism' (ibid., 45).

The big questions as Fromm sees them are about what stops human beings from resisting authority and pursuing love and freedom. In trying to answer them he uses Reich's character theory, but in a truncated and ineffective form. Although Fromm emphasizes that he sees humanity as '*primarily* a social being', and therefore that 'individual psychology is fundamentally social psychology' (1960, 247), he actually offers no real social analysis, no picture of how character structures are implanted in the individual; he specifically rejects the analytic account that links individual development and social structure through the family.

> As long as we assume, for instance, that the anal character ... is caused by certain early experiences in connection with defecation, we have hardly any data that lead us to understand why a specific class should have an anal social character. However, if we

understand it as one form of relatedness to others ... we have a key for understanding why the whole mode of life of the lower middle class, its narrowness, isolation, and hostility, made for the development of this kind of character structure. (Fromm 1960, 249–50)

Fromm seeks to explain character structure by appealing to – character structure, in a wholly circular argument. The link between social and individual levels of reality was already a relatively weak point in Reich's theory; Fromm, intending to strengthen that link, dissolves it altogether.

Working within the ego-psychology approach, Erik Erikson tries to develop a theory of character formation which incorporates the social and cultural element. To do so – in a way which will be acceptable to American social policy-makers – Erikson abandons two crucial elements of psychoanalysis: sexuality and infancy. He proposes a theory of development which continues throughout the entire life cycle, rather than focusing like Freud on the events of early childhood; and also, like Fromm, he reinterprets the Freudian developmental stages in a way which de-emphasizes libidinal pleasure. Thus, for example, his description of the oral phase emphasizes not so much breast-feeding and weaning, but more speech as a psychosocial accomplishment:

This intrinsic relationship of speech not only to the world of communicable facts but also to the social value of verbal commitment and uttered truth is strategic among the experiences which support (or fail to support) a sound ego development. It is this psychosocial aspect of the matter which we must learn to relate to the by now better known psychosexual aspects. (Erikson 1980, 124)

Erikson creates a powerful and moving rereading of the Freudian/Reichian character model in terms of social accomplishment and (his central concept) identity formation. Although much is taken away, much of value is added to round out the picture of human growth – and to 'depathologize' character (cf. Totton 1998, 194–6). What he also does, though, is to assume that healthy development is about adaptation to society as it is constituted. 'The growing child must derive a vitalizing sense of reality from the awareness that his individual way of mastering experience ... is a successful variant of a group identity' (Erikson 1980, 21). That 'must' is meant both descriptively and prescriptively. But what happens if group identity and individual needs conflict?

As Poster puts it, Erikson 'simply assumes that the patterns the adults use in raising children have a built-in social wisdom' (Poster 1978, 70); and then seeks to give advice on how to optimize these patterns. There is little room in his picture for the innate clash between society and the individual which is central for Freud or Marcuse. Both his clinical and his psycho-historical work is focused on the idea that 'the individual's mastery over his neurosis begins when he is put in a position to accept the historical necessity which made him what he is' (Erikson 1980, 50). Erikson is thus in a position to study very sensitively 'the ego's relation to changing historical reality' (ibid., 45), how 'the historical prototypes which determined infantile identity-crises appeared in specific transferences and in specific resistances' (ibid., 28). What he cannot do is question society's legitimacy as the co-creator of individual identity.

PSYCHOCLASSES

Lloyd deMause's 'psychogenic theory of history' is perhaps the most intellec-
tually coherent attempt so far at a psycho-historical theory and methodology. It
is explicitly based in the object relations school of psychoanalysis (whereas
Marcuse and Brown are both classical Freudians, focused on the individual and
their drives rather than on relationship).

> I call this theory 'psychogenic' ... because it views man [*sic*] more as *homo relatens* than
> as *homo economicus* or *homo politicus* – that is, as searching for *relation*, for *love*, more than
> for money or power. The theory states that it is not 'economic class' nor 'social class'
> but '*psycho*class' – shared child-rearing modes – that is the real basis for understanding
> motivation in history. (deMause 1982, ii)

DeMause offers a developmental historical sequence of child-rearing modes,
together with their psychosocial consequences. In order, the modes are: infanticidal, abandoning, ambivalent, intrusive, socializing, and helping – the names
are sufficiently descriptive for our immediate purposes. Each gives rise to a
typical psychic structure in the individuals exposed to it – for example, the
'infanticidal' mode produces typically schizoid structures, the 'intrusive' mode
typically compulsive, and so on; and each structure can exist in a 'normal', 'neurotic' or 'psychotic' version (deMause 1982, 132ff.).

However, these structures are not only individual, but *collective* and *cultural* for
a given society and era. In deMause's picture child-rearing modes are overlapping, with older modes surviving long after new ones arise; any given era will
exhibit a unique mix and interaction of different child-rearing patterns. The key
stage in historical development is the 'ambivalent' mode:

> up until then progress is achieved by internalization and repression of previously pro-
> jected parts of the personality (magic), whereas after ambivalence is able to be toler-
> ated (the Kleinian 'depressive position'), progress is achieved through the reduction of
> repression and the increase in ego activity. (Ibid., 136–7)

'Progress' is hardwired into deMause's scheme of history, leading ineluctably
towards liberation and transcendence of history.

> Freud's idea that civilization proceeds by 'progressively greater renunciation of
> instinct' was precisely backward; civilization proceeds only through progressively
> greater acceptance of the drives of children. ... Hegel's idea that history is 'man's
> nature achieving itself' is closer to the truth, but only because each generation tries to
> help their children achieve their own desires. ... (Ibid., 137)

The motor of history is the child-rearing mode, constantly pressing towards
greater acceptance of the child's impulses through the adults' increasing ability
to identify with their children, rather than project their own intolerable 'bad-
ness' into them. If this is the motor, the transmission belt is the 'group-fantasy',
collective modes of defence against childhood anxieties: those who share a particular child-rearing mode – members of the same 'psychoclass' – will tend to
share group-fantasies. 'Each generation brings a new psychoclass to the historical stage, disturbing the group fantasies of the older psychoclasses and producing periods of rebellion, triumph and reaction' (ibid., 139).

This in a nutshell is deMause's theory of psycho-history; it has clear similarities to Reich's ideas, in the central role attributed to collective character

structures, and how these arise out of child-rearing modes. However, deMause emphatically does *not* attribute these structures to socio-economic sources; his child-rearing modes appear to arise spontaneously out of human psychobiological nature. The only causative element is the 'fetal drama' of birth and pre-birth patterns, 'the basis for the history and culture of each age, as modified by evolving child-rearing styles' (ibid., 245). The traumatic nature of the fetal drama explains the drive to psychotic violence and destruction in human history, 'cycles of death and rebirth … which even today continue to determine much of our national political life' (ibid.).

What makes deMause's theory more than intriguing speculation is its potential testability, through the methodology he offers for analysing historical and contemporary manifestations. A key tool is 'Fantasy Analysis' (ibid., 193–230), which picks out from any text 'the metaphors, similes, body terms, strong feeling words, repetitive phrases and symbolic terms', and explores their thematic content. DeMause stresses that this is not as easy as it sounds: for example, our language is full of dead or sleeping metaphors, and strongly charged language can be subliminal:

> Often a meeting which is deciding on going to war spends much of its time discussing procedural matters in a very dull, emotionless language, but just as everyone is about to fall asleep, slips in a term like 'killing the outstanding bill' or 'progress on the bill has come to a dead halt', and the psychohistorian must be alert enough to pick up just the words 'killing' and 'dead'. (Ibid., 194)

Clearly the listening skills of the psycho-historian are very similar to those of the therapist – including ignoring all negatives (as Freud says, the unconscious does not understand 'not'), and all subjects and objects.

While Fantasy Analysis is not wholly 'objective', since it involves qualitative evaluations, deMause has shown that different readers following the rules of the process will come up with extremely similar results. From his analysis of texts such as the Nixon Tapes or material from the Cuban missile crisis, striking patterns of imagery of a primal nature emerge. As deMause says, the *interpretation* of this imagery is subjective, and therapists working from different models will each understand the imagery in their own fashion. His own interpretations are based on the 'fetal drama' which he sees acted out in American politics, and he shows the emergence of traumatic birth imagery in American political language *before* the Cuban missile crisis as part of an unconscious build-up of destructive impulses. For example, at a news conference in July 1962, Kennedy is 'talking about' quite ordinary, undramatic domestic issues, but a Fantasy Analysis reveals: 'danger … danger … plunges … disastrous … drain … drain … weakened … chaos … chaotic … dangerous … blast' (ibid., 21–17)

– 'even though the only thing he could refer to as "disastrous" was a vote on medicare'. It is important to grasp that this is not understood as Kennedy's *personal* material, but as expressing a collective theme: 'Leaders are personalities able to become containers for the bizarre projective identifications of group-fantasies' (ibid., 138).

DeMause and his colleagues, then, have made a strong case for the idea that unconscious primal fantasies appear in national and international politics (deMause's work with political cartoons is even more convincing – ibid., 301–17). The public reactions of wild fury to his discussion of current group-fantasy themes during the Carter presidency have all the hallmarks of resistance (ibid., 300–1).[19] His detailed *interpretation* of the fantasy material is open to argument, just as with an individual client; and – as with a client – must surely depend upon an empathic openness to the unconscious themes.

DeMause's reduction of history to the single dimension of psycho-history is more dubious, as is the dogmatic onwards-and-upwards optimism of the scheme. Poster (1978, 154) criticizes both this optimism, and what he sees as deMause's individualist approach, separating child-rearing from the whole social structure in which it is embedded. He also argues that the psychic mechanisms of deMause's scheme are not flexible enough to account for the variations in form and intensity of parental responses to their children.

DeMause is passionately clear about the political implications of his work on 'the evolution of childhood' (ibid., 1–83): the need to press in every way for a collective shift to the 'helping mode' of child-rearing, which, he argues, 'results in a child who is gentle, sincere, never depressed, never imitative or group-oriented, strong-willed, and unintimidated by authority' (ibid., 63) – strikingly similar to Reich's 'genital character', in fact! He also hints at the direct political uses of his analysis of group-fantasies: 'With time, we may yet come to know *consciously* the historical group-fantasies we unconsciously share, communicate, and act upon together – a first step, one would think, in decreasing their delusional hold upon us' (ibid., 239).

10

Gender and Sexuality

Psychotherapy has had perhaps more interaction with the politics of sexuality than with any other political issue. The reasons for this are apparent: sex and gender are *par excellence* the material of psychotherapy sessions. They are also the building blocks of many therapeutic accounts of people's problems. Here I shall look at some of the ways in which this theoretical and clinical concern has influenced the taking of political positions – positions on the power relations between the genders and between different sexual orientations.

PSYCHOANALYSIS DECONSTRUCTS SEX AND GENDER

We saw in Chapter 8 that for Freud, sexual repression creates culture – but at the same time, creates neurosis. He frequently expresses doubt as to whether this is an acceptable price to pay. He is ambivalent, though, about how repressive civilization *has* to be in order to *be* civilization,

> particularly if we are still so much enslaved to hedonism as to include among the aims of our cultural development a certain amount of satisfaction of individual happiness. It is certainly not a physician's business to come forward with proposals for reform; but it seemed to me that I might support the urgency of such proposals. ... (Ibid., 55)

At the end of his *Five Lectures on Psycho-Analysis*, he tells of the citizens who tried to break a horse of the habit of eating by gradually reducing its rations to nothing (Freud 1909, 87). The horse, of course, dies; just as, Freud implies, we will all be unable to survive properly without adequate sexual expression.

Mainstream psychoanalytic theory has tended to assume Freud is right that repression is inevitable. Often, unlike Freud himself, it has assumed it to be *desirable* – that heterosexual genitality is preferable to any other kind of sexual expression, and in some sense 'natural'. Freud, however, was emphatic about the artificial nature of human sexuality, describing the complex processes whereby 'the combination of the component instincts' of sexuality 'and their subordination under the primacy of the genitals' is gradually effected (Freud 1905, 118), and the diverse forms this can take. But as Laplanche and Pontalis point out in their influential psychoanalytic lexicon, 'the fact remains that Freud and all psychoanalysts do talk of "normal" sexuality' (Laplanche and Pontalis 1988, 308). And since psychoanalysts are widely regarded – not least by themselves – as experts, their views on sexual normality have been highly influential.

One area in which Freud's emphasis on the construction of sexuality continues to be important is that of gender. Despite his confusions around gender (see e.g. Totton 1998, 200ff.), Freud steadily and powerfully asserts that it is not a 'natural' attribute that one is born into, but something a human being *takes on*, during their initiation into culture (e.g. Freud 1905, 141–4). Although someone born with male genitals is highly likely to take on a masculine gender position, this is not certain or automatic; their identity has to go through many 'vicissitudes' in order to reach this point – vicissitudes around their identification with and relationship to the parent of each sex. (See e.g. Freud 1925; Freud 1931.)

PSYCHOTHERAPY AND FEMINISM

For Freud, the same is even more true of someone born with female anatomy, because the feminine gender position is far more fragile, contradictory and insecure than the masculine (Freud 1925, 342; 1931, 374ff.). His emphasis on the construction of gender has been taken up by many feminist writers as a starting point for an account of female identity as the subjective side of political oppression – fragile and contradictory because *imposed* by patriarchal culture. Thus although many feminists, particularly before Juliet Mitchell's book (1975), criticized Freud for his sexism,[20] many recent thinkers, while acknowledging the sexism, use him as a resource: as Frosh says, 'psychoanalysis can be used to undermine claims to fixedness or authenticity, in sex and gender as in everything else' (Frosh 1997, 189).

However, another important figure in psychoanalytic feminism is, like Freud, a man. Lacan (e.g. 1977) offers an account of gender differentiation which embeds it in the fundamental structure of social relations and of language, arguing that the positioning of women as 'lacking' is crucial to human culture. Despite his phallocentrism, Lacan's ideas about gender have formed a crucial bridge between Freud and feminism for many theoreticians (Brennan 1989). One of the first feminist groups to use these ideas was the famous French *Psychanalyse et Politique* collective (Roudinesco 1990, 518–20).

As with psycho-politics generally, psychoanalysis has contributed significantly to feminism, without learning very much from it; while humanistic psychotherapy has learnt a great deal from feminism without contributing very much to it (except perhaps some of the early impulse towards discovering the 'political' in the 'personal'). A number of practitioners have chosen to put therapy in the service of a feminist project – as in the following passage from a 1975 Women's Mental Health Workers Conference in San Francisco:

> Just about everyone … was raised in a sexist society, by a nuclear or extended family which had a strict division of labor by sex, and an ideology which includes sex-role stereotypes. Insofar as psychologically based therapy helps the client to reject these, it is good. Therefore, feminism is intrinsically therapeutic and all good therapy whether done by and for men or women, must be feminist – in other words, it must include a feminist analysis of the clients' thoughts and behavior patterns and an effort to help the client overcome her or his own internal sexism, which is so self-crippling. (Wolman 1975, 4)

In a *non sequitur* marked by the hopeful 'therefore', Wolman maintains that because therapy can be feminist, feminism is necessarily therapeutic. Like many politicized therapists, she does not consider the ethical problem of imposing one's own viewpoint on the client's material. The use of 'must' in the phrase 'good therapy ... *must* be feminist' shows how politics takes priority over psychotherapy, which she treats as a political tool.

> As women working for the mental health of women, we have an important job – to heal our battered sisters and strengthen each other for the fray. But we must remember that therapy only helps individuals, it doesn't change the system. In order to do that we must work together – collectively and politically. (Ibid., 5)

Even among humanistic therapists who do not privilege feminism in this way, there are many – men as well as women – who fully accept a feminist analysis of current gender relations. For example, Arnold Mindell writes: 'I believe that the Third World War has been going on since the early part of the 20th century. The Third World War is the war between women and men' (Mindell 1992, 118). Mindell does not seek to give an account of femininity, but simply to encourage men to listen to women as he feels all 'mainstream' groups need to listen to the disempowered.

Many Jungian women analysts have dialogued with feminism, tending always to support some degree of essentialism – belief in 'the feminine' as a fundamental category. In fact, Jungians often see this as their key contribution to feminism, drawing from Jung's emphasis on distinct masculine and feminine natures. Some, like Wehr, simultaneously use feminism to critique aspects of Jung's thought, 'bringing the light of liberation theory to bear on analytical psychology' (Wehr 1988, xi), and then applying 'liberated' Jungian concepts to feminist ends. Others, like Rutter, are influenced by Jungian theory towards a conservative view of femininity.

> Some feminist schools of thought reject the spirit inherent in women's biological gift of life on the grounds that such valuing reinforces the patriarchal wish to keep women at home.... I believe it is a great loss to deny the essence of woman's nature – her relation to her body and its wisdom.... (Rutter 1993, xvii)

A number of therapists from both psychodynamic and humanistic traditions – including several Jungians – have taken up the complex project of creating a specifically feminist *form* of psychotherapy, considered in Chapter 17.

Conservative Views on Gender and Femininity

The image of the archetypal heterosexual coupling, Man and Woman, exerts a powerful hypnotic influence even on those with access to the tools for criticizing it. We see this equally in humanistic psychotherapy and in the traditions deriving from Freud; and perhaps especially in Jungian theory (with the honourable exception of Andrew Samuels: Samuels 1993, 167–70). In language typical of much growth movement thinking, for example, Danaan Parry argues that 'our next journey in awareness', after getting beyond the conventional understanding of masculine and feminine, 'is not towards androgyny, rather to deeper levels of maleness and femaleness' (Parry 1989, 153). He envisions a 'natural' progression of psychological growth from 'Personality Man / Woman' – the alienated gender identities of ordinary culture – through 'Integrated Man / Woman', where each gender learns to take on its missing complementary qualities, Yin for men and Yang for women – to a culmination in 'Natural Man / Woman':

When women and men have tapped this rich force of *natural* woman-power and man-power, they are free to express that force in their own unique, *natural* way. The point is that the outward physical expression of that force, no matter what one's sexual preference, will come from a deep, grounded, *natural* part of us, rather than the surface, reactionary, societal role. (Parry 1989, 147, my italics)

The enormous amount of work demanded from the concept of 'naturalness' is evident from its appearance no less than three times in this last passage! But with the best will in the world, there is a limit to how much work 'nature' can do; 'natural' ends up signifying whatever we personally like and agree with. This is also the case with much of the 'men's movement', which has been influenced by popularized versions of humanistic and Jungian therapy in its search for new models of masculinity. Psychoanalytically influenced forms of therapy, especially in their popularized forms, are equally susceptible to this collapse into empty versions of 'normality'. Denise Riley's *War in the Nursery: Theories of the Child and Mother* (Riley 1983) brings out how leading object relations analysts, by being 'the authors of their own "popularisations"', were taking active sexual-political initiatives (1983, 85).

The most famous of these was Winnicott's series of wartime radio talks, firmly and authoritatively presenting a narrative of psychoanalytically inflected normal family life: 'Every now and then the child is going to hate someone and if father is not there to tell him where to get off, he will hate his mother and this will make him confused, because it is his mother that he most fundamentally loves' (quoted in Riley 1983, 88). Riley also quotes Ribble 1943: 'Two parents who have achieved maturity and happiness *in their respective biological roles* are the native right of every child' (Riley 1983, 87; my italics). Riley argues that Kleinian-influenced analysts such as Winnicott and Bowlby are proposing an account of 'motherhood' which demands that the mother devote herself wholly to the child; and points out how well this fitted with the economic requirement that women vacate the workplace after World War II (ibid., 7–8).

Certain statements by psychotherapists on gender are clearly relics of a bygone age, as this from the prominent early American analyst Smith Ely Jeliffe:

Let us have done with this silly prattle about the injustice of separate laws for separate types. ...The cry for equality is merely a delusional projection of the female wish to be a man ... the result is the deluge of mannish, bespectacled female lawyers, artists, politicians. ...[T]he imitation has produced results far short of man, even at his most emasculated. (Jeliffe, quoted in Herman 1992, 406)

This was written in 1927, contemporaneously with highly radical statements on gender, many from within the analytic world; it is extraordinary how the most varied and opposed social views could coexist there. Another contestant in the sexist old codger stakes was Carl Jung:

I asked myself whether the growing masculinisation of the white woman is not connected with the loss of her natural wholeness ...; whether it is not a compensation for her impoverishment; and whether the feminisation of the white man is not a further consequence. The more rational the polity, the more blurred is the difference between the sexes. The role homosexuality plays in modern society is enormous. (Jung 1963, 247)

PSYCHOTHERAPY ON HOMOSEXUALITY AND 'PERVERSION'

Conservative accounts of gender are closely linked to conservative accounts of homosexuality and 'perversion' – as the *non sequitur* of Jung's last sentence above (implying a familiar false equation between male homosexuality and effeminacy) emphasizes. The link is underlined in a quotation from the well-known French psychoanalyst Jeanne Chasseguet-Smirguel, which directly bundles together modernism, perversion, and gender politics.

> [S]houldn't we associate historical ruptures which give an inkling of the advent of a new world, with the confusion between sexes and generations, peculiar to perversion, as if the hope for a new social and political reality went hand in hand with an attempt at destroying sexual reality and truth? (Chasseguet-Smirguel 1983, 293)

'Sexual reality and truth' here refers to the difference between the genders, and what Chasseguet-Smirguel, like many other analysts (cf. McDougall 1995; Stoller 1968) regards as the necessity (social, biological, metaphysical?) for each individual to identify with one gender – the anatomically given one. 'Perversion', whatever its complexities, is identified with uncertainty about or rejection of gender identification: a refusal to be a proper man or woman. The talismanic role of 'sexual difference' in a number of psychoanalytic accounts is striking, as the apparent guarantor of (depressive) normality in not only sexual but general social relations.

Again we see how conservative accounts depend upon a reading of 'normality' and 'reality' – which can be extended to manifestations like marriage: 'Prostitution and homosexuality are clear cases of schizoid compromise in their evasion of the *real* relationship of marriage. That is the reason why they are so hard to cure' (Guntrip 1977, 303, my italics)[21]. The category of 'normality' can be maintained around gender and sexuality even while acknowledging Freud's point that all human sexuality is constructed.

> [N]either homosexual nor heterosexual object choice is constitutionally determined, that is, hereditary in origin, biologically innate. Both are learned behaviours, the perverse act constituting 'abnormal learning' and the heterosexual act a normal form of sexual expression. (Socarides 1996, 264)

This may strike us as a breathtaking piece of false reasoning – if no sexual orientation is innate or biologically founded, how can one be defined as 'abnormal learning'? Abnormal compared with what? Socarides does in fact base his concept of normality on biology – 'male–female sexual pairing is determined by two-and-a-half billion years of evolution' (ibid., 252). Unfortunately billions of years of evolution can apparently go wrong rather easily; and Socarides is concerned to convince his homosexual patients that, since their orientation is not hardwired, it can be 'put right'. Sometimes, however, he encounters difficulties:

> The worst prognosis in my homosexual patients are those ... who demonstrate severe splitting of the ego with projection more prominent than repression, and a tendency towards paranoid thinking of an insistent and intractable nature. They evidence ... chronic inclination to misunderstand others, and continually feel the analyst is letting them down. (Ibid., 266)

In other words, one imagines, these are homosexual patients who dispute Socarides' theories ('misunderstand others'), suspect his agenda ('paranoid'), and express anger and disappointment at his treatment of them ('projection ... letting them down').

Socarides' views are mainstream (although vigorously contested by other therapists – e.g. Friedman 1988; Isay 1993; Samuels 1993). In the same volume as Socarides' paper (cf. Socarides 1988), Limentani identifies homosexuality as a 'syndrome' – that is, pathological – with three 'types': one using homosexuality to 'prevent the emergence of heterosexuality' (Limentani 1996, 218); one using it to 'ward off overwhelming separation and psychotic anxieties, a dread of mutilation and even of disintegration' (ibid., 219); and one, 'bisexuality', showing 'a severe dissociation between the male and female parts of the personality' (ibid., 222), together with 'an imperfect super-ego formation' – that is, they don't feel guilty about it, because someone in authority has 'actually encouraged *or ignored*' (my italics) bisexual behaviour (ibid., 223).

His account of bisexuality shows the same profound confusion between sexual object and gender identity which we have already mentioned, and which is endemic in psychotherapy, particularly in its conservative wing.

> Choosing a man to love does not necessarily mean that the man who does so does it as a sort of woman. The homosexual man is usually sure that he is a man ... not only homosexual men can sense themselves unconsciously to be women.... (Samuels 1993, 196)

Despite sharing the confusion which Samuels points out, Freud's line on homosexuality was radical and accepting. In a famous letter to the mother of an American homosexual man, Freud stresses that homosexuality is 'nothing to be ashamed of, no vice, no degradation, it cannot be classified as an illness. ... Many highly respectable individuals of ancient and modern times have been homosexuals, several of the greatest men among them' (Grotjahn 1951, 331). He expressed this view not only in private, but also in his theoretical writings: 'Psychoanalytic research is most decidedly opposed to any attempt at separating homosexuals off from the rest of mankind as a group of special character' (Freud 1905, 56n., added 1915). Freud certainly attempted to *explain* homosexual object choice, rather than treating it as simply given – but did exactly the same thing with heterosexual object choice: 'the exclusive sexual interest felt by men for women is also a problem that needs elucidating and is not a self-evident fact' (ibid.).

Freud's viewpoint has been sustained by analysts such as Robert Stoller, who writes that 'I do not find heterosexuals in the mass to be any more normal than homosexuals' (Stoller 1985, 97) – putting the category of 'normality' itself in question. Along the same lines, Nancy Chodorow has argued cogently that *all* sexual positionings, heterosexual as well as homosexual, are 'compromise formations', symptoms of distress (Chodorow 1992); this is also one way in which Lacan's theory of gender and sexuality has been interpreted (cf. Verhaeghe 1996).

Much more typical, though, are the anti-gay views of Socarides, which have an important source in the earlier work of Sandor Rado (1949). Lesbianism tends to be subsumed under male homosexuality, or, if differentiated, to be regarded as almost not a real sexuality at all, with a supposed function as an escape from the rigours of heterosexuality (Frosh 1997, 201; on lesbianism and psychoanalysis in general, see O'Connor and Ryan 1993). Adam Jukes justifiably concludes that psychoanalysis and its derivatives today function largely as 'social guardians, rooting out deviant identity and adjusting it to the demands of oedipal normality. ...[T]he family and heterosexuality [are] the criteria, latent or otherwise, against which to measure mental health' (Jukes 1993, 254).

Some humanistic therapies have taken over the conservative analytic view of homosexuality; particularly, perhaps, bodywork therapists, inheriting Reich's genital supremacist thinking, and combining a strongly affirmative attitude towards 'normal' heterosexual activity with an equally strong pathologization of homosexuality. Lowen portrays 'the homosexual' as 'one of the most tragic figures of our times', and refers to 'the inner deadness of the homosexual personality' (Lowen 1965, 75). In his view 'love can be fully expressed only in a heterosexual relationship' (ibid., 120), and 'what the homosexual doesn't know is that even masturbation is better than the homosexual experience' (ibid., 110). If 'the homosexual' doesn't know this, it is hard to see how 'the heterosexual' can, but no matter. Like Limentani, Lowen's view is that '[t]he body of the homosexual individual cannot tolerate strong heterosexual feelings. It fights them by "going dead". ... The homosexual act is a reaction to this paralysis and deadness; it is an attempt to regain genital sensation' (ibid., 97).

In the prominent Reichian therapist Elsworth Baker's view, 'the basic cause of homosexuality is fear of heterosexuality. Extensive therapy is usually required to cure this condition' (Baker 1967, 89). Another well-known body psychotherapist, Stanley Keleman, joins the chorus, although taking precisely the opposite view to Lowen's of sexual excitement and homosexuality:

> In talking with homosexuals, I hear that sexual excitement is something to be gotten rid of. 'I have so much sensation that I've just got to relieve myself of it.' His excitation is rarely pleasurable feeling; it is relief, but not satisfaction. (Keleman 1975, 38)

This contradicts Lowen's view that homosexuals have difficulty getting charged up at all, and that the purpose of gay sex is to reaffirm the existence of the genitals (Lowen 1965, 97). The topic of homosexuality gives therapists freedom to fantasize to their heart's content!

In Chapter 16 we examine gay critiques of heterosexist therapeutic practice.

PERMISSIVENESS

Just as therapists tend to follow their own personal prejudices – or perhaps their own neurotic patterns – around homosexuality, so with the growth of sexual freedom and experimentation in general. We have quoted Chasseguet-Smirguel's implicit comparison of modern culture with the last days of Rome or Babylon. Another therapeutic critique of permissiveness is Levitt's and Rubinstein's brave but muddleheaded investigation of the 1970s American counter-culture (Levitt and Rubinstein 1974). Here the counter-culture is measured against the yardstick of genitality – and found wanting.

> Since psychoanalysis regards genitality as the sine qua non of health, it is worth noting that in the counter-culture there is little concern with this consideration. ... Issues of oedipal conflict, castration, jealousy and rivalry are crucial matters in

normal development and are resolved in the acquisition of productive skills which lead to a sense of identity. (Levitt and Rubinstein 1974, 330)

Levitt and Rubinstein make some valid criticisms of the counter-culture's claims of gender equality; and go on to argue that the sexual life of the youth they investigate 'has a child-like pregenital quality' (ibid.) – which is regarded *prima facie* as a negative judgement. They conclude:

> The transient coupling of the counter-culture and its characteristic flattening of affec-tive response creates real wonder as to whether youthful sexual reactions are truly genital in nature. ... Perhaps the prevalence of sensory stimulation in the psychedelic culture is related to a diminishing of genitality. If this is so, the final expression of adaptation in the struggle against technocratic rationalism may well be bisexual inter-changeability and a return to pregenitality. (Ibid.)

It seems that again, any alternative (real or imagined) to heterosexual penetra-tive sex tends to be viewed by some therapists as threatening – not only to their personal world-view, but also to human society in general, which is experienced as founded on the heterosexual embrace. Samuels is one of the few directly to oppose this view, arguing that the 'primal scene' – the image of the parents in bed together – is 'completely congruent with homosexual experience' (Samuels 1993, 168).

The growth movement, where one might expect to find strong support for permissiveness, tends to assume more than it spells out. Carl Rogers argues that '[a]n individual who is attempting to live his [*sic*] life in a person-centered way brings about a politics of family relationships, and marriage or partner rela-tionships, which is drastically different from the traditional model (Rogers 1978, 29). But Rogers does not tell us what this 'drastic difference' is. Schutz argues that '[h]onest marriage, rather than monogamy or an open marriage, is the ideal' (Schutz 1979, 195).

As for Fritz Perls, he is explicitly critical of over-permissiveness, in a way reminiscent of Marcuse's theory of 'repressive desublimation':

> [T]he increase in the quantity of fairly unrestrained sexuality has been accompanied by a decrease in the excitement and depth of pleasure. ... [T]his particular desensitiz-ing [is] similar in kind to the rest of the desensitizing, contactlessness and affectless-ness now epidemic. They are the result of anxiety and shock. ... [R]elease of sexuality has come up against a block of what is not released ... the inhibition of aggression. (Perls et al. 1973, 390)

Perls et al. criticize sex education and opt for letting 'nature' take its course. 'It is now taught that sexuality is beautiful and ecstatic and not "dirty"; but of course it is, literally, dirty.... It is far better, permitting everything, to say noth-ing at all' (ibid., 390–1).

BEYOND GENDER?

Andrew Samuels has written 'in praise of gender confusion', arguing that

> to the extent that gender confusion is usually taken to be a mental health problem or a neurosis, we are making a colossal mistake here and even playing a most destructive con trick on those supposedly suffering from gender confusion. The problem is, in fact, gender certainty. (Samuels 1996, 86)

He suggests that particularly for men, uncertainty or fluidity about gender-appropriate behaviour is politically radical and creative; and that the apparent certainty about what constitutes masculinity offered by much of the 'men's movement' – even if it offers a 'new vision of masculinity' in place of the traditional one – is actually counter-productive, and only adds to men's confusion.

This aligns with new currents of feminist thinking, which emphasize plural and fluid identities – no one is *just* 'woman' or 'man', but also a whole range of overlapping categories like 'black', 'white', 'middle class', 'working class', with different facets significant at different moments – and which have begun to deploy Freudian ideas in a new way. The American analyst Jessica Benjamin, for example, has been trying to theorize a move beyond the simple binary system of feminine/masculine – a move which parallels the new voices of the 'transgender' movement (e.g. Bornstein 1994).

> If sex and gender as we know them are oriented to the pull of opposing poles, then these poles are not masculinity and femininity. Rather, gender dimorphism itself represents only one pole, the other pole being the polymorphism of the psyche. (Benjamin 1996, 120; cf. Sinfield 1994)

This sort of thinking has only just begun to be heard within psychotherapy; but it seems likely to represent the mood of the future, dovetailing as it does with a huge interest in accommodating and tolerating difference of many kinds.

11

The Roots of Hatred

According to Jacqueline Rose (1993, 37), in the 1930s the British diplomat Lord Davies asked the prominent psychoanalyst Ernest Jones how long psychoanalytic research needed to find a way to end war. Jones said about 200 years. Lord Davies said he'd take a short cut, and went to the League of Nations. However, neither the League of Nations nor any subsequent international body seems to have got very far in solving the problem – certainly not in understanding the sources of power-seeking, aggression and hostility in human behaviour. Perhaps it is time to turn back to psychotherapy for some ideas.

Why do people seek power over each other? Are power-seeking and aggressivity innate human traits, or are they conditioned by particular cultural or individual circumstances? Answers tend to imply a particular political alignment – with some exceptions, the right believes in innate aggression while the left believes that a non-aggressive society is possible. We can also to distinguish between creative and destructive forms of power and aggression (Perls 1955; Steiner 1981). Many styles of therapeutic groupwork have explored conflict and ways to work creatively with it – for example Tavistock-influenced methods, and Arnold Mindell's World Work.

Closely linked with questions of power and aggression are questions of sexism and racism. Although these phenomena clearly have causes in the external world – economic and social factors which favour their development – most of us would agree that there are also important *internal* causes involved, that sexist and/or racist attitudes serve a psychological function for those who hold them as well as, perhaps, a political function for the dominant class.[22] Again, psychotherapy seems a useful place to look for explanation.

In all of these areas, the key contribution from psychotherapy so far relates to a psychological mechanism described by many theoreticians under different names – most commonly, as *projection*. We shall see in what follows that projection is a powerful concept for understanding the form and function of sexist and racist beliefs, or indeed of any 'ism' which identifies a dangerous and despicable 'other'.

THE SOURCES OF VIOLENCE

According to Freud, aggression is an innate human characteristic.

[M]en [*sic*][23] are not gentle creatures who want to be loved ... they are, on the contrary, creatures among whose instinctual endowments is to be reckoned a powerful share of aggressiveness. ... In consequence of this primary mutual hostility of human beings, civilized society is perpetually threatened with disintegration. (Freud 1930, 302)

The control of aggression is, in fact, Freud's primary justification for civilization's repression of sexuality. 'Civilized man [*sic*] has exchanged a portion of his possibilities of happiness for a portion of security' (Freud 1930, 306). In a rare explicitly political statement, he attacks communism for its denial of innate aggression (ibid., 303–4).

Wilhelm Reich thought that *Civilisation and its Discontents*, from which I have been quoting, was written specifically to oppose his own views (Reich 1967, 44). Reich certainly takes a very different position from Freud – precisely that humans *are* 'gentle creatures who want to be loved', who seek the 'natural pleasure of work and activity' (Reich 1983, 8). The evident presence of violence, malice and hatred in the world he ascribes entirely to the distortions of culture: 'Antisocial actions are the expression of secondary drives. These drives are produced by the suppression of natural life' (ibid., 7).

By 'secondary drives', Reich means the intermediate character layer between the superficial, inhibited 'niceness' which is enforced on us, and our natural core. He does not specifically address the obvious question: If human beings are innately kind and loving, how is it that we create such oppressive cultures? How did it all go wrong? Presumably, his answer would be that oppressive social structures arise in response to scarcity, and to the economic pressures this creates.[24]

The contrasting positions of Freud and Reich, with correspondingly contrasting implications for social activism, are the poles between which most other psychotherapists have placed themselves. Reich's view of human nature is one factor which attracted so many radicals in the 1960s and 1970s. Freud's version of aggression, however, was taken up strongly by Melanie Klein, and has influenced many attempts to understand social behaviour from a therapeutic viewpoint. Klein traces out a complex sequence of introjections and projections, splittings and recombinations, whereby the infant, and later the adult, attempts to manage the (in Klein's view) terrifying 'innate conflict between love and hate' (Klein 1975, 180). We try to get rid of our own hate by treating it as not ours, but belonging to *other people* – whom we can then freely hate. Writing about the threat of nuclear war, Hannah Segal puts it like this: 'First we project our destructiveness into others; then we wish to annihilate them without guilt because they contain all evil and destructiveness' (Segal 1988, 51). Or in the words of the old joke: 'Stamp out intolerance'!

For Klein, the desirable outcome is the 'depressive position', where we can integrate our positive and negative feelings and experiences. She links this with the task of 'reparation' – 'the variety of processes by which the ego feels it undoes harm done in phantasy, restores, preserves and revives objects' (Klein 1975, 133). These ideas have been used to develop a politics which claims to be both radical and realistic, based on a continuous mature compromise between our loving and destructive impulses (see e.g. Alford 1990; Frosh 1987; Young 1994, 133ff.).

REHABILITATING AGGRESSION

There is a trend within humanistic psychotherapy in particular to revalue aggression itself: to treat it not as a dark and damnable primal force, but as a normal and acceptable guest at the human table. For example Fritz Perls (1955, 28) argues that 'morality and aggression ... are essentially linked' – the discrimination of good from bad, in the organismic sense that what is conducive to survival and flourishing is 'good', involves an aggressive guarding of the boundary of self. '[A]ggression is essential for survival and growth. It is not an invention of the devil, but a means of nature' (ibid., 33). As elsewhere (Perls 1969, *passim*; Perls et al. 1973, 386ff.), Perls links aggression with *eating*; and thus identifies it as a natural bodily function. 'It is not aggression, any more than sex, that is responsible for the neuroses, but the unfortunate organization of aggression that occurs in our institutions and families' (Perls 1955, 35).

In his presentation of aggression as a natural force, Perls is influenced by his own therapist, Reich:

> Every positive manifestation of life is aggressive, the act of sexual pleasure as well as the act of destructive hate, the sadistic act as well as the act of procuring food. Aggression is the life expression of the musculature, of the system of movement. (Reich 1983, 156)

And the Jungian analyst Andrew Samuels even gives a specifically political function to aggression:

> We may come to see aggression as a politically reparative drive, understanding that aggression often incorporates not only intense wishes for relatedness, but equally intense wishes for participation, in a more cooperative and communal mode, in political activity. To be authentically aggressive, angry in the belly, and still able to be part of social and political processes, is a psychological and ethical goal of the highest order. (Samuels 1993, 56–7)

Samuels suggests that, as with many other psychological states, the problem is not aggression itself but 'being trapped in one particular style of aggression. Much fear of the consequences of aggressive fantasy can be understood as fear of playing permanently on one aggressive note' (ibid., 155).

CONFLICT

These more positive versions of aggression can be developed into a positive reading of conflict itself, on both personal and political levels. Conflict can be seen as the necessary precursor to growth, through its signal that the current situation is incomplete and needs to change. I have already quoted Arnold Mindell's statement that 'engaging in heated conflict instead of running away from it is one of the best ways to resolve the divisiveness that prevails on every level of society' (Mindell 1995, 12).

In Mindell's view, what makes conflict unproductive is (much as Samuels says above about aggression) the fixedness of our roles.

> The typical structure of a minority-majority conflict is that there is no *metacommunicator*, no neutral witness to the conflict. ... Neither side feels able to occupy the metacommunicator position of neutrality or fairness because, regardless of the issues, everyone identifies only with their feelings of hurt, anger and victimization. ... The

outside world fails to see its own position as a role in the conflict. Thus, there are no local battles. Every local battle is a world war in which everyone is a part. (Mindell 1992, 100–1)

Mindell's approach is therefore to support all participants in pushing their own role to the fullest extent, while providing a 'metacommunicator', in the expectation that, having been heard, the role will then be completed and shift into a new perspective. He seeks to welcome even the 'terrorist' roles in conflict, both literally and metaphorically:

Some therapists categorize an inclination towards terrorism as a 'narcissistic disorder'. Rebellion is often seen as evidence of 'paranoia'. By diagnosing terrorist behavior as inappropriate, deviant, sociopathic or psychopathic, psychology and psychiatry lull the mainstream into deeper complacency. ... Insisting that psychological work take precedence over social change is abusive and undemocratic. The terrorist arises in all of us when we feel unheard or unable to protect ourselves. ... So-called 'pathological, borderline, dysfunctional, or psychotic' people who disturb or threaten the mainstream are potential world-changers. We need to find value and not just the pathology in symptoms. (Mindell 1995, 91–2)

Samuels also argues that political conflict and discontent is a natural human phenomenon: since it never corresponds wholly to our wishes, 'there is an innate desire in humans to change political and social reality'. However, this cuts both ways: 'At times of rapid social and political transformation, the desire for change can take the form of opposing and obstructing whatever political activity is going on' (Samuels 1993, 58).

SEXISM

The obscurity of femininity, that 'dark continent', both reflects and is symptomatic of unconscious male intent rather than feminine opacity. (Jukes 1993, 256–7)

It is mainly psychoanalytic writers who have gone beyond the critiquing of sexism and patriarchy to ask how and why they arose. Several feminist authors in the 1970s tried to use Freudian ideas to address these questions; and, as so often in psychotherapeutic politics, have looked for answers in the structure of the family.

Freud's contribution has radically deepened our awareness of ... the immense strain imposed on both male and female personality by the fact ... that the main adult presence in infancy and early childhood is female. In this sense, Freud is revolutionary. What is conservative is his assumption that this structural defect constitutes a fixed condition of our species' existence. ... (Dinnerstein 1978, xii)

Simply stated, Dinnerstein's thesis is that antagonism to women (in both men and women) originates in the total dependence of babies on their primary carer – almost always a woman.

[A] woman is the helpless child's main contact with the natural surround, the center of everything the infant wants and feels drawn to, fears losing and feels threatened by. ... She is this global, inchoate, all-embracing presence before she is a person.... When she does become a person, her person-ness is shot through for the child with these earlier qualities. And when it begins to be clear that this person is a female in a world of males and females, femaleness comes to be the name for, the embodiment of, these global and inchoate and all-embracing qualities. (Dinnerstein 1978, 93)

As Dinnerstein sees it, each human being needs to find a way of escaping from the painful dependency of infancy; and we do this by identifying infancy with femaleness, and femaleness in turn with something less than human. 'Women can be defined as quasi persons, quasi humans; and unqualified human personhood can be sealed off from the contaminating atmosphere of infant fantasy and defined as male' (ibid.). Her straightforward remedy for patriarchy and sexism, then, is that we find ways for men to share equally in childcare.

Dinnerstein's influential, but rambling and repetitive book has a minute bibliography in which the only psychoanalytic references are to Freud's *Civilisation and its Discontents* and *The Future of an Illusion*; Norman O. Brown's *Life Against Death*; Erich Fromm's *Man for Himself*; and Melanie Klein's *Envy and Gratitude*. Nonetheless, she defines her two main influences (ibid., xi) as psychoanalysis and Gestalt psychology (as distinct from Gestalt psychotherapy).

Juliet Mitchell's *Psychoanalysis and Feminism* (1975) is on an altogether different plane of scholarship and intellectual grip. Her main concern is to rehabilitate Freud's work for feminists.

> Freud's analysis of the psychology of women takes place within a concept that is neither socially nor biologically dualistic. It takes place within an analysis of patriarchy. His theories give us the beginnings of an explanation of the inferiorized and 'alternative' ... psychology of women under patriarchy. Their concern is with how the human animal with a bisexual psychological disposition becomes the sexed human creature – the man or the woman. (Mitchell 1975, 402)

The Freud whom Mitchell describes is one heavily influenced by Lacan's re-reading (although Mitchell's understanding of Lacan is incomplete). Sexism originates from the Oedipus complex, treated by Mitchell as a *political* conflict:

> At first both sexes want to take the place of both the mother and the father, but as they cannot take *both* places, each sex has to learn to repress the characteristics of the other sex. But both ... want to take the father's place, and *only the boy will one day be allowed to do so*. Furthermore ... *both* children desire to be the phallus for the mother. Again, *only the boy can fully recognise himself in the mother's desire*. Thus *both* sexes repudiate the implications of femininity. (Ibid., 404, original italics)

Mitchell is clear that (at this stage in her career – she later trained as a psychoanalyst) her interest in Freud is an instrumental one: his theory alone cuts sufficiently deeply into the muscle and bone of society to offer feminists an effective strategy.

> Women have to organize themselves as a group to effect a change in the basic ideology of human society. To be effective, this can be no righteous challenge to the simple domination of men ... but a struggle based on a theory of the social non-necessity at this stage of development of the laws instituted by patriarchy. (Ibid., 414)

A third influential work from the 1970s, Nancy Chodorow's *The Reproduction of Mothering* (1978), draws more on the object relations schools of psychoanalysis to explain how

> [w]omen, as mothers, produce daughters with mothering capacities and the desire to mother. These capacities and needs are built into and grow out of the mother-daughter relationship itself. By contrast, women as mothers (and men as not-mothers) produce sons whose nurturant capacities and needs have been systematically curtailed and repressed. (Chodorow 1978, 7)

With some variations of detail, Chodorow's core argument is similar to Dinnerstein's: it is women's central role in parenting that leads to male domination. In a sense, as her title indicates, Chodorow is not attempting to describe the *origins* of sexism but only its *reproduction* from one generation to another. Again like Dinnerstein, and far more than Mitchell, Chodorow's account exists pretty much in a social and economic vacuum – Elliot characterizes both theories as 'a discourse of narcissism' (Elliot 1991, 134), focused wholly on a free-floating mother-baby pair, without much input even from father, let alone from the wider society.

Many later feminist writers – therapists and others – have developed various of the 'psycho-feminist' ideas pioneered by Mitchell, Chodorow and Dinnerstein; and those of Irigaray, Kristeva, and others. Ernst and Maguire (1987) is a useful compendium of different therapeutic views on the relationship between individual and social aspects of gender. Adam Jukes puts succinctly the difficulty of the entire project: 'The problem of attempting to explain male sexism and misogyny is that of trying to find an explanation which does not assume the existence of gender identity' (Jukes 1993, xxiii). For feminists, or indeed anyone trying to understand these matters, there is a constant struggle to maintain a critical distance from the discourses of gender, rather than surrendering to some form or other of essentialism or naturalism.

Out of the wealth of relevant material, I will consider a book by the Kleinian therapist Adam Jukes which explicitly brings together the themes of aggression, power and sexism - beginning with its title: *Why Men Hate Women* (Jukes 1993).

> My central thesis is that men exist in a state of perpetual enmity with women which they express overtly and covertly, by controlling and dominating them (Jukes 1993, xiv).

Jukes believes that 'even normal heterosexual relations are characterized more by sadism inflicted by men on women than by love' (ibid., 62); and denies the frequently asserted idea that women have 'an active, collusive investment in the present gender arrangements' (ibid., 64), or that female masochism is a collusive factor in male oppression (ibid., 223–57).

Like the other writers we have considered, Jukes looks to family life for his explanation, invoking the Kleinian concept of 'ambivalence' – that the infant fuses its positive and negative experiences of the mother into a single figure of the 'good/bad mother' (ibid., 51ff.).

> [T]his 'bad' mother is terrifying. The conflicts she provokes in the infant arouse his fear and hatred, and are very difficult to cope with. This decision – never again to allow a women to have such power over him – is a momentous one. I believe it is made by all men. ... It is the individual psychological root of misogyny, whatever its social or biological significance. ... (Ibid., 53)

Jukes goes on from this relatively familiar analysis to paint a picture of masculinity as founded on the projection outwards on to women of unacceptable feelings and experiences – in particular, weakness. 'For a man the essential quality of femininity is its "otherness" [which] is constituted from projected parts of the self' (ibid., 105). Since 'men need an excluded other in order to define the male self' (ibid., 117), Jukes is pessimistic about the possibility of dissolving 'the male encapsulated psychosis from which misogyny derives' (ibid., 94); he finally concludes that 'men have too much to lose and too little to gain by sharing power with women' (ibid., 322).

In Jukes' view, the debate about whether hatred and destructiveness are innate to human beings is not relevant. Whether or not misogyny is innate, 'every man suffers from it (albeit sometimes to quite a minor degree...), and ... the social and psychological conditions which precipitate and reinforce it occur in every man's life' (ibid., 106). As he points out, this still leaves plenty of room for social activism to ameliorate the effects and expression of misogyny. He argues that greater awareness – though not necessarily acting out - of homosexual feeling between men might lead to greater capacity for intimacy; helping to bring to consciousness the roots of misogyny, though not to weaken its force (ibid., 140).

Jukes also expresses a position held in common by Kleinian and Lacanian analysts: gendered identity 'does not fall into the individual's cognitive/perceptual field as an object of knowledge, but is actually the most important principle of meaning by which we order perception and make sense of the social world' (Jukes 1993, xxiii). Gender, according to this point of view, is not a category available for our conscious examination, but one of the building blocks which makes up our humanness. Thus Lacan argues that culture, like language, is structured around a binary division which has the effect of privileging the masculine over the feminine. This is nothing to do with choice or oppression, in Lacan's view, but simply an unavoidable aspect of our existence in language. Jukes summarizes this in a way which brings together Kleinian and Lacanian ideas:

> The female unconscious is different from the male because it is predicated largely on the woman's relationship to the absent penis, whereas the man's is predicated on fear of its absence. These anxieties derive from the fundamental significance of the phallus as a symbol in the structure of language, and not from any fundamental – that is, innate – female anxieties about not having one. (Jukes 1993, 320)

We may observe a slide within this passage between the *penis*, as an anatomical feature, and the *phallus*, as a symbolic entity which can be *represented* by the penis; and ask, as many people have asked of Lacan, why the two must necessarily be identified with each other. In other words, because a woman does not have a penis, does this mean that she cannot have the phallus?

The idea that gender is a feature of the unconscious as well as the conscious mind, a way in which we structure *all* our experience, can be powerful in helping us comprehend how deeply sexism grips us. It can also encourage the sort of slackening of attention which I mentioned earlier, a slide into acquiescence to sexism. This is what seems to be happening in the following passage by two prominent feminist therapists:

> Gender is inextricable from our notions of subjectivity. The ordering of the sexes is a fundamental characteristic of human development. In enabling her infants to assume a gendered sense of self, the mother relates to them in gender-appropriate ways. (Eichenbaum and Orbach 1987, 57–8)

– in other words, she introduces them to the culture's sex-role stereotypes, and 'presents the psychological possibilities' of gender roles (ibid., 58) through the mothering relationship.

RACISM

The first significant attempt to think psycho-politically about racism was the black African Franz Fanon's important work of the early 1950s, *Black Skin, White Masks* (Fanon 1986). Fanon uses the central concept of The Other, which he derives from the French analyst Jacques Lacan, to account for the way in which white culture identifies the black man with what it fears in sexuality - its 'dark', 'animal' quality. He draws not only on Freud, but also on Adler and Jung, to construct his account.

> European civilization is characterised by the presence, at the heart of what Jung calls the collective unconscious, of an archetype: an expression of the bad instincts, of the darkness inherent in every ego, of the uncivilised savage, the Negro that slumbers in every black man. (1986, 187)

It is this same basic theory which has been repeated and developed by other writers – notably Rustin (1991) and Kovel (1988, 1995). The increased sophistication of later versions is partly a matter of defining the psychological mechanisms involved in racism more closely; and partly of relating the psychological aspects of racism more clearly to the economic and political aspects. An analysis has been developed which is, at least in principle, capable both of identifying the *common* elements in different examples of negative social projection – sexism, racism, anti-semitism – and of *distinguishing* their particular forms and structures in terms of the particular social and psychological function they serve.

Kovel and Rustin both argue that the real source of racism is in the destructive effects of capitalist society on its own members, leaving many people alienated and desperately needing some object on which to project their own unbearable feelings – to put it simply, someone to blame. Kovel sees white racism as inseparable from capitalism: 'The core of capitalism has always been the same quantification that reaches into the psyche to structure white racism. What is dark and clotted in the interior of the western mind appears shiningly rational on the surface' (Kovel 1988, c). In his latest approach to the topic, Kovel implicates the particular quality of the Western psyche. 'Until the bourgeois West introduced its notion of a unified personality, all other societies had regarded the psyche as essentially polycentric' (Kovel 1995, 207) – that is, each individual awareness as open to other people and to the natural world in general. 'Could it be', Kovel asks, 'that as the western mentality began to regard itself as homogeneous and purified – a *cogito* – it was also led to assign the negativity inherent in human existence to other peoples, thereby enmeshing them in the web of racism?' (Ibid., 212).

In a subtle and passionate analysis, Kovel portrays a convergence of economic and psychological factors through the institution of slavery: 'the animality projected onto the black by virtue of his or her role in slavery became suitable to represent the vitality split away from the world in Puritan capitalist asceticism' (ibid., 217). He insists that racism is not just a contingent feature of our society, but essential to its structure, so that we experience 'a continuous reinstitutionalization of the material basis of racism and a continuous reproduction of racism itself' (ibid., 218–19), often in new forms and guises. Racism, Kovel argues, 'plays a vitally important part in the establishment of what might be called the psychological economy of the West. Just as the races became segregated physically by neighbourhood, so did they come to embody segregated mental essences' (ibid., 218). Of course, precisely the same can be said of the genders. The 'segregated essence' of femininity is in some ways parallel to that of blackness, with its qualities of earthiness and darkness; and when the two come together in white male fantasy, as in the image of 'blacks screwing our women', the result is an explosive cocktail of fear and rage.

DIFFERENT KINDS OF POWER

The rapprochement of psychotherapy and political activism which occurred in the 1970s gave birth, among other things, to a new analysis of power, and a very practical application of ideas about group dynamics to the field of political organizing. An important expression of this thinking is Claude Steiner's book, *The Other Side of Power* (Steiner 1981). We have already met Steiner as a significant figure in the California Radical Therapy/Radical Psychiatry scene; this book is a distillation of what he felt he had learnt from his practical political and therapeutic involvement.

The book is founded on a distinction between 'a specific form of power I call Control, which depends on exploiting and manipulating others', and 'the other side of power, which we all have within our reach: the substantial, tangible, usable, durable powers of love, intuition, communication and cooperation which can get us what we want and make us genuinely happy' (Steiner 1981, 18–19). Steiner employs the theoretical concepts of Transactional Analysis (TA), which he helped to create, to understand 'that important difference in people's character which determines whether they will accept domination or challenge it' (ibid., 54). In other words, a new question is being asked here: not 'where does aggression come from?' but 'where does *submission* come from?'

Developing TA founder Eric Berne's division of the ego into Parent, Adult and Child states (Berne 1967), Steiner attributes both domination and submission to 'the controlling, oppressive Parent which is also called the Enemy or the Pig Parent' (Steiner 1981, 56). It is this internalized negative figure in us which both seeks to control others, and tells us that we must submit to others' control. Steiner also develops Berne's concept of 'games' to look at political interactions: 'It became clear that all human injustice could easily be analyzed in terms of transactional sequences which I called power plays' (ibid., 212).

Another TA concept which Steiner uses to understand political reality is the 'stroke' – described by Berne as 'the unit of social recognition' (Steiner 1981, 88): a 'stroke' can be physical touch, or by extension any way in which we show affection, recognition or approval. Steiner develops the concept of 'the Stroke Economy' (ibid., 88ff.), which he sees as parallel to the capitalist economy:

> Strokes could be freely available; except for limitations imposed by time, the supply could be virtually limitless. Yet strokes are in great scarcity because an artificial economy has been imposed on them which reduces their circulation and availability. (Ibid., 88)

He suggests that the rules of the Stroke Economy are as follows:

Don't ask for strokes.
Don't give strokes.
Don't accept strokes you want.
Don't reject strokes you don't want.
Don't give yourself strokes. (Ibid., 89)

The 'power plays' which Steiner analyses generally consist of manoeuvres around the exchange of strokes.

Steiner believes that 'every power play has an antithesis: a tactical procedure which can be used to neutralize it' (ibid., 98). This is not a matter of fighting fire with fire, but of a sort of judo which disarms the 'Pig Parent', 'a form of verbal martial art which like Aikido teaches only defense and knows of no offensive moves' (ibid., 98). His recipe for social progress is simple, at least in theory:

When we take time to figure out the power play and to recall the antithesis and co-operative response to it, we gain the strength and the practice to exercise the dis-obedience and opposition to other people's manipulations which is necessary to replace Control with Cooperation. (Ibid., 167)

In the latter part of the book, Steiner moves his focus from how to *resist* Control, to how to *give up* Control (ibid., 171), recognizing that at least in certain circumstances, we can all be the oppressor.

Two other works from the same period can represent many efforts to apply some of the hard-won insights of psychotherapy to political organizing, and to escape from the knots of domination and depression which so frequently strangled radical initiatives. Interestingly, both draw on co-counselling, which we will examine in Chapter 18. *Clearness* (Woodrow 1976) is one of several documents created by Movement for a New Society, a loose alliance of various co-operatively run households and enterprises on the East Coast of the USA. There is an obvious influence from psychotherapy in the emphasis placed on space for emotional expression:

in a clearness meeting there often needs to be space for feelings to be expressed. …The facilitator needs to watch for people who are having strong feelings or who are getting upset … so that they can be given support or space to share what is happening for them. (Woodrow 1976, 9)

Clearness is wholly practical in its intention, offering new but tried and tested structures for people who do not want to use traditional hierarchical methods of organizing. *Co-operative and Community Group Dynamics: Or Your Meetings Needn't be so Appalling* (Randall, Southgate and Tomlinson, 1980), is a British book of text and cartoons with the same purpose, but more theoretical ambition. It synthesizes ideas from Paulo Freire, Wilhelm Reich and W.R. Bion to develop a picture of what can work well or badly about groups.

Randall and her colleagues use Reich's concept of the 'creative orgasmic cycle' (which he intended purely as a description of sexual intercourse) and argue that it can be applied to any creative activity, including the dynamics of meetings (Randall et al. 1980 6–7). Reich's cycle consists of four elements: nurturing, energizing, peak, and relaxing. Randall et al. identify a corresponding 'destructive cycle', with its own form of each element (ibid., 10–11); also an 'intermediate' or everyday average cycle (ibid., 12–13). So for example in the 'creative nurturing' phase, 'people help and let themselves be helped, give information, talk about how they feel' (ibid., 13); in the 'destructive nurturing' phase, 'helping becomes smothering, patronising, paternalism, refusing help; people are dependent, tantalised or complaining' (ibid., 10). In the 'intermediate nurturing' phase, a halfway house between the two poles, 'people talk politely but without real interest ... some nurture themselves; the rest just sit and wait; "business" is started and nurturing ignored; one or two people try to do the nurturing for everyone' (ibid., 13).

Randall et al. also discuss the different forms of leadership in the three cycles. In a creative group, 'leadership goes to those who can help the process best at the time; those who have the skill and knowledge for the current phase' (ibid., 24). By contrast, in the destructive group, 'leadership is with aggressively sadistic figures who will identify an enemy indiscriminately and take immediate action to fight or flee' (ibid., 27). In the intermediate group, one may find the 'founder's syndrome' where everyone depends on the original leaders; the 'charismatic leader'; the 'compulsive collective', where an overwhelming emphasis on equal responsibility stops anyone coming forward at all; the 'bureaucrats and the bored', divided between a minority who do all the work and a passive majority; 'love is all', where a focus on emotional needs excludes organizational planning and leadership; or conversely, 'nothing but the task', where the emotional and relational aspect is excluded (ibid., 28–9). This account is somewhere between a description and an explanation of group dynamics, since no underlying principle is offered to account for why different groups choose different options. The second half of the book offers practical steps to move from destructive or intermediate structures to creative ones.

Conclusions to Part II

Several central issues start to emerge in Part Two. The overarching one, perhaps, is 'human nature'. What are people *like*? What do we *have* to be like, and what can be changed by upbringing, by education, by general social or material environment? These are key questions of political theory, setting up the framework within which it is meaningful to argue over goals, strategies and tactics. And they are clearly questions on which psychotherapists might be expected to have views.

It is arguable, in fact, that psychotherapists *necessarily* have views on these issues: it is scarcely possible to undertake the activities of psychotherapy without them. Mostly these consist of beliefs about which qualities and activities are 'natural' and 'healthy', and which are 'abnormal' and 'pathological' (even if therapists try to avoid using such terms, they are generally implied). If this is true, then it may be more productive for therapists to be open and conscious about their line on 'human nature' than to be unaware that they have one. The writers quoted in this section have generally taken up this challenge.

Within the general theme of human nature, some specific issues predominate – notably, the question of whether repression of individual desire by social restraints is contingent or inevitable. In Part Two we have examined the whole spectrum of views on this, ranging from Freud's belief that repression is the price we pay for security from violence, and that only the most minor tinkering is possible; through Marcuse's suggestion that repression is a social variable, and that several different 'reality principles' are possible; to the assertion that social repression is unnecessary and undesirable, and should give way either to polymorphous perversity (Brown) or to free genitality (Reich).

Another key question, often linked to the previous one, is about aggression: is this an innate human trait, or something produced by environmental pressures, either directly or as mediated through parenting? If aggression is innate, can we distinguish between 'healthy' and 'unhealthy' forms? Similarly, are domination and submission hardwired into us, or can we trace out the mechanisms whereby they come into being, and imagine a human society without them?

A further question which occurs for the first time here, but which will be increasingly important as we continue, is: 'Who decides?' In other words, who is the arbiter of reality? By what right do psychotherapists establish themselves as experts on general human questions? Certainly it is appropriate that they have views, but it is not clear that their views should be given any particular weight by the rest of us – or certainly not because they come from psychotherapists, rather than for their innate worth and incisiveness. This issue is particularly important when practitioners try to impose their social views on individual clients.

A difference on social-political thinking has emerged between the attitude of psychoanalysis and that of humanistic psychotherapy. By and large, analysis sees itself as contributing to political theory – but is not very interested in learning from it. By contrast, humanistic therapists have been much more willing to learn from politics – taking on the analyses of various marginalized groups, for example; but have not generally contributed much on a theoretical level. Humanistic therapy has, however, made some contributions of a more practical kind, in its influence on group dynamics – a general recognition that people *feel* as well as thinking and acting.

Part III
Politics of Psychotherapy

12

Psychotherapy under Totalitarianism

This chapter brings together accounts of therapy in Nazi Germany, Latin American dictatorships, and the Soviet Union. In each of these different forms of 'closed society', therapists attempted to continue their work, with varying degrees of success and compromise.

GAULEITERS

'Where the history of psychoanalysis under Nazi rule in Germany is concerned', writes Chasseguet-Smirguel,

> it is almost as if one had quite literally obeyed the order: 'You are requested to close the eyes' appearing in one of Freud's dreams. ... One must not see. A most tenacious legend, the validity of which, because of its very great likelihood, was not questioned for a long time, holds that analysis was 'liquidated' under the Third Reich. (Chasseguet-Smirguel 1988, 1059)

This 'likely legend' was based on the authority of the prominent analyst Ernest Jones (Jones 1964, 619), and had obvious value for psychoanalysts after the war, in defusing some of the potential for blame and counter-blame in the story of analysis under the Nazis. At the first post-war Congress of the IPA, one of the two dominant figures in wartime German psychoanalysis furiously attacked the other. The next Congress had the planned theme 'National Socialism and the Second World War in their Long-term Consequences for the Analytical Movement and Practices': this was changed – presumably to avoid further confrontation – to 'The Return of the War and Persecution in the Analytical Cure' (Chasseguet-Smirguel 1988, 1060).

Once Hitler took power in 1933, a programme was undertaken to 'Nazify' every part of German life and culture. Psychotherapy was no exception. All forms of psychotherapy were brought together into a 'Reichs Institute for Psychological Research and Therapy', under the direction of M.H. Goering, an obscure practitioner thought to have been appointed partly for his right-wing politics, and partly for the surname he shared with his distant relation Hermann. (For all of this see Chasseguet-Smirguel 1988; Cox 1985; Samuels 1993.)

Despite his political beliefs, Goering seems to have worked to protect the practice of psychotherapy to the maximum extent – even psychoanalysis. Although Jewish practitioners (the majority) were long gone, psychoanalysis continued to be practised at the Reichs Institute; analysts made up Section A of a three-section structure (oddly reminiscent of the arrangements in the British Institute for Psycho-Analysis), the other two being Jungians, and followers of Schulz-Encke's revisionist form of analysis. Psychoanalysts could not mention Freud's name (hence the anonymous 'Section A') or 'Jewish' concepts such as the Oedipus complex. They could, however, continue practising and training students – including Goering's own wife, but certainly very few Nazis (Chrzanowski 1975, 495).

Freud seems to have acquiesced in this situation, reportedly saying of the German analysts, 'I have nothing to forbid them and nothing to demand of them' (Chasseguet-Smirguel 1988, 1064). This sounds marginally more plausible than the other, hagiographic remark attributed to him:

> 'Quite enough! We Jews have suffered for our convictions for centuries. Now our Christian colleagues must learn to suffer for theirs. I attach no importance to my name being mentioned in Germany, so long as my work is presented correctly there.' (Spiegel 1975, 489)

Chrzanowski and his colleagues interviewed several wartime German analysts. He reports that

> we found a group of idealistic, nonpolitical individualists who banded together under a situation of extreme external stress and strain. ... Not one person ... expressed the slightest doubt that he had continued to function as a psychoanalyst throughout the Hitler years (Chrzanowski 1975, 495–6)

He describes a degree of resistance to authority, some sense of a free space offered within analysis:

> We learned that many people were saved from the Gestapo through the use of pseudo diagnoses. For instance, some people who were reported to the S.S. ...were saved when a fictitious diagnosis of 'schizophrenia' was pinned on them. One of the recurrent problems existed in the mandatory response to the Nazi salute – raising one's right arm and saying 'Heil Hitler.' ... Analysts connected with the Institute circumvented this by informing their patients about the usual therapeutic set-up in which handshakes, salutations and other personal communications are avoided. (Ibid., 499)

Alongside these jolly japes, the report suggests the more chilling side of the situation: '[B]oth analysts and analysands lived in potential fear of each other. Patients frequently were afraid that the analysts would betray confidences. Psychoanalysts were concerned about being denounced by their patients' (ibid.). One analyst was in fact executed as a spy, though apparently not through a patient's actions.

How seriously can we take Chrzanowski's picture, based on the report of participants in the Nazified analytic community? As he says,

> it is difficult to conceive of an ongoing psychoanalysis in the setting I have briefly described. It is also hard to appreciate how people could work on intrapsychic problems in the midst of socio-personal chaos, destruction and inhumanity. (Ibid.)

This makes it also hard, then, to accept his conclusion that 'something related to the spirit of psychoanalysis survived in one fashion or another even if it defies our conceptualization of the analytic process in general' (ibid., 499–500).

Several other writers take a similarly upbeat approach. Cox characterizes the effect of the Nazi period on psychotherapy as follows:

> [I]t is manifestly not the thesis of this book that Nazi Germany provided a positive environment for the practice of medical psychology ... or that psychotherapists in the Third Reich were unsung heroes and martyrs. It is the thesis ... that the Third Reich witnessed not only the survival but also the professional and institutional development of psychotherapy in Germany. ... (Cox 1985, 4)

This leads to the extraordinary claim that '[t]he establishment of the Göring Institute ... constitutes an important part of psychotherapy's past as a landmark in its continuing evolution as a profession in Central Europe and throughout the world' (ibid., 23).

Spiegel (1975) leans rather more towards the 'unsung heroes and martyrs' version.

> The aim of Group A was to maintain rigorously the theory and practice of the Freudian mode of analysis, with the meticulous dedication that puts one in mind of the oral tradition for historical accuracy in preliterate societies. Understandably, in those perilous times the analytic functioning of the Institut was kept low-keyed. Issues of trustworthiness and caution in communication were of paramount importance. It was life 'in the catacombs.' (Spiegel 1975, 489)

It seems as though the legend of the liquidation of psychoanalysis to which Chasseguet-Smirguel refers has been succeeded by the legend that psychoanalysis, and psychotherapy in general, kept some sort of lamp alight through the darkest days of Nazism – a lamp of freedom or, more modestly, of professionalism.

Chrzanowski acknowledges that

> [i]n many respects, it does defy logic to contend that the Goering Institute retained a humanistic haven in the midst of an infrahuman inferno. I do not believe that the people inside of the analytic fortress were unaffected by the events in the mainstream. (Chrzanowski 1975, 496)

This defiance of logic, however, is maintained by many of writers on the topic – as wish-fulfilment does so often go against all reason.

GENERALS

Janine Puget's account of psychoanalysis under the 1970s Argentinian junta (Puget 1988), gives a different, bleaker, and perhaps more convincing picture of how totalitarianism can impact on the practice of psychotherapy. Here there was much less direct state intervention in what therapists did – nothing like Nazi officials sitting in on all meetings of the institutions. Yet Puget describes an all-pervading damage to the ability of analysts and analysands to *think* together: an extension of the general situation,

> which we may call 'social chaos'. In this state an attack is made on all referents capable of facilitating the social awareness of a crisis, and the implementation of coherent modes of action to resolve it. The social space for the recognition and discussion of data is abolished. (Puget 1988, 88)

Since both analysts and patients are affected by the general fear of speaking, and even thinking, freely, 'free association' in every sense becomes impossible.

[T]he consulting room ... was divided into two different spaces. There was one in which patients talked about their fear, searching for realistic indicators of it, attempting to get away from the confusion created by the repressive social discourse. ... There was a second where political repression exerted such a notable effect that treatment took place in what seemed like an aseptic capsule. Any mention of events outside the intrapsychic and transferential world was rejected as irrelevant, as something that happened to others or that put the psychoanalyst's power in question. (Ibid., 90–1)

In the attempt to preserve the therapeutic space as a safe one, exactly that which needed to be explored was excluded.

As fear, terror and panic were not included in the analytic space, evident and unconscious corrupt pacts between analyst and patient were created. On some occasions some analysts denied treatment to 'guerrilla' fighters; on other occasions they did provide treatment but only after they had accepted the patient's wish not to refer to this area. (Ibid., 91)

What is very striking is that the banishment of 'events outside the intrapsychic and transferential world' described by Puget is already a part of much analytic practice – and thus *available* as a tactic for terrified analysts under the Junta.

In many consulting rooms the internal world of the family and its historico-genetic problems became a bastion. The more one analysed a certain type of fantasy, it was felt, the more one would feel protected and the more defences against violence there would be. (Ibid., 112)

The therapy *group* developed an important role in this situation as apparently the 'only effective method of fighting, of doing something, of thinking and avoiding mental disorganization' (ibid., 107). Such groups were therefore attacked by the dictatorship:

At the public level ... anything connected with groups or community work was abolished, and the groups also disappeared as therapy alternatives from the minds of the professionals. Certain types of rationalization were even heard in favour of abandoning this type of work. (Ibid.)

Jimenez (1989; cf. Berenstein 1987) gives some vignettes from working in Chile under the Pinochet regime.

A patient ... told the analyst that he was not Pedro Soto, the identity under which he had requested the interview, but Juan Carrasco, a middle-ranking political leader at the time of Allende. ... [A]fter the coup he had to go into exile, but ... had decided to return ... to work in the political opposition. ... [T]he political work was slow and left him a good deal of time to think out many things afresh and to do something he had always wanted – namely, to get psychoanalysed. He then recounted his personal history, describing his symptoms, and there was no doubt that he was suffering from a character neurosis. The therapist was shocked. (Jimenez 1989, 497)

The analyst suggested to his patient that there was a problem inherent in doing psychoanalysis when he had dangerous secrets to keep. The patient responded that he did not think he had any dangerous secrets. 'The therapist objected that the patient did not seem to realize that the mere fact of having returned secretly to the country put him in a dangerous position' (ibid.).

There was also the identity problem: was it possible to analyse someone who came to treatment with a false identity? ... There was also the immediate aspect of the danger.

Did the analyst feel capable of tolerating an illegal situation, of complicity with a wanted man? How could he estimate the possible dangers of this? Why did the patient not go into analysis while he was in exile? Were not many politicians people with a strong tendency to act out, perhaps with a psychopathic nucleus? All these are questions which the therapist put to himself. (Ibid., 497–8)

Unfortunately, Jimenez does not tell us how he answered these fascinating and complex questions, But he does refer to another interview with an underground activist under threat of death who

said that during these years of undercover life ... [he] had ended up not knowing what he believed in or what he expected from life. He felt trapped. In this way he described a profound mid-life crisis – he was about 40 years old – a crisis of identity, an affective crisis and certainly also a political crisis. (Ibid., 498)

Asked by the patient whether he was afraid, '[t]he therapist said yes, he was afraid, but added that anyone would be afraid in his position, like the patient himself, who was terrified'. The patient accepted this striking example of self-disclosure, and went on to say that although he realized he had to leave the country, he could not bear the guilt this would entail. Asked whether he had killed anyone, he said that he was not capable of armed struggle, but only of political work.

The therapist told him that all he could offer was four psychotherapy sessions, which would focus on the need to flee, his guilt feelings, and his grandiose fantasies of being a hero and a traitor. ... The sessions were held in a tense and difficult atmosphere. The patient finally decided to leave the country, and did so. (Ibid.)

Jimenez offers further clinical vignettes to illustrate both 'politics as a metaphor for the transference' and, more unusually, 'transference as a political metaphor' – situations in which the therapeutic relationship can offer a way of thinking about social power relationships. He also considers 'political reality as an escape' from the anxiety of analysis – activism as acting out; and moments when political reality irrupts directly into the analytic space, for instance general strikes, when the analyst's decision whether or not to work will necessarily be construed politically by his patients. 'At the time of the socialist government, I knew of a training analysis that was broken off because the analyst and the candidate got into a violent political argument' (ibid., 501).

This leads on to a discussion of 'sociopolitical reality as a countertransference burden' (ibid.), and to a presentation of what Jimenez sees as the fundamental problem posed for analytic work by 'extreme political conditions', in the light of the crucial need for analysis to create 'a space and time which will allow distance to be gained from the original traumatic events so that they can thus be worked through again within the framework of a new experience'. For this to happen, 'some degree of distancing from current, present-day reality is necessary' (ibid.); yet clearly a psychotic denial of current circumstances is not therapeutic.

COMMISSARS

In the early Soviet Union, psychoanalysis was very popular, as a sort of parallel to Bolshevism in the creation of a new society. Indeed, it took on a quasi-official role: 'All members of the first, officially recognized Russian psychoanalytic society occupied important positions within the state apparatus ... the Russian society was as much a political group as it was a psychoanalytic organization' (Nobus 1998b, 11). Under Stalin the situation changed drastically: from 1936 analysis was banned and went underground – associated, ironically, with the sorts of radical views on the family and sexuality from which Western analysts were simultaneously dissociating themselves! With the new pro-family Soviet ideology, psychoanalysis 'acquired a morally depraved character' (ibid., 12). From the mid-1930s, psychoanalysis was 'considered "a direct product of a certain stage in the development of capitalist democracy". "Its extreme individualism, pleasure drives, eroticism – all these are characteristic features of the ideology of the decaying bourgeoisie"' (Balint 1952, 64, quoting from Wortis 1951, 77–8).

Harmat (1987) describes the persecution of Hungarian psychoanalysis during the Stalin era: the leaders of the analytic society 'had to sign a statement declaring that psychoanalysis was a product of capitalism in decay and an anti-state ideology. Works by Freud, Adler and Jung were destroyed, two psycho-analysts were arrested and, no doubt, subjected to brutal treatment in prison' (Harmat 1987, 505–6). Even allowing for the 'no doubt', we can recognize the real catastrophe of the situation:

> The former psychoanalysts tried to get rid of their patients; the patients of their psychoanalysts. Hundreds of patients found themselves out on the street. It will never be known how many reacted with a deterioration in condition, how many committed suicide. (Ibid., 506)

Harmat acknowledges that psychoanalysis was not actually banned, and that some analysts continued to practise throughout – 'it was necessary to earn a living' (ibid.).

During the Stalin period two other things happened. A specifically Soviet approach to psychotherapy and psychiatry developed; and psychiatry began to be used as a weapon of state control over political dissidents. There had earlier been two isolated, failed attempts to incarcerate female opponents of the Bolsheviks in sanatoria (Bloch and Reddaway 1977, 49–51); but Stalin developed a 'systematic policy of internment' (ibid., 52) which continued up until the late 1980s, although with periods of greater or lesser severity.

There were several aspects to this process. As Bloch and Reddaway point out, the Soviet physician's oath is 'in all my activities to be guided by the principles of communist morality'; and there is a logic to the idea that an opponent of communism must necessarily be mentally sick, suffering from (in the terminology of the diagnoses given to dissidents) 'paranoid reformist delusional ideas', 'poor adaptation to social environment', 'over-estimation of own personality' (i.e. believing oneself capable of changing society), 'moralizing' (ibid., 251). One can find parallels to this pathologization of social deviance in Western psychiatry and psychotherapy – the concept of 'adjustment' in American psychoanalysis (Hartmann 1939a), or the psychiatrist William Glasser's 'Reality Therapy' which holds that 'all patients have a common characteristic: they all deny the reality of the world around them. Some break the law, denying the rules of society...' (Glasser 1965, 6). Again, Coles describes how when I was working in the South[ern USA] with children going through school desegregation and particularly with youth in the sit-in movement ... I saw one young student after another being carted off not to jail but to mental hospitals ... with diagnoses like adolescent adjustment reaction, psychoneurotic disturbance, borderline personality. ... The doctor saying 'And how long have you felt rebellious?' (Coles et al. 1971, 161)

The parallel with Soviet treatment of dissidents is extremely clear. Indeed, the radical psychiatrist David Cooper accuses Western psychiatrists of having 'the self-justifying hypocrisy to criticize their Soviet fellow-culprits for using but a selection of their routine procedures. An impertinence that cannot be as naive as it seems' (Cooper 1980, 135).

Soviet psychiatry, naturally enough, was based on Marxist-Leninist principles. Western observers are often horrified or uncomprehending that psychiatry can be based on a general world-view. But of course it always is; the advantage, perhaps, of the Russian approach is that this is explicit. Marxist-Leninist psychology criticizes psychoanalytic theory as individualist and philosophically idealist. D. Fedotov, Director of the Soviet Institute of Psychiatry, echoes in Marxist terms a criticism often made in the West:

> The psychoanalytic schools cling to the notion that the unconscious is a separate subdivision of the psyche, essentially independent of the external world.... Man [*sic*] is thus fenced off from the world, from the reality of which he is a part and outside of which ... he is inconceivable. (quoted in Friedman 1963, 277)

Hence Balint, reviewing a book on Soviet psychiatry, can say that 'one is struck by ... the almost complete absence of psychotherapy in the Western sense' (Balint 1952, 64). He explains this by the underlying theoretical position:

> It is above all man's [*sic*] relationship to his work that determines whether he is content, happy, and healthy. Consequently every psychotherapy must aim first and foremost at restoring the patient's ability to work and thus establishing his confidence as a useful member of the community. (Ibid.)

Soviet psychotherapy, thus, divided naturally between a biological approach closely equivalent to Western psychopharmacy and psychosurgery (ibid.); and an 'educative' verbal therapy very similar to much Western psychotherapy before Freud.

> The persuasive force of the spoken word seems to be the leading therapeutic device used.... For example, Platonov uses the term 'speech therapy' to refer to 'the immediate curative influence of the physician's words in his dealing with the patient'. (Friedman 1963, 274)

The aim of Soviet psychotherapy was 'the gradual promotion of an attitude of optimism in the patient' (Bloch and Reddaway 1977, 41). According to Sosland (1997, 229), several Western forms of psychotherapy were officially accepted by the Soviet regime from Stalin's time onwards: these included autogenic training, hypnosis, 'rational therapy' (according to Sosland nearly the same as modern cognitive therapy) and what he calls 'conditioning-reflective [reflex-conditioning?] therapy'. These are all methods of persuasion and re-education.

Valery Tarsis, in his novel about psychiatric internment (Tarsis 1965), describes three main groups of patients in 'Ward 7', apart from Tarsis himself, a politically dissident writer, and one individual whom Tarsis regards as actually mentally ill. These are failed suicides, mostly young; people who had attempted or enquired about emigration ('the Americans'); and young people with unconventional lifestyles. We can see that these people's problem is, from our point of view, political and social, rather than psychological; and also, how a Soviet psychiatrist could sincerely believe otherwise. However, it is certain that at the heart of Soviet psychiatric policy was a deliberate hypocrisy, using diagnosis – mainly of an 'extremely broad and loose' category of schizophrenia (Bloch and Reddaway 1977, 225) – as a means of disposing of awkward individuals whose trial might create negative publicity. 'Although this form of misuse has sometimes occurred elsewhere as well, in no other country ... has it become widespread and systematic, the expression of a deliberate government policy' (Bloch and Reddaway 1977, 31; cf. Cohen 1989).

While those incarcerated in an ordinary mental hospital were perhaps no worse off than in a third-rate Western institution (and better off than someone in the Soviet gulags – there is evidence of criminals bribing psychiatrists to diagnose them as mad: Cohen 1989, 30), the regime of the 'special psychiatric hospitals' (secure units) was atrocious, 'so pathological and harsh that there must be few institutions to rival it' (Bloch and Reddaway 1977, 219). Bloch and Reddaway argue (ibid., 186) that even if one accepted the diagnosis of mental illness, most of the treatment given to dissidents was 'wholly inappropriate and often punitive and harmful'.

The consciously punitive side of Soviet psychiatry was the work of a small core group of practitioners in senior positions (Bloch and Reddaway 1977, 220). An even smaller group of courageous psychiatrists actively opposed the system – some of these being imprisoned or having to flee the country (ibid., 234f.). The vast majority were passive, perhaps often unaware – and, I would argue, perhaps often genuinely sympathetic to the argument that social nonconformity is *prima facie* evidence of pathology.

Since the end of the Soviet system, psychoanalysis, along with a charivari of Western systems of psychotherapy and everything else, has had a new freedom in Russia. In 1996 Yeltsin even issued a decree on 'the revival and development of philosophical, clinical and applied psychoanalysis' (for the text see Sosland 1997, 232) – perhaps the first ever announcement on the subject from a head of state. Nobus describes the competition between different branches of psychoanalysis:

> Whereas the IPA has been building strongholds in Moscow and St Petersburg, managing to fight off the Lacanians quite successfully, the latter are attacking the capital via former Soviet republics such as Moldavia, Armenia, Georgia and Belorussia. None of the competing associations seem to bother very much about ... the actual demand of the Russian people. (Nobus 1998b,14)

Currently Russia has a glut of psychotherapy. According to Sosland (1997, 230), Moscow has three psychoanalytic associations, three Gestalt institutes, and schools of psychodrama, humanistic psychotherapy, NLP, Ericksonian hypnotherapy, transpersonal work and body psychotherapy. Five or six institutions offer eclectic courses. He points out (230–1) that because of historical circumstances, different forms of psychotherapy coexist in Russia as equals – so that NLP or Process Work have equivalent status to Freudian or Jungian analysis, for example. 'Psychoanalysis ... is merely one among many theories and techniques that are being rediscovered' (Nobus 1998b, 14). Apparently one can find advertisements from practitioners offering 'psychoanalysis and massage': a service not available in the West since the days of Georg Groddeck (Totton 1998, 75).

13

Psychotherapy in the Public Eye

In democracies, psychotherapy and counselling have not had to struggle for existence and identity in the same ways as in totalitarian societies. However, psychotherapy still has a public existence, a representation of itself by itself and by others, which can often be problematic. In totalitarianism, we might say, psychotherapy is a foreign body, intrinsically alien to its environment. In open societies, it frequently finds itself playing an important role *on behalf of society*. That role, though, can be an ambiguous one, a site where some of society's deep tensions and splits express themselves – and are sometimes mirrored in the splits and tensions of psychotherapy itself.

The Medical Model

A recurring example is the ambivalent relationship between psychotherapy and medicine. Psychoanalysis was created by a medical doctor; yet Freud argued very clearly that his creation was not a branch of medicine – 'I do not see how it is possible to dispute this' (Freud 1927, 355). However, large numbers of practitioners always *have* disputed it, starting with a majority of Freud's colleagues, who for the only time overruled his stated view, and made medical qualification a requirement for training as an analyst in the United States.

From that point, the extent of medicalization in psychotherapy has varied wildly. It is important to bear in mind that treating psychotherapy as a medical activity has little intellectual foundation. The concept of 'mental health' is essentially a metaphor, considering the psyche *as if* it was a dysfunctional bodily system. Some of the key theoretical advances of psychotherapy have been redefinitions of its activity which make this medical metaphor increasingly inappropriate: for example, focusing on belief patterns, on relationship, on family systems and social context.

A physiological or biochemical interpretation of emotional distress involves closing one's eyes and ears to the greater part of human experience – like someone who insists that love is just a matter of glandular secretions. Certainly glandular secretions accompany love; but if we wanted someone to fall in love with us, would we try to develop a pill to affect their glands? From the point of view of most psychotherapy, then, treatments of a medical nature are the equivalent of a love potion: dubiously effective, but more than that, *missing the point*. (The

Viagra phenomenon comes to mind.) Psychoactive drugs may well be indicated in emergency situations; but drugs can no more remedy our psychological difficulties than they can teach us mathematics, render us witty, or turn us into Buddhists.

How, then, do psychotherapists so often find themselves in or actively seek out medical roles? The reasons are generally political, economic or both. The American analysts who sought to bar lay practitioners did so for reasons of status and income (Jacoby 1986, 146). Doctors hold one of the highest social roles available in Western society; any group which stands a chance of joining them will probably try to do so – and logic can go hang. This medicalization is currently underway in both the USA and the UK; and in both cases, it is largely a matter of clients (Totton, 1997b). Bluntly, there are currently not enough clients willing or able to pay for private therapy; or, the other way round, there are too many practitioners seeking clients. In each country, therefore, there is a need for therapy to be paid for by a third party. In the USA, this third party is the insurance company; in the UK, the National Health Service.

Managed Care

Reasonably enough, American *medical* insurers have required that the psychotherapy treatment they pay for is *medical* treatment: that the client is defined not as unhappy, or seeking to grow, or in existential crisis, but *ill*. This requirement has been greatly sharpened by a general shift towards 'managed care': insurance companies employ specialized agencies to oversee treatment, solely to minimize the insurer's outlay – hence, the number of allowable sessions. The managed care company demands that each client is assigned a 'DSM number' – a psychiatric definition, based on the *Diagnostic and Statistical Manual* (American Psychiatric Association, 1994), of the supposed disease entity from which they are suffering. Each DSM number is in turn allotted a fixed number of authorizable sessions, irrespective of the individual client's needs as perceived by themselves or by their practitioner.

The whole issue of 'diagnosis' actually demonstrates the huge difference between psychotherapy and medicine. No two forms of psychotherapy will understand the client's issues in the same way; in fact, it has often been suggested that a fundamental activity of psychotherapy is the construction of a satisfying narrative about those issues (e.g. Schafer 1983). It is as if Western medicine, Chinese traditional medicine, homeopathy, Christian Science, chiropractic and voodoo got together to agree on a set of diagnostic categories. The arguments would be not only about which categories were appropriate, but about what kind of thing constitutes a category.

Any diagnostic system for psychotherapy, thus, is necessarily a *political* entity: the product of a series of power battles, alliances and trade-offs. This is extremely clear with the *DSM*, which shifted between one edition and another from psychoanalytic to psychiatric categories of diagnosis, as the power balance shifted within its parent body. It became even clearer in the battle over whether or not homosexuality should be listed as a disorder, which was eventually won by gay rights groups. As one might expect, many of the diagnostic categories of *DSM IV* are masterpieces of circularity and vacuity – for example '312.9: Disruptive Behavior Disorder'. This basically asserts that disruptive behaviour is caused by a condition called Disruptive Behavior Disorder, the main sign of which is disruptive behaviour. The only significant statement being made here is that to be disruptive is to be *sick* – rather than, for example, angry or oppressed.

Many American practitioners have expressed outrage and disgust at the distortions of therapeutic relationship and process entailed by managed care (see e.g. O'Hara 1997, 24–8; Totton 1997b, 113–14). However, little effective resistance has emerged, largely because of the power of the medical-insurance complex in American society – possibly as great in its own way as that of the military-industrial complex which people talked about in the 1970s. Some therapists have taken a principled stand against working with managed care companies; their financial situation is often now precarious.

The NHS

We in the UK have our own version of managed care: the positioning of counselling and psychotherapy in the National *Health* Service, which, although it lets therapy reach large numbers of people who would not otherwise get it, also means that audited, cost-effective, time-limited therapy becomes central (House, 1996; Totton, 1997b). Therapy, in other words, finds itself required – again, quite reasonably from the point of view of those doing the requiring – to answer a different set of questions from those which might otherwise seem relevant: because it is claiming a role for itself in a medical service, it needs to present itself as a medical enterprise, within the scientific/technological style of medicine currently acceptable in our society.

There are strong reasons for doubting whether therapy can or should really be fitted into such a model. Persaud puts some of the arguments succinctly, making a comparison with alcohol: 'most people feel better after a drink following a stressful day, but does that render alcohol a healthcare enterprise...?' (Persaud 1996, 201). The analogy with an activity which is harmful in excess is probably mischievous; but the conclusion that counselling is best categorized as a 'leisure activity' rather than a form of health care has much to be said for it.

Probably most of those offering counselling within the NHS (especially in GP practices) would not agree with a hardline medical-model approach. They see their work more as a practical opportunity to help a lot of people who need it but cannot afford to pay, and who they believe should be entitled to help from the state. In some cases, they also see a chance to influence from within (cf. House 1996). In other words, whether or not they know it, they are practising a political activity known as 'entrism'. This generally encounters one major problem: while we are trying to alter the system from within, it is also doing its best to alter us!

Although there is evidence that counselling does cut the number of people seeking doctors' appointments (which is the justification for its use), much of the pressure for counselling to be available comes directly or indirectly from training organizations seeking work for their graduates. Meanwhile, of course, the NHS benefits in turn from the inflation of therapy and counselling training beyond the real demand for such services: GP practice counsellors are frequently paid well below the going rate. They accept this because they are either trainees working out their required hours, or graduates who cannot find better paid clinical work.

COMPETITION AND CONFLICT

> Because of its ambiguous epistemological status (is it a psychological practice or medical treatment?) as far as ownership is concerned, psychotherapy has been at the centre of important boundary disputes and conflicts between professional groups inside the mental health services over the past twenty years. (Pilgrim 1990, 12)

These 'disputes and conflicts' have not only been in the mental health services. Competition, rivalry, and dominance games have played a major part in relations between, for example, psychoanalysis and psychotherapy; psychotherapy and counselling; psychotherapy and psychiatry; and the humanistic and psychodynamic branches of both psychotherapy and counselling. Van Deurzen-Smith predicts that because of 'human nature' (which, as we are finding, is a complicated and slippery concept), practitioners will always continue to 'build new walls between themselves sooner than having to admit equality and parity' (van Deurzen-Smith 1996, 14). As Hinshelwood puts it:

> One of the most striking features of the profession is its fragmented state, in which rivalrous groups claim allegiance to different theoretical orientations, and protect themselves by arcane terminologies that restrict the possibility of interchange. Each group prizes its own orientation above all others. (Hinshelwood 1985, 16)

Hinshelwood attributes this 'intensely felt siege mentality' to 'collective defensiveness' (ibid.), but does not really ask where this defensiveness comes from. Some of it may stem from the 'one down' position of almost every psychotherapy and counselling practitioner. In the minds of its practitioners – even those who strenuously oppose this situation – psychotherapy is a pyramidal hierarchy. Psychoanalysts are at the top; followed by cascading angelic orders of those not allowed to call themselves analysts, but who have received what is basically a psychoanalytic training; followed by the lower orders of psychodynamic psychotherapists. One's ranking in this system depends mainly, though not entirely, on how many times per week one has been trained to see one's clients:

> the received wisdom is that 'more means better'. Analysts go for five times a week, the elite organizations recommend that but accept three, and those further down the pecking order accept as little as one or two sessions per week for training therapy and for supervised training cases. (Young 1996, n.p.)

In fact, the question is seriously posed: 'if a training organization does not require its trainees or training cases to attend for three times per week, should its graduates be allowed to call themselves psychotherapists?' (ibid.).

For those within this hierarchy, non-psychodynamic therapists (who generally see their clients – whisper it – only once a week or even less) are often virtually invisible – the term 'psychotherapist' is used in common parlance to mean 'psychodynamic/psychoanalytic psychotherapist'. And analysts can treat analytic therapists with an extraordinary degree of condescension:

> Throughout the conference [on the relations between psychoanalysis and psycho-analytic psychotherapy] there was a recurring imagery in which psychoanalysis was referred to as 'pure', 'pure gold', and so on … and psychotherapy as 'alloy', 'debased', 'copper'…. [S]omeone spoke of his fear that unless they found a way of opening the back door, the shit would come up through the drains. (Ibid.)

Those outside the analytic/psychodynamic realm can be equally dismissive of those within it – and deeply ignorant of what they in fact do. For example, this is a remark by a prominent member of the British Association of Humanistic Psychology Practitioners:

> [P]sychoanalytically-based modalities don't threaten the status quo. Their goal is merely to make you less miserable; their model of relating is the familiar and reassuring one of parent/child; and their view of the human is the reductive one found in every GP's surgery. (Coulson 1998, 11)

One frequently hears this kind of thing said in humanistic circles, though it is less common in print: it is many years since humanistic approaches explicitly defined themselves over and against psychoanalysis – for example, Fritz Perls' extensive critique of analytic ideas (Perls et al. 1973, Book Two, *passim*), or Carl Rogers', who in 1972 spoke of the need to 'release clinical work from the dying orthodoxy of psychoanalytic dogma' (Rogers' 1980, 236). Equivalent prejudice on the analytic side more often takes the form of lofty silence about the very existence of humanistic work. There is little actual debate between the two camps.

There is, however, a striking convergence between many on both sides, with some analysts adopting the humanists' holism and emphasis on human contact (e.g. Arden 1998; Lomas 1994), and some humanists adopting the analytic emphasis on transference and counter-transference (e.g. Soth 1999). Of course there are those in both groups who reject such alien seed – for example Mowbray's robust defence of the distinction between psychotherapy and 'human potential work' (Mowbray 1995, 172ff.). The convergence can be enriching for all, but can also foster a bland illusion of 'generic psychotherapy'.

In my own experience, most people have only the haziest understanding of the different terms so important to therapists. One distinction which *is* often important to clients, however, is between psychotherapy and counselling. Many people feel that seeing a psychotherapist defines one as mentally ill, whereas seeing a counsellor does not. Thus some of my clients have insisted on calling what we do 'counselling', even though the term forms no part of my own background!

If only the distinction were that easy to define. In an often-quoted epigram, Dryden reports that 'Whenever I am asked what is the difference between a counsellor and a psychotherapist, I reply "About £8,000 a year"' (Dryden 1996, 15). Certainly there is no research evidence of consistent differences in the style, content or depth of work offered (ibid., 16). The terms are in any case differently used in the UK and the USA. Jacobs (1996, 6) believes that some counsellors are at least as competent as some psychotherapists, and that the relevant distinction is between experienced and inexperienced 'or even pedestrian' practitioners. Even the financial difference that Dryden suggests is by no means universal, applying much more to public employment than to private practice. Van Deurzen-Smith offers a phenomenological account:

> Counsellors tend to feel superior to psychotherapists about being more able to work short-term; more pragmatic, streetwise and better tuned in to the problems of ordinary people; and more broad-minded about the relevance of competing theoretical models. They are scornful of psychotherapists, whom they often see as unrealistic, arrogant and ignorant of ... crisis situations. ... Psychotherapists are generally convinced that they are superior to counsellors by virtue of their longer, more thorough training, their higher fees and the exclusivity of their theoretical models. (van Deurzen-Smith 1996, 11)

The truth seems to be that the differences between psychotherapy and counselling are largely ones of *culture*: those who assemble under each banner (perhaps in the first instance largely by chance) tend to share a common language, a set of networks and organizations, a particular relationship to theory and research. However, there is a very definite tendency to rank psychotherapists higher than counsellors – one which van-Deurzen-Smith argues that it is taboo to make explicit (ibid., 10). The distinction is thus very like that between modern social classes: hard to define, uncomfortable to talk about, but nonetheless very apparent.[25]

Scandals and Public Alarms

Matching the prominence of psychotherapy and counselling in contemporary Western culture is the prominence given to scandals around abusive behaviour by individual practitioners. Every time one of these stories unfolds – and sometimes they are horrific – it is accompanied by concerned articles asking whether anything can be done, and sometimes questioning whether therapy is actually a beneficial activity. More recently in the UK, each such article has been followed by sober, responsible letters from those involved in forming accrediting bodies, pointing out that – as it is often phrased – 'anyone can set themselves up as a psychotherapist', and promising that if they have their way, such abuse will be a thing of the past.

All of this is closely equivalent to the sorts of moral panic identified in Geoffrey Pearson's important book *Hooligan: A History of Respectable Fears* (Pearson 1983). Pearson demonstrates clearly that, so to speak, things have *always* been getting worse, society being always – in the eyes of the media – on the verge of collapse. Similarly, vulnerable people have always been exploited by some of those in positions of influence and authority, and there is no evidence whatsoever that regulation can stop this happening (cf. Mowbray 1995, 108ff.). Concerning sexual exploitation, which is generally the highlighted issue, Mowbray stresses that 'practitioner–client sex occurs in professions that are *already* licensed and have specific sanctions against it' (ibid., 112, original italics). Nonetheless, public alarms have played an important role in the development of a lobby for psychotherapy regulation in the UK. It was media coverage of Scientology in the 1960s which led to the Foster Report, the first initiative towards the statutory control of psychotherapy (ibid., 35ff.).

More complex is the massive public debate over child sexual abuse, which has intertwined with concerns about the role of psychotherapy. Therapists have been placed squarely in the cross-fire, massively attacked *both* for creating false memories of abuse in their clients (e.g. Ofshe and Watters 1994; Showalter 1997, 144f.), *and* for refusing to believe clients' accounts of abuse (e.g. Masson 1990; Miller 1984). In 1994, the media claimed to have discovered a group of psychotherapists in the United Kingdom who based their work on the belief that virtually everyone has been sexually abused (Palmer and Rogers' 1994, 8).

Without exploring the subtleties of the issue (see for example Scott 1996; Sinason 1998), it is apparent that psychotherapists are carrying the can for something with which society is unable to deal: the fact that very large numbers of people *claim* – rightly or wrongly – to have been raped and sexually mis-treated as children. Since we don't know what to do with this, we blame those who we feel *should* know – psychotherapists and counsellors, who of course can no more solve this problem than they can the problem of war. (In a rather par-allel way, therapists sometimes seem to get the blame for divorce.)

14

The Institutions of Psychotherapy

As well as struggles between different bands of practitioners, there are also power struggles within therapeutic institutions: therapists seem no less aggressive and power-seeking than any other human group. An excellent and well-documented example is the International Psychoanalytic Association; but similar processes of exclusion, faction-forming and manipulation occur across the board. Why do therapists apparently find it so difficult to apply their understanding of human motivations and relationships to their own institutions? As Robert Young asks:

> Why do the leaders – as distinct from the followers, patients and supervisees – behave badly? Why aren't they stopped? Why is it so hard to take account of issues of power, patronage and economics? Why, when we do, can we not provide an account which integrates such matters with those of individual and group unconscious dynamics? (Young 1996, n.p.)

Certainly many of the 'founding fathers' of psychotherapy were notoriously authoritarian, manipulative, in some cases even abusive. The list would have to include Freud, Jung, Lacan, Reich, Perls, Berne, and probably many others. But as psychotherapy itself has discovered, we cannot blame leaders for the problems of groups: the group creates the leader it requires. Kennedy offers some suggestions as to why it might be that practitioners have problems working together well in institutions:

> One may wonder whether the general need for restraint [during sessions] accounts for the way that analysts at times can be so unrestrained in their institutional behaviour, when they come together in group settings. ... Also analysts are notoriously prone to particular sorts of character problems which limit their capacity to be ordinarily human and sociable. ... (Kennedy 1998, 121)

These 'character problems' are the shadow side of the very qualities which enable people to carry out this peculiar job – qualities such as self-motivation, reserve, inner-directedness, sensitivity.

THE IPA

Freud wanted to establish an organization which would present a unified face to the world, and preserve his discovery intact against all attempts to compromise it. The structure which emerged, the International Psychoanalytic Association (IPA), has survived many storms and struggles, and shown its effectiveness as a 'big boat' containing many different groups of passengers (Wallerstein and Weinshel 1989); at the same time, it has never shown much compunction in throwing awkward customers to the sharks.

We have already looked at the exclusion of Wilhelm Reich. Other important cases are the silencing of Sandor Ferenczi (Gay 1995, 578–85), and the exclusion of Jacques Lacan, discussed in the next section. Perhaps even more important is the overall atmosphere of analytic training and institutions, which according to many critics makes it enormously difficult for anyone to take a dissident or even a strongly original stance[26] (Kernberg 1986, 1996; Szasz 1958; Wallerstein 1993).

In the post-war years the IPA was increasingly dominated by the United States,[27] where psychoanalysis became far more widespread than anywhere else on the globe: in 1952, 64 per cent of IPA members were American (Kurzweil 1989, 54).[28] Already in 1936, the Americans had declared that they would veto any IPA resolution that tried to control psychoanalysis in the USA (ibid., 53). By sheer numbers, the Americans were bound to conquer; however, American psychoanalysis was also increasingly mainstream, medicalized, and conservative. 'Psychoanalysis [in the USA] had finally become legitimate and respectable, perhaps paying the price in becoming sluggish and smug, hence attractive to an increasing number of minds which find security in conformity and propriety' (Oberndorf 1964, 207). This tendency, although most developed in the USA (where it went together with the socially conservative theoretical trend towards ego psychology, discussed above in Part Two), was not restricted to it:

> By the 1940s ... the European and American intellectual community had reached substantial agreement on the fundamentally conservative nature of Freudian theory. ...Psychoanalysis had become a branch of the medical profession, and the typical practising psychoanalyst carefully distinguished the discrete precepts and techniques of his therapeutic science from the ambitious metahistorical adventures in which Freud had indulged. (Robinson 1970, 147–8)

The shift in the sociocultural position of psychoanalysis inevitably affected its organization. A key aspect was the exclusion in America – unlike most other parts of the world – of non-medical (lay) analysts.

> Several motives induced American analysts to exclude non-medical practitioners. They believed psychoanalysis required medical expertise in order to distinguish somatic and psychological disorders. The lack of prestige besetting psychoanalysis in its earlier years grieved them. By limiting analysis to medical doctors they ensured its respectability. Nor can the more cynical motives be excluded: eliminating the lay practitioners guaranteed them a larger and more lucrative trade. (Jacoby 1986, 146)

Jacoby connects this with the arrival in the United States during World War II of so many European refugees. He quotes Walter C. Langer, a lay analyst trained in Vienna: 'I cannot help but think back on the remark that the President of the New York Psychoanalytic Society made when I approached him for affidavits [for refugee analysts fleeing Vienna]: "what in the world would we do with all these additional analysts?"' (Jacoby ibid.). To eliminate the lay analysts put some control on the numbers of immigrant competitors.[29]

By the late 1950s, Thomas Szasz describes the situation as one of wholesale professionalization, with training calculated to intimidate and control the candidates in every way possible. He argues that the training – like a medical one – becomes a rite of passage, where endurance, rather than originality or excellence, enables one to qualify (Szasz 1958, 599). Szasz argues that the whole structure of psychoanalytic training – including the requirement of personal analysis – is determined by the establishment's need for power over new recruits. He roundly dismisses arguments that this is for the good of those recruits, or of their patients:

> The important element of truth in the argument obscures its aggressive character toward those who do not comply with the group's authority. ... [A]ltogether different criteria of acceptability are used: (1) On the part of an authority-group toward those who aspire to join the group; and (2) on the part of members of the same group toward one another. (Ibid., 599n.)

Szasz is known as a maverick, and so his arguments are often ignored. Otto Kernberg, however, one of the most eminent American analysts, takes a possibly even more critical attitude towards training, describing 'the paranoid atmosphere that often pervades psychoanalytic institutes and its devastating effect on the "quality of life" in psychoanalytic education' (Kernberg 1986, 803–4). In a later satirical paper, 'Thirty Methods to Destroy the Creativity of Analytic Candidates' (Kernberg 1996), he 'proposes' measures that combine bureaucracy, intimidation, authoritarianism and indoctrination.

> Convey clearly ... that critical thinking is welcome as long as it leads to a confirmation of your dominant leader's views. Make sure to reward those students who are excited and fully convinced by what you assign to them.... Raise delicately but early the question as to what extent candidates' attempts not only to present papers but to have them published (!) may reflect unresolved oedipal competitiveness or narcissistic conflicts. ... Another perfectly legitimate method for increasing paranoid fearfulness in candidates is simply not conveying full and adequate information about requirements, expectations, rules, regulations and channels for redress of grievances. (Kernberg 1996, 1032–7)

Kernberg's earlier paper identifies a major discrepancy between the aims of analytic training and the methods used (Kernberg 1986, 812), and argues that institutes should shift from a structure modelled on 'a combination of the technical school and the theological seminary' to one 'combining the features of the art school and the university college' (ibid.). Kernberg suggests that the causes go further than power-seeking and poor group dynamics:

> [T]he therapeutic process of psychoanalysis liberates radioactive products and the dispersal of this radioactive fallout, which ordinarily occurs in psychoanalytic treatment carried out in an open social setting, is interfered with by the constraining and amplifying effects of the closed environment of the psychoanalytic institutions. (Ibid., 813–14)

This corresponds with Steltzer, who left analytic training when he became convinced that 'the training process could be described as a kind of narcissistic illness, both of the candidates and of the institution' (Steltzer 1986, 59). Among the causes that he assigns are 'the decathexis of external reality' (ibid., 67) – in other words, everything is ascribed to internal factors – and 'the loss of the dream experience and the transitional space' (ibid., 69) as the trainee *analyses* rather than *experiences* her own psychic life. In Steltzer's view, trainees and then psychoanalysts become 'a special kind of schizoid-alexithymic population' (ibid., 72): they lose touch with their own feelings and fantasies through too much intellectual processing.

Steltzer suggests that psychoanalysis, and psychotherapy in general, are *inherently* damaging to their practitioners. But the problems of training can be more concretely located in current circumstances and structures, as do Szasz and Kernberg, and also Arlow, who identifies, among other problems,

> recurring splits of institutes. There have been about half a dozen such in the American Psychoanalytic Association,[30] with almost as many splits threatened but fortunately averted. ... During the past eight years alone the [IPA] Central Executive Committee ... has had to deal with identical problems in France, Spain, Brazil, Venezuela, Columbia, and Australia. (Arlow 1972, 558–9)

Arlow derives these splits from conflicts over 'who shall have the right to train, that is, who shall be training analyst' (ibid., 559). Like many authors he emphasizes the 'ever-present problem' of the division between ordinary psychoanalysts and training analysts, who alone have the right to analyse trainees and report on their suitability. The position of training analyst is

> endowed with charismatic implications. The training analyst is regarded as possessing the psychoanalytic equivalent of omniscience. It is from the training analyst that candidates claim their descent. In many places the professional career of an individual may be determined by who his training analyst was. (Ibid., 559)

We shall see how Lacanian analysts tried to address this problem after splitting away from the IPA. The IPA itself has continued on a path of multiple and often painful compromise,[31] its guiding star always the spread and survival of psychoanalysis, and its primary method always the committee. Sometimes even IPA committees have been unable to stay together. In Portugal in 1967, the visiting IPA committee initially rejected two of the four candidate analysts before them – one as too rigid, the other as apparently a paranoid schizophrenic. It turned out that the Portuguese training institute was well aware of these problems, but hoping to nod through candidates whose connections with the Salazar dictatorship would help strengthen the position of Portuguese analysis. Three of the committee members acceded to this; the fourth – Paul Parin, an important figure in the Platform group – resigned (Kurzweil 1989, 206–7).

The different national groupings which are federated as the IPA currently pursue very varied clinical, theoretical and institutional approaches (ibid., 225–6; Joseph 1980). Many of the IPA's rules are more honoured in the breach than in the observance – on admission requirements for training, personal analysis, supervision and clinical experience, for example. Each local grouping, and even more the IPA as a whole, steers a flexible, politically conscious course.

Currently there seems to be a trend throughout psychoanalysis towards pluralism and acceptance of diversity.

> We are all more willing today to acknowledge the diversity of theoretical perspectives ... as well as the different regional, cultural, language and thought conventions within which psychoanalysis is expressed ... to see each theoretical perspective as a legitimate framework within which respected colleagues can organize the clinical encounters in their consulting rooms and interact therapeutically with their patients. (Wallerstein and Weinshel 1989, 358)

Cautious and informal negotiations are even underway for the rejoining of the IPA and the Lacanian schools. One can praise this as a far-sighted ecumenism; or treat it with more suspicion as a bureaucratic fudge responding to contracting markets for psychoanalytic work.

THE EXCLUSION OF JACQUES LACAN

A major crisis in the IPA occurred with the expulsion of the French analyst Jacques Lacan in the early 1950s.[32] Like Reich, Lacan was got rid of by shabby administrative procedures rather than direct confrontation. Unlike Reich, Lacan continued to call himself a psychoanalyst; and in fact there are said to be more Lacanian than IPA psychoanalysts in the world – mainly outside the Anglo-Saxon countries.

Also like Reich, Lacan was a difficult and autocratic personality, or so it seemed to many around him (see Roustang 1986); this may be why his presence as a senior figure in the French analytic organization, known for historical reasons as the Société Psychanalytique de Paris (SPP), could not be tolerated. There were certainly other provocations, such as Lacan's championing of lay analysis and his use of the 'variable session' – calling an end to the session at a moment of his own choosing, rather than after 50 minutes.[33] Nobus concludes that

> The rulers of the SPP considered Lacan a renegade, who was not willing to subject himself to the agreed standards of psychoanalysis, and who was suspected of trying to exhort people to undermine the established structures of power. (Nobus 1998a, 59)

The crisis began within the SPP's training institute, where Lacan was elected provisional president, then summarily removed in a row over different drafts of the institute's articles. According to Nobus,

> Lacan vigorously opposed an Institute in which all the power was centralized in one person or in one committee, and whose primary aim was not to train and to assure the transmission of psychoanalysis, but to dominate people and to dismantle opposing forces as much and as quickly as possible – in short to produce a large number of strictly conforming individuals. (Nobus 1998a, 58)

Removed from the Institute, Lacan was then elected SPP President, but almost immediately a campaign began for his expulsion on charges which included (like those against Socrates) inciting the students to rebel, and violating the rules of the society. Lacan and others broke away to form the Société Française de Psychanalyse (SFP), and Lacan soon began his famous series of Seminars which ran until his death. 'From then on the ... SPP publicly ignored the Lacanians' (Kurzweil 1989, 221).

The IPA therefore had to deal with two competing French analytic organizations; and in 1959 the 'Lacanian' SFP asked for affiliation to the IPA. After some slow grinding of bureaucracy, in 1962 the SFP was accepted as a Study Group – but only if Lacan and his colleague Françoise Dolto were progressively excluded. This became an ultimatum: the SFP would lose its affiliation unless it excluded Lacan as a training analyst by the end of 1963. A majority of the SFP acquiesced, leading Lacan the next day to break off his seminar on 'The Names-of-the-Father' in its first session, with the words:

I am not here in a plea for myself. I should, however, say that – having, for two years, entirely confided to others the execution, within a group, of a policy, in order to leave to what I had to tell you its space and its purity – I have never, at any moment, given any pretext for believing that there was not, for me, any difference between yes and no. (Lacan, 1990, 95)

The SFP's acquiescence in Lacan's removal led very quickly to a further scission and the creation of not one but two new analytic groupings – one, the École Française de Psychanalyse – shortly renamed the École Freudienne de Paris (EFP) – founded by Lacan. In 1969 some analysts resigned from the EFP to form the Quatrième Groupe, subtitled Organization psychoanalytique de langue française (Roudinesco 1990, 470–7).

There is a clear resemblance between these analytic fissionings and the sort of splits and recombinations of 'groupuscules' so common on the ultra-left.[34] Certainly there was a *political*, as well as a clinical-theoretical, radicalism to the project of Lacan and his colleagues – a rejection of the hierarchy of analytic institutions, where 'a sovereign body of self-nominated members not only sets out the theoretical lines, but also decides over the selection, training and promotion of candidates' (Nobus 1998a, 60). We shall see in Chapter 15 how the Lacanians tried to put this political programme into practice. In early 1980, shortly before his death, Lacan brought the fissioning process to a climax by unilaterally dissolving the EFP itself.

I mentioned in Chapter 3 that Lacanian analysis entered the university after May 1968, when student pressure led to the setting up of a Department of Psychoanalysis at the University of Paris VIII, staffed under Lacan's auspices and with a substantial number of non-analytic teachers (Turkle 1979, 174) – a move which 'established for the first time in a French university a psychoanalytic teaching stripped of any debt to medicine or psychology' (Roudinesco 1990, 552–3). A number of political projects met at this point, including the government's wish to de-fang the student radicals by giving them some of what they wanted in a sterilized environment, and the Lacanians' wish to assert their authority as the voice of psychoanalysis in the academy.

In the immediate postwar period, psychoanalysis had to achieve a status for itself through its own institutional movement, whereas in 1968, it was, on the contrary, a matter of psychoanalysis seeking refuge from societies which had become overgrown, dogmatic, or sclerotic. (Roudinesco 1990, 550)

The Department became a shambles, however, dragged this way and that by competing forces, until in 1974 Lacan suddenly conducted a *putsch* from above. With no formal authority, he took personal charge of the Department, installed his non-analyst son-in-law Jacques-Alain Miller as Chair, and renamed the Department *'le Champ freudien'* – 'the Freudian field'. All scheduled courses were cancelled, and anyone – staff or otherwise – who wanted to give a course had to present it as a research project to a small Scientific Committee with Lacan as a member. Many were rejected (including the prominent feminist analyst Luce Irigaray), and many people resigned.

In a further innovation the Department, having argued for some years, against student pressure, that study at Vincennes could not authorize anyone to practise analysis, suddenly announced a *clinical* programme. To translate this from the private language of psychoanalysis, it has always been held (a) that only analysts are in a position to teach about analysis, and (b) that the key to becoming an analyst is to undergo a training analysis. The existence of 'non-analyst psychoanalytic practitioners' (Turkle 1979, 187) on the teaching staff at Vincennes was already an issue; now a course about analytic practice was to be run partly by non-analysts, and partly for the non-analysed. As we shall see in Chapter 15, these issues reflected an ongoing struggle to create a new, Lacanian form of analytic training and accreditation.

INSTITUTIONALIZING PSYCHOTHERAPY AND COUNSELLING IN THE UK

You could call this a rich culture and see it as a tribute to human tolerance and coop-erativeness that they have continued to work together. I think it is those things, but it has also been hell and hilarious to hear all the shenanigans about who is and is not willing to get into bed with whom. Snobbery, denigration, and slavering sycophancy have co-existed with patience, integrity and remarkable feats of containment. (Young 1996, n.p.)

The history of British psychotherapy and counselling since the start of the 1970s provides rich examples of the many ways in which therapy and politics intersect. The period has seen a determined and sustained effort on the part of many eminent practitioners towards 'forging a new profession of adult non-medical psychotherapists' (Pedder 1989, 219). It has also seen the gradual and at first confused emergence of what is now an equally determined *opposition* to professionalization (House and Totton 1997).

The professionalization process began in 1970, with the Standing Conference for the Advancement of Counselling (Jones 1996, 7). Out of this emerged in 1977 the British Association for Counselling (BAC), which '[s]ets standards for train-ing and supervision; monitoring the skills and resources of qualified counsellors; codes of practice and ethics; and complaints procedures. ... It is coming to view itself as a professional body with elements of a Learned Society in the making' (ibid., 8). In the process, several of the BAC's most senior and influential members, some deeply involved in the institutionalization of counselling, have become disaffected with aspects of that process (e.g. Feltham 1997; Thorne 1997).

In an odd reversal of the usual relationship between psychotherapy and counselling, BAC provided the initial facilities and administrative back-up for the United Kingdom Council for Psychotherapy (UKCP) (Jones 1996, 9). BAC convened the 'Rugby Conference' on the professional status of psychotherapy and counselling in 1982, from which it later gracefully withdrew, leaving the UK Standing Conference on Psychotherapy (formed in 1989) which in 1993 became the UKCP (Mowbray 1995, 49–50). UKCP and BAC now stand side by side as the two self-defined professional bodies for psychotherapy and coun-selling in the UK.

The motor force for recruitment to both bodies has always been insecurity. Practitioners and trainees have been given to understand that they are in danger of being unable to practise if they do not conform to BAC and UKCP requirements. Much of this focused for several years on '1992' – the date of the establishment of a free internal market in the European Community, and the supposed date by which the EC would impose regulatory standards on UK practitioners (Heron 1997, 12; Mowbray 1995, 20ff.). It was claimed that after 1992 'we can expect new laws to come into force within the next few years, standardizing the regulations for psychotherapy in all member countries' (Boadella, 1991, 33); and that for the UKCP to become the single voice for psychotherapy would prevent 'the atrocious repression which has taken place in most countries of Europe, where only such psychotherapy as is approved and controlled by the psychiatric establishment is allowed to take place' (Rowan 1991, 33). Wild stories circulated that, after 1992, unregistered therapists would be fined hundreds of pounds.

Almost all of this was fantasy, serving the interests of regulation. Mowbray (1995, 23) discusses the creation, in the minds of those writing on the subject, of imaginary EC bodies with imaginary goals of control; and stresses the reality that the EC was 'not seeking to harmonise the regulation or training of *any* profession' (ibid., 25), quoting a European Parliament document of November 1993 to the effect that '[t]he Commission does *not* plan to make specific proposals for psychotherapists' (ibid., 26, my italics).

Once the EC bogeyman disappeared in a puff of smoke, the UKCP performed an astonishing U-turn: from being a defensive union in the face of external pressure for regulation, it began itself to press for the regulation of psychotherapy: 'the next big step is to get a law passed and achieve statutory registration' (Pokorny 1995, 421). A number of little articles and letters started appearing in the press telling horror stories about abusive practitioners, and suggesting that the UKCP, backed up by statute, was the solution.

Unfortunately the UKCP found itself struggling against the government's enormous unwillingness to act in an arena so strewn with landmines. This had been a consistent position since the 1970s, when a private member's bill to set up a statutory register of psychotherapists failed due to lack of government support: the government said then what its successors have said ever since, that 'unless the profession could agree there was nothing that the government would do' (Pokorny 1995, 415; cf. Heron 1997, 11; Mowbray 1995, 42–5). The UKCP has been trying to position itself as the united voice of psychotherapists; in this it has failed, as a government spokesperson again stated as recently as 1997 (Richardson, 1997).

Why have successive governments and their civil servants taken this line? Essentially, it is because the apparent unity of the UKCP, and therefore its claim to speak for 'the profession of psychotherapy' is a fiction. The claim operates on three levels: first, that there is a single specifiable activity called psychotherapy, whose practitioners are psychotherapists; second, that those practitioners are meaningfully represented by the UKCP; and third, that the UKCP is the only body to represent them.

Ann Richardson of the Department of Health briskly demolished the first claim in the statement mentioned above.

> There are no plans to regulate what after all we have to call an activity, rather than a title. I mean, psychotherapy is something that people do. It's something doctors,

psychologists, nurses, social workers, lay psychotherapists do. ... Another thing that
militates against [statutory regulation] is the increasing evidence of the effectiveness
of a variety of approaches.... (Richardson 1997)

This attacks one fundamental justification for the UKCP: the idea that there is
a single activity of psychotherapy. The UKCP has always been an uneasy coalition of people who do very different things: analysts, humanistic practitioners,
behaviourists, hypnotherapists. What precisely do they have in common? In
1991, Rowan accurately stated that '[t]he reason why this [the UKSCP as
it then was] has been possible is that it is not agreement on theory which is
being attempted, but *agreement on staying together*' (Rowan 1991, 33). He clearly
approves of this, but from another point of view it can be seen as a fatal flaw in
the elaborate balancing act which constituted UKCP.

I write 'constituted' rather than 'constitutes' because the coalition has begun to
come apart: in 1992 a number of senior analytic organizations broke away to form
the British Confederation of Psychotherapists (BCP) (Pokorny 1995, 418–19).

It was particularly ironic that among the objections made by [the BCP] was that certain procedures in the UKCP were excessively democratic, with full voting rights in
the hands of organizations which they thought did not merit them. (Young 1996, n.p.)

The groups which formed the BCP demanded a veto over decisions of the
UKCP as a whole as their price for staying. 'They claimed to be senior to all
other psychotherapeutic practitioners and referred to the device they advocated
as "the Security Council model"' (ibid.). It appears that several of these groups
acted undemocratically in relation to their own membership, which was often
not properly consulted about the break with UKCP (ibid., Samuels 1997b, 47).

The existence of the BCP, together with that of the Independent Practitioners Network (Chapter 16), refutes the UKCP's claim to be *the* representative body for psychotherapy. But how representative is it in any case? The
UKCP has no individual membership: its members are therapy *organizations*,
each of which must have 'enough people in it to make sense' (Pokorny 1995,
416). In 1993, 90 per cent of member organizations were training bodies
(Mowbray 1995, 55). It is these training bodies which have banded together to
control access to the profession, and to ensure that their trainings alone will
admit practitioners to the National Register of Psychotherapists which the
UKCP established in 1993.

As Mowbray puts it, 'the UKCP is essentially an exclusive club for psychotherapy trainers – a political lobby for the psychotherapy training business'
(Mowbray 1995, 57). It includes no representation of the public interest, consumer groups, students, or non-training practitioners, the great majority of
psychotherapists. It is also constructed so as progressively to close off access
even for new training organizations. The requirement that a candidate organization must have 'enough people in it to make sense' means that a training has
to attract a sizeable number of students before it can apply for UKCP membership, with no guarantee that it will be accepted. If the UKCP succeeds in its
declared intention of dominating the practice of psychotherapy, so that those
not on its register have difficulty getting work, then who will be prepared to
sign up for a non-UKCP training?

The UKCP has achieved a great deal in terms of getting the different forms of psychotherapy to talk to each other – not an easy task. It has also put on the agenda the question of practitioner accountability, which had previously been seriously underemphasized – although the UKCP's approach may not be the best one. However, despite all the good will and effort invested in the project, it suffers from the serious flaws which I have outlined. Its central project is inevitably to safeguard the interests of its members; and its members are those who run established psychotherapy trainings.

15

Challenging the Institutions of Psychotherapy

There have been several attempts over the years to challenge and reform the styles of organization which exist in the field of psychotherapy and counselling. In this chapter, we shall looks at three of these, corresponding to the three sections of the last chapter: the Platform group as a response to the IPA, the *passe* as a Lacanian method of accreditation, and the Independent Practitioners Network as a response to the UKCP and BAC.

THE PLATFORM GROUP

The Platform movement began at the 1969 World Congress of the International Psychoanalytic Association, in Rome (Langer 1989, 111–13). This Congress tried to make sense of the stirring revolutionary events of 1968; according to Langer, though, its attempts were 'totally disappointing. Once again, the thread-bare rhetoric of an "Oedipal generation gap" served only to irritate many of the participants' (ibid., 111).

Into this charged atmosphere came a banner in the lobby of the Rome Hilton announcing 'PSYCHOANALYSI$'. Underneath, a blackboard invited delegates to a 'Para-congress' in a nearby working-class bar. Behind this initiative were a number of candidate analysts from Austria, Switzerland and Italy: 'young, attractive people in hippie clothing … carrying on the climate of 1968 in Paris' (ibid., 112). The Para-congress debated two issues: training and ideology. A series of complaints were drawn up to present to the official congress, concerning the cost of training, enrolment criteria, texts used, and so on: a 'platform', in fact. As a result, 'Platform' groups were established in the three countries mentioned above, and also in Argentina.

According to Modena (1986, 9), the Swiss Platform group, based in Zurich, 'consisted of physicians and psychologists who had learned by participating in the student movement that no science could be politically neutral'. In the face of strong opposition, they developed their criticism of analytic training structures and proposals for democratization. 'Thanks to the support of a few progressive training analysts … a model of self-government was eventually achieved' – in the shape of the 'Zurich Psychoanalytical Seminar', which was given passive recognition by the local IPA group, the SGP (Swiss Society for Psychoanalysis).

According to Modena (ibid.), the 'strongest weapon for democratization' was that several analysts who could have joined the SGP chose to stay with the Seminar. Writing in 1986, he describes the structure of the Seminar as a radical extension of the *passe* (see below): 'Everybody is an analyst-in-training by self-declaration' (ibid., 10). Every analysis can be a training analysis – no distinction is made between this and an ordinary analysis. Modena gives vignettes (ibid., 12–15) of patients changing their minds in both directions during analysis as to whether or not they wanted to become analysts.

Since analysts and analysands coexist as peers within the Seminar, many situations of dual relationship arise. Modena is rather sanguine about the effects of this on analytic work, or vice versa: 'In most cases negative consequences are easily avoided; indeed these "disturbances" can even enrich the analytic process' (ibid., 21). However, he does recognize that such a 'disturbance' can be severe, and that

> in … exceptional situations, the analysand must decide which is more important, personal analysis or the organization's activities. It would, however, also be conceivable that the analyst, in the interest of the patient, might temporarily avoid the Seminar. One way or the other a reasonable resolution can usually be found by two adult people who have complementary interests in the continuation of their common work. (Ibid.)

We are perhaps entitled to be surprised by this formulation: 'two adult people', according to psychoanalytic theory, are precisely not going to be available to negotiate at many points in an analysis. Modena's optimistic account is reminiscent of many humanistic practitioners' attitude to transference (e.g. Mowbray 1995, 172ff.); and perhaps for similar reasons – it *should* be possible, therefore it *must* be possible. Two outcomes are likely: either transference is suppressed, or chaos ensues. However, the opposite extreme is the already existing norm in the IPA, where as Kernberg satirically recommends,

> [w]ithin a small psychoanalytic society, it is always possible to justify forbidding candidates to attend … meetings because such a small group might not be able to avoid contacts between candidates and their analysts outside the sessions, and this justifies perfectly the isolation of the institute teaching from the active scientific world of psychoanalytic thinking. (Kernberg 1996, 1037)

In Argentina, the 'Plataforma' group began in 1971 with a declaration that 'the undersigned psychoanalysts … have decided to make public their separation from the International Psychoanalytic Association and its Argentinian affiliate' (Langer 1989, 243). Addressing 'mental health workers', the group explained their view that psychoanalysis 'has been distorted and arrested' by bourgeois ideology (ibid.), and their intention to put 'our knowledge at the service of ideologies which uncompromisingly question the system' of capitalism (ibid., 244). Their disagreement with 'psychoanalytic societal organization' was 'at all levels: theoretical, technical, didactic, investigative and economic; but here we want to emphasize the one that is decisive, the ideological' (ibid.).

The declaration goes on to argue that the institutional structure of psychoanalysis reflects its obedience to capitalist ideology – specifically, in the oligarchic distribution of power within analytic organizations, and in particular the exclusion from decision-making of analytic students.

This vertical order, in which hierarchical authority does not necessarily coincide with a higher scientific level but with seniority and bureaucratic experience ... not only perverts the Institution's specific function ... but also replaces it with the search for prestige, status and economic achievements. (Ibid., 245)

More decisive, though, according to the declaration, is the way in which such hierarchical/bureaucratic structures 'encase psychoanalysts, with their acquies-cence in their long wait for promotion, in the bastion of a strictly apolitical and a social profession'. As a result, they proclaim a decisive break with the IPA: 'From now on ... psychoanalysis is wherever psychoanalysts may be' (ibid., 246).[35]

The Plataforma group came together with other radical Argentinian mental health groupings to create a training organization, the Teaching and Research Centre, with a programme that combined Marxism and psychoanalysis. The training cut across sacred distinctions between analysts, psychologists and other psycho-practitioners, in 'an epistemological effort to separate the strongest nuclei of psychoanalytic theory from those that had important ideological con-notations or that were mere rationalizations of the only esteemed practice: indi-vidual, protracted psychoanalysis' (Langer 1989, 123). This lasted from 1971 until the growth of right-wing terror in Argentina in 1974, and offered, accord-ing to Langer, 'the proof that serious high-level training can be provided and acquired outside the official psychoanalytic institutions, for a minimal eco-nomic contribution which serves for the upkeep of the premises' (ibid.).

THE *PASSE*

All the companions in arms were agreed on at least one point. They did not want to reproduce the kind of instruction and the hierarchy in effect in the societies affiliated with the IPA ... that they regarded as contrary to the manifestation of an authentic desire to be an analyst. They all wanted to found a Freudian republic that did not resemble an association of notables and functionaries. But they did not know how to make the transition.... (Roudinesco 1990, 443)

When Lacan left the IPA, alongside his theoretical and clinical project of the 'return to Freud' there was also an institutional project: the creation of 'the ideal psychoanalytic society, an institution in which power is decentralized and in which the juniors just as much as the seniors have the power of decision' (Nobus 1998a, 61). In practice, however, 'the more Lacan's influence grew and the more his institutional initiatives expanded, the more he was regarded as an autocrat, tolerating only those who were absolutely loyal to his cause and who did nothing else but parrot his ideas and sell his name' (ibid.). The core of the Lacanian group's position on analytic training was that there was no distinction to be made between psychoanalysis to treat some psychological problem, and psychoanalysis for the purpose of becoming an analyst.

[I]f somebody came with a demand for analysis because he or she wanted to become an analyst, this demand could be treated as a symptom. Sometimes it might even turn out that this demand was a very nasty symptom indeed, and that it had nothing to do with the desire of the analyst as such. (Ibid., 62)

This hits directly at the power structure of psychoanalytic institutions, the sin-gling out of an elite group of 'training analysts' who, like bishops, are alone able to create new analysts. Under this new dispensation, any analysis might produce a new analyst, though no analysis could be guaranteed to do so. The emphasis shifts from the creation of psychoanalysts to their *recognition* by their peers.

The institution of the *passe* in 1967 (Lacan 1990; Nobus 1998a, 63) formalized this shift. It was enshrined in a lengthy document, part history and part theory: 'The whole', Roudinesco tells us – with what degree of irony it is hard to judge – 'was of a singular beauty, and once again revealed the genius of its author' (Roudinesco 1990, 444). To be recognized as an analyst within the École Freudienne de Paris (EFP), an analysand must discuss her analysis, in particular its ending, with two – later three – other analysands, the *passeurs*. These three inform a *jury d'agrément* of what they have heard; and this jury decides whether or not the individual has demonstrated her 'ability to theorize the training experience transmitted by way of the couch' (Roudinesco 448), and should therefore be recognized as an analyst.

> The candidate does not have to prove to his or her seniors that he or she would be a valuable analyst ... he or she has to testify to an experience in front of three people who are his or her equals. The jury does not judge any kind of knowledge presented by the candidate, but a knowledge spoken by people who have nothing to gain or to lose in the entire procedure. (Nobus 1998a, 63)

This is clearly a radical process, breaking with the traditions of the IPA, parallel to those of general professional training. 'Lacan ... laid claim to the ultra-traditional notion of a "training analysis". But he used the term in an unprecedented way ... he defined the training analysis in terms of a personal vision of the personal analysis' (Roudinesco 1990, 445). However, the *passe* was not very successful, creating violent arguments over the jury's decisions, and accusations that they were dominated by Lacan – 'working under the multidimensional gaze of a master who in fact continued to be the analyst of one and all' (Roudinesco 1990, 463).

Roudinesco sums up the outcome as follows:

> [Lacan] was unable to keep the new distinctions in rank from being more or less similar to what had prevailed before. Moreover, he had conflated his role as intellectual master with his position as director of the École. ... Hostile to the constitution of centers of power ... he had eliminated them by Draconian means and ... done away with those who had been loyal to him in favor of a cohort of epigones devoted to his person. (Roudinesco 1990, 443)

This failure may in part be attributed to Lacan's personal shortcomings. It may also be argued that the *passe* was bound to fail, since it constituted an unsatisfactory halfway house between formal accreditation, and the more radical position which Lacan expressed in a later version of the *passe* proposal: 'The psychoanalyst derives his authorization solely from himself' (quoted Roudinesco 1990, 444).

However, it is also possible to identify structural difficulties with democratic psychotherapy training of any kind: difficulties related to the phenomena of transference and counter-transference on which psychotherapy is largely founded. Nobus describes this in Lacanian terminology as

> the fundamental drama of an analytic society that tries to organize itself according to the principles of the discourse of the analyst: Where members are not supposed to exert power, but rather to cause the desire of the other, the effect is that the other is

hystericised and in turn installs the other as a master, whether he or she likes it or not. (Nobus 1998a, 64)

Nobus also indicates that the *passe* is being threatened by pressures to conform with the new accreditation bureaucracy. 'These will certainly affect the future of psychoanalysis, if only because many analysts, even Lacanian ones, are more than willing to exchange what they have achieved for a large-scale social recognition and a batch of new loyalties' (ibid., 63).

THE INDEPENDENT PRACTITIONERS NETWORK

The Independent Practitioners Network (IPN) in the UK is not primarily a challenge to the *content* of psychotherapy practice or training; like the *passe*, it represents a demand for that content be taken seriously, for theory be applied to the institutional forms of therapy (cf. Nobus 1998a, 64). It originated in response to the pressure for compulsory registration of therapists described in the last chapter. This response, however, has developed from an essentially *defensive* banding together of practitioners to protect their right to practice, into a more proactive initiative for a new model of accountability and a new way to relate to each other.

In late 1994, a proposal appeared for 'an alternative model of accountability and validation ... which actually makes use of what we know as therapists about human interaction'. Concerned individuals and groups were invited to a conference which would set up a network composed of *groups* of therapists – rather than either individuals or training organizations – involved in mutual self and peer assessment and accreditation: a network where

> there will be no distinction of more or less qualified or 'registered' members, since we recognise that therapeutic ability is not based on hours of training or numbers of essays written. Nor will we be scrutinising each others' qualifications. In other words the structure will be horizontal and multi-centred rather than vertical/pyramidal. (Totton and Edmondson 1994)

The aim was 'to provide intending clients with a context of basic security within which they can make their own decisions about which practitioner is valuable for them' (ibid.). The Network would 'not attempt to define terms like "therapy", or to distinguish between different styles of work, since we see a richly pluralistic and multi-skilled ecology as the ideal' (ibid.). Above all, the Network would not be a 'trainers' club' like the UKCP: accreditation would be mutual and horizontal, rather than trickling down from the top. Sixty people attended this meeting, and most of them agreed to set up a Network along these lines. There was strong emotion – many people spoke of feeling that they had found a home, a place to belong.

The Network which has evolved consists of a number of groups of usually between five and ten practitioners. Some of these already existed – centres or group practices, for example; some have formed specifically to join the Network. For this, they need to formulate an ethical statement which is made freely available; and to form links with two other groups participating in the Network.

The members of a group agree to stand by each others' work – a much debated phrase which essentially means that they take responsibility for processing any problems that arise, for example, conflict with a dissatisfied client. Similarly, linked groups agree to stand by each others' process as a group: that is, they satisfy themselves that the other group is genuinely monitoring and challenging its members' practice. The foundation of the Network, therefore, is face-to-face relationship and experience, in direct contrast to the formal qualification basis of UKCP or BAC accreditation. IPN is very much smaller in membership than UKCP; however, all its members are active participants, while the great majority of UKCP-accredited practitioners have a passive involvement, being written onto the books by their training organization.

The safeguard for clients is that they can take their grievance to any of fourteen or more people – or indeed to anyone in the Network; and that if the group their practitioner belongs to fails to resolve the conflict to the satisfaction of its link groups, those links will be withdrawn and the whole group will lapse from membership. (As a balancing factor against trivial disputes, the group withdrawing its link would itself no longer be a full member, and would have to find a new link. The structure encourages groups to assure themselves of each others' integrity, but not to fall out over details.)

Participation in the Network is open to anyone (IPN 1996, 1). There is no shared position on therapeutic methods, theory or training: the Network supports diversity and plurality, and recognizes that there are many ways of becoming an effective practitioner. There is no one shared ethical code; but each member group must publish its guidelines (and the names of its members) to the whole Network. The central goal of the Network is given in the constitution as 'furthering and supporting good practice' (ibid.). The question of what 'good practice' is, however, does not have a single answer; but openness about practice allows a wide and ongoing debate, including criticism and challenge. The Network's whole ethos is that there is no centre to give authoritative judgement; individuals must take responsibility for their own definition of what good practice means, and share this definition publicly.

So far IPN seems to be functioning well; but potentially problematic areas have emerged. To begin with, the Network has experienced the usual difficulties over leadership and conflict which every organization has to face; and has not always dealt with them well. However, to an extent participants have been able to use their skills and awareness as therapists to find ways forward. The next problem is also fairly familiar: the Network tends to divide into a minority who do the work and know what is going on, and a majority who are relatively passive, relatively out of touch, and sometimes resentful about this. IPN cannot function successfully without the active participation of most of those involved. But it is not yet clear whether that participation can be achieved and maintained.

The test which IPN has yet to meet is a major conflict between a participating practitioner and a client – what more orthodox institutions would call a 'complaint'. The intention is to approach such a situation using a conflict resolution model, rather than an adversarial, 'guilty/not-guilty' one. The practitioner's group will be able to draw on the help of its two link groups, and ultimately on the entire network. IPN's resolution is not to formalize a procedure, but instead to rely on the intelligence and creativity of all those involved to create a good outcome.

Conclusions to Part III

It is clear that, as a group, psychotherapists and counsellors can claim no special political qualities – except, conceivably, an above-average degree of argumentativeness. We have seen therapists adapting with greater or lesser success to the demands of totalitarian regimes; competing viciously with each other for power, prestige and income; and manipulating institutions and training programmes in order to maintain hegemonic control.

Does this undermine the claim of psychotherapy to have some insights into political processes? Not intrinsically – one can understand a problem without being able to surmount it. But the evidence is certainly not encouraging, if we are hoping for psychotherapy to show us some means of progress in human affairs: it cannot even organize itself politically in a way which conforms with its own theory. Lacanian discourse theory, to which Nobus refers in the last chapter, offers a theoretical basis for arguing that this is structurally impossible:

> Where members are not supposed to exert power, but rather to cause the desire of the other, the effect is that the other is hystericised and in turn installs the other as a master, whether he or she likes it or not. The major difficulty ... has to do less with taking up the position of the analyst ... than with preventing the analysand from attributing the position of master to the analyst. (Nobus 1998a, 64)

A rough equivalent of this in more familiar language would be to say that psychotherapy works (according to most practitioners) through utilizing the transference – that is, by deliberately allowing profound feelings to arise in the client towards the therapist. The intention is to illuminate the client about their own process; but the experience leaves a residue of feeling for the therapist which, in the context of an organization where almost everyone is someone else's ex-client, is bound to be politically explosive.

These thoughts connect with two issues that have been touched on above, and to which we will return in Part Four. In discussing the Soviet Union, we mentioned the power of the therapist to define what is 'healthy' or 'pathological' in the client (the medical terminology underlines the point): a power which is at the least capable of exploitation, and possibly innately corrupting. One form in which it is employed is what we have characterized as the exclusion of external reality from the consulting room; so that if the client introduces political themes, for example, these are immediately pathologized, treated as symptoms, or as attempts to damage the therapy rather than to enrich it. As so often, what is portrayed as a protection of the client or the therapeutic space may actually protect *the therapist* from having to face difficult but important conflicts.

Part IV
Politics in Psychotherapy

16

Challenging Bias and Ideology

Psychotherapy and counselling have been massively and often justifiably criticized for treating some behaviour as 'normal', 'healthy', etc., and other behaviour as deviant and 'neurotic'. Issues cited include gender; sexual orientation; ethnic group and culture; and class.

These matters are still being fought out in therapy, just as in the world in general: it would be wrong to expect therapy to solve them in isolation. But one criticism we will encounter is precisely of therapy's unwillingness to give up this isolation and *engage* with such issues – to exist 'in the real world'.[36] In Jeffrey Masson's words:

> Every therapy I have examined … displays a lack of interest in social injustice. Each shows a lack of interest in physical and sexual abuse. Each shows an implicit acceptance of the political status quo. In brief, almost every therapy shows a certain lack of interest in the world. (Masson 1990, 283)

This says something about the therapies Masson chooses to examine – as we have demonstrated, there are plenty of therapies and therapists concerned with these matters. But Masson is accurate about the majority trend in psychotherapy and counselling towards social disengagement. Arnold Mindell, very much with the engaged minority, adds to the list of therapeutic prejudices the belief that everyone should be a therapy-head:

> [M]ost therapists assume that the only conscious human beings are ones who think about themselves all the time. Such apparently 'harmless' assumptions are so full of naive prejudices that it is not surprising that our Western therapies and group and organizational practices are not solving city and international problems. (Mindell 1992, 4–5)

FEMINIST AND GAY CRITIQUES

As Eichenbaum and Orbach argue,

> Psychoanalysis, humanistic psychology, transactional analysis, phenomenology, existential psychotherapy, gestalt psychotherapy and psychosynthesis, loudly declaim their

political indifference and lack of bias. They rarely concede that their discipline, like feminist psychotherapy, expresses a particular world view. (Eichenbaum and Orbach 1987, 49)

To make the point again: the assertion that one is apolitical often masks political conservatism. And psychotherapists are often conservative in their view of women and gays. In an elegant piece of research, Broverman et al. (1970) asked therapists to list those characteristics which they regarded as defining a normal male, a normal female, and a normal person. Normal males and normal persons were ascribed similar characteristics – including 'intellectual', 'rational', 'aggressive', etc.; normal women, however, seen as 'normally' passive, nurturant and emotional, were thus not regarded by the psychotherapists involved as normal persons.

Many authors (e.g. Dutton-Douglas and Walker, 1988) have comprehensively criticized psychotherapy from a feminist perspective for its inbuilt sexist assumptions. In the 1970s and 1980s feminists frequently challenged the sometimes extreme sexism of growth movement facilitators and therapists.

> We have found some leaders who assumed that nonconformity to feminine norms was neurotic. Group leaders have felt at liberty to make such sexist remarks to women as, 'You could be attractive if you tried', 'Do you want to grow breasts?' ... If a woman has been sexually insulted in the street and brings her distress to a growth movement group she may be told: 'It's only because you feel bad about yourself that this incident bothers you'. (Ernst and Goodison 1981, 312–14)

There has been a genuine education of humanistic practitioners on issues of sexism – partly through the general cultural shift over the past few decades away from *overtly* exploitative and oppressive attitudes. However, just as for the culture as a whole, sexism in the growth movement has to some extent gone underground rather than disappeared.

Feminists have also criticized specific types of therapy – for example, Waterhouse claims that 'women coming into counselling can be particularly harmed as a result of the person-centred [i.e. Rogerian] emphasis on self-transformation [which] gives unwarranted weight to the individual's power to effect change in their everyday lives irrespective of material and socio-political constraints' (Waterhouse 1993, 63). This is part of a more general criticism of psychotherapy for its over-emphasis on the individual and the internal at the expense of the social and external.

Feminists have also often criticized the *style of relationship* which they see in psychotherapy, using ideas about power which have developed within the women's movement. A sophisticated critique of psychotherapy in its application to adolescent girls is offered by Gilligan et al.:

> Adolescent girls have emerged as key figures in our study of women's psychological development.... Resistance in clinical practice has meant obscuring or burying psychological truths or avoiding key memories and feelings, and thus has been seen as an impediment to the creation of a working therapeutic relationship. ...We elaborate the concept of resistance by joining girls' struggle to know what they know and speak about their thoughts and feelings. In doing so we acknowledge the difficulties girls face when their knowledge or feelings seem hurtful to other people or disruptive of relationships. Thus the word 'resistance' takes on new resonances, picking up the notion of healthy resistance, the capacity of the psyche to resist disease processes, and

also the concept of political resistance, the willingness to act on one's own knowledge when such action causes trouble. (Gilligan et al. 1991, 1–2)

Several forms of specifically feminist therapy have been developed over the last decades – some in a psychodynamic style, both Freudian (e.g. Ernst and Maguire 1987; Prozan 1993) and Jungian (e.g. Young-Eisendrath and Wiedemann, 1987), some humanistic (e.g. Chaplin 1988); and psychotherapy as a whole has to a limited extent been shifted in its views and procedures by feminist interventions. Betty Prozan identifies 'three major areas where feminists have crusaded and where psychoanalysis and psychotherapy have been influenced and have responded, although with some defensiveness and resistance: battered women, childhood sexual abuse, and therapist–patient sexual relations' (Prozan 1993, 209).

Even though there has been plenty of sexism in the field of psychotherapy, it has always been something of an equal opportunity employer *vis-à-vis* women (Appignanesi and Forrester 1992, 6). However, until quite recently there was a widespread view in the analytic world that homosexuality is a disqualification for analytic training, backed by the argument that homosexuality is *perverse* in the technical sense of the word, and entails an incapacity to hold a positive fantasy image of the copulating parental couple, which many analysts see as vital to psychological wellbeing (Cunningham 1991, 62).

Thus the report of the IPA's 'Study Commission on the Evaluation of Applications for Psychoanalytic Training' states that

> the first serious disqualification proposed was homosexuality, followed by other forms of perversion. …[O]pinion was sharply divided. On theoretical grounds it was argued that homosexuality *per se* (a symptom) was not the relevant issue but that the attendant narcissistic personality disturbance would interfere with analytic work, and therefore the selection would depend on the assessment of the analysability of the narcissistic disturbance. Some of the group felt there was no theoretical justification to disqualify a homosexual if his 'analytic sector' remained intact, but others could not envision, for example, sending a son to a homosexual analyst. (McLaughlin 1978, 81–2)

For some years, even to argue against this position was experienced as dangerous to one's professional standing. Thus 'Cunningham' (1991) finds it necessary to write under a pseudonym when arguing, not even that perversion should not disqualify from analytic training, but only that homosexuality is not strictly a perversion; while in the early 1970s a gay psychiatrist who came out to members of the American Psychiatric Association did so wearing a mask and using a voice-disguising microphone (Sinfield 1994, 246).

As one might expect, though, increasingly voices have been raised against both the practical policies of exclusion, and their theoretical underpinnings. Some of these accept, at least implicitly, the argument that a perverse personality structure is unsuited for psychotherapy training, but argue that homosexuals may not fall within this category. Samuels insists that 'the fruitfulness signified in the primal scene, and the problems therein, are completely congruent with homosexual experience' (Samuels 1993, 168). Cunningham, among others, points out that the exclusion of gays is based upon

> the heterosexual ideal: the person whose heterosexuality is stably organized, who harbours no envy of the opposite sex, who gladly houses in his/her inner world a

benign notion of parental intercourse. [T]his particular ideal is in fact attained only partially or sporadically even by emotionally mature heterosexuals. It seems that because this ideal is unattainable as a whole a sense of failure and self-criticism is 'pushed out' onto homosexuals. (Cunningham 1991, 62–3)

Similarly, Mendoza says that: 'Many homosexuals are so perverse in their organization that they are not suitable to train as psychotherapists, and so are many heterosexuals' (Mendoza 1997, 394).

A distinction started to emerge between gay *clients* and gay *practitioners*. Thus the American Psychiatric Association agreed in 1973 to list in the *Diagnostic and Statistical Manual* only homosexuals who were unable to accept their own homosexuality. But while other homosexuals were thus no longer officially sick, that did not mean they were well either – certainly not well enough to practise psychotherapy. Homosexuality was left in a sort of limbo, neither saved nor damned.

Slightly more positively, Isay, a gay psychoanalyst, proposes a 'gay affirmative' therapy, describing a *normal* developmental pathway for a homosexual identity (Isay 1993, 10; ct. Cornett, 1995). However, Isay describes normal male homosexual development as bound up with effeminacy. Although this leads him to call for a society where feminine traits are valued equally with masculine ones (ibid., 129), it still leaves him firmly within a binary system of gender-linked qualities. As Sinfield asks, in reference to Isay's work, 'do we not have reason to suspect any concept of the normal? May not some kinds of gayness involve not having "a well-integrated personality", and will it be legitimate to "cure" or discriminate against them?' (Sinfield 1994, 252). Here psychotherapy encounters Queer Theory, which poses a robust challenge not only to 'the entire masculine/feminine binary model' (ibid., 248) underlying therapy's – and of course the whole culture's – thinking about homosexuality, but also to the very concept of psychological 'health' and 'normality'.

In an article entitled 'Opening the Profession' (Ryan and Samuels 1996), Joanna Ryan and Andrew Samuels describe a piece of direct action which had major effects upon the practice of British training organizations around homosexuality. In 1995, the Association for Psychoanalytic Psychotherapy in the National Health Service (APP) proposed to invite Charles Socarides to give its annual lecture. As we have already seen, Socarides can be accurately described as 'a virulent campaigner against moves for lesbian and gay rights, on the grounds that the homosexual rights movement constitutes a serious threat to Western culture' (Ryan and Samuels 1996, 36).

The founding group of the organization Psychotherapists and Counsellors for Social Responsibility (PCSR), which we have already encountered, asked Ryan and Samuels to develop a response to the fact of this invitation; they produced a 'Letter of Concern', which

connected the APP's invitation to two problematic issues concerning psychoanalytic psychotherapy in this country: first, the alleged discrimination against lesbians and gay men who try to train at the Institute of Psychoanalysis and some other psychoanalytic psychotherapy organizations; second, the privileged status given to graduates of the Institute ... when it comes to appointment as consultant psychotherapists in the NHS. (Ibid.)

This was signed by about 200 'registered[37] psychotherapists'. However, journals approached to publish it responded rather ambivalently; eventually it appeared in the *British Journal of Psychotherapy* in March 1996, and summaries were placed in two other journals.

The Letter called not for cancellation of the lecture, but for proper debate about the issues it raised, and for the APP to distance itself from Socarides. In the event the APP did cancel the lecture, on the grounds of an alleged threat of disruption. It then 'became possible for the issues to be swiftly converted into a problem of free speech, thus enabling numerous colleagues to decline support' (ibid., 37). According to Ryan and Samuels, 'some people told us they were simply too scared to sign' (ibid.).

Nonetheless, the authors characterize the campaign as 'highly successful' (ibid.), leading to a productive meeting with NHS officials, and gaining a positive response from politicians, together with support from the British Psychological Society and the UKCP. 'It seems possible that a number of organisations which may have been operating discriminatory policies have begun changing them' (ibid., 38). The Society for Analytical Psychology (the main Jungian training body), the Tavistock Centre and the Institute for Psychoanalysis all produced equal opportunity statements specifically mentioning sexual orientation. However, Ryan and Samuels are cautious in their enthusiasm: 'Even now, it is possible that grounds will be found to exclude lesbians and gay men, by for example demanding higher standards of "mental health" from them' (ibid.).

SOCIAL CRITIQUES

Psychotherapy and counselling have frequently been criticized, both from inside and from outside the field, as politically reactionary and mystifying. (This is said perhaps roughly as often as the opposite, that psychotherapy is intrinsically progressive and demystifying.) I shall focus here on critiques from within. For example, the British clinical psychologist David Pilgrim (1992) argues that both psychodynamic and humanistic therapies downplay the significance of social and material factors, though in different styles: in psychodynamic therapy, clients are expected to 'suffer forbearance in the face of oppression' and 'notions of external reality are chronically questioned' (Pilgrim 1992, 230), while humanistic work is 'permeated by a whole set of ideas about the growth or transcendence of the human spirit or mind unfettered by material reality' (ibid., 232). In other words, both devalue practical struggle, the former from a pessimistic and the latter from an optimistic perspective.

Pilgrim suggests that '[a]ny attempt to privilege a psychological explanation over a social one is a victim-blaming insult and a comfort to reactionary elements who sustain poverty in their own interests' (ibid., 252). He attacks 'professional special pleading and the mystification of outsiders ... that it entails' (ibid., 237), and reserves his worst spleen for the ways in which therapists constantly suggest that they have the answer to everything, showing 'an unending ingenuity in preying on each new manifestation of human anguish' (ibid., 251). He argues that '[i]f the therapy trade is to continue ... it is crucial that its associated rosy glow of humanism and moral rectitude ... is dispersed' (ibid., 241).

Ann Kearney (1996) focuses on the claims to political neutrality of much contemporary counselling and psychotherapy.

> I suggest that counsellors are, like everyone else, political beings with a political ideology ... which has direct and indirect consequences for their clients. ... [C]ounselling is informed by a set [of] political values and beliefs which are part of the dominant political ideology of the society in which counselling is being practiced. (Kearney 1996, 9)

She describes her puzzlement 'as I read or listen to what are clearly political views framed in non-political ways' (ibid., 58). 'When we try to be politically neutral, not only do we end up being "conservative" (in the sense of not challenging the status quo) but even more importantly we do this "out of awareness", by default' (ibid., 59). Kearney attributes the current apolitical stance of counselling and psychotherapy to the impact of Thatcherism (ibid., 67–75). She quotes Thatcher's famous statement that 'there is no such thing as society, there are individuals and their families' (ibid., 67), and points out how this applies to certain styles of therapy. This perception could clearly be generalized to include North American therapy as impacted by Reaganism.

Kearney claims that 'the issue of class is almost never referred to in counselling at any level' (ibid., 9). However, class has major effects on the therapy relationship, in several ways – Kearney focuses on different language styles, using the socio-linguistic work of Basil Bernstein (e.g. Bernstein 1971; Kearney 1996, 32–44), and on economics.

> Poverty affects. ... whether counselling is accessible ... and where it is (for instance, with GP fund holding practices) the client has no choice of counsellor, no control over the duration of the counselling and no control over the choice or type of counselling available. (Ibid., 52)

As Pilgrim succinctly puts it, '[p]ersonal growth is reserved for the rich' (Pilgrim 1992, 233). And at this point, the social critique of therapy divides into two: one wing arguing that therapy is a very *good* thing which should not be given on an elitist basis,[38] and the other arguing that perhaps therapy is *not* such a good thing, and should be treated with suspicion as diversionary and mystifying.

Kearney argues that Rogerian counselling, her own form of practice, '*does* have the potential to radically transform external social and political structures as well as individual people ... is *not* inherently conservative' (Kearney 1996, 80, original italics); and that it is possible to inject society into the model, so to speak, and 'focus on "the self-actualising tendency of the socially-positioned individual"' (ibid., 82). However – and this is crucial for many left-wing critics of psychotherapy –

> so long as class issues are seen to be something external and irrelevant in a client's counselling we will not facilitate the client's awareness of the social constraints that exist and the possible personal costs of trying to overcome them. (Ibid., 53)

ANTI-RACIST CRITIQUES

In its early days, psychotherapy was, generally speaking, as racist as the society around it. We have already looked at examples in the work of Freud and Jung.

As late as 1930, the *International Journal of Psycho-Analysis* found it appropriate to publish Colonel C.D. Daly's paper using analytic concepts to 'interpret' the Indian struggle against racism and colonialism:

> such sensitiveness [by Indians] to any suggestion of inferiority could only arise from a deep-seated sense of inferiority, the unconscious source of which we will endeavour to shew. ... [T]he mental mechanism familiar to psycho-analysts as the 'displacement of ideas' accounts for [hostility to British rule], and ... the problem which presents itself to us is the unmasking of the repressed unconscious ideas of the Hindu people, one which entails among other questions a correct valuation of their reactions to the 'Oedipus phase' of development, and an understanding of the anal-sadistic and pre-genital sources of their character traits. (Daly 1930, 193–4)

The racial attitudes of psychotherapists have generally improved in line with those of society as a whole. But there is plenty of evidence, and wide awareness, that ethnic minorities in Europe and North America are still not well served by psychotherapy and counselling (e.g. Mays 1985; Sue 1977). This is usually ascribed to:

> the inability of therapists to provide culturally responsive forms of treatment. ...[M]ost therapists are not familiar with the cultural background and styles of the various ethnic-minority groups and have received training primarily developed for Anglo, or mainstream, Americans. (Sue and Zane 1987, 37)

The ways in which this can be situated range from the extremely politically conscious to the totally 'apolitical'. An example of the first is Sue and Sue (1990), where 'counseling and its relationship to the culturally different are seen within the political framework of the larger society. The racist and damaging effects that current mental health practices and standards are having on minorities are revealed' (Sue and Sue 1990, vi). An essentially apolitical approach is that of Pedersen (1976, 1985; Pedersen and Ivey 1993) who focuses on the technical problems of cross-cultural therapy without considering the broader socio-economic context of racism and disadvantage – although he acknowledges that

> Increasing evidence suggests that professionally trained counselors may not be prepared to deal with persons from different racial, ethnic or socioeconomic groups whose values, attitudes and general life-styles are different from their own or perhaps threatening. (Pedersen 1976, 48)

Nonetheless, his solution is quite simply to create a new expert profession of cross-cultural counsellors and therapists.

At the opposite extreme, Fulani, in her introduction to a collection of papers on black women's therapy, argues that work with minorities demonstrates the need

> to create a fundamentally new form of psychology ... which challenge[s] the traditional bottom line commitment to adaptation and [seeks] to replace it with a commitment to the empowerment of an entire community through the practice of an empowerment therapy. (Fulani 1988, xvi)

She rejects approaches which aim to *include* minorities in the mainstream culture: 'the society that patients are being adapted to or assimilated into remains racist, classist, homophobic and sexist to its core' (ibid., xiii).

From somewhere in the middle of this range, Krause suggests that

> [i]n psychotherapy there is always a tension between the need for the therapist to understand clients as much as possible from the inside and the need for the therapist

to be receptive to the aspects of the client's life and self-perceptions which the client herself does not see. One could say that creative psychotherapy takes place from within this tension. ... This may not present significant problems when the social and cultural background of therapist and clients are more or less similar. However, when the gap ... is wide, whether it is for reasons of culture, class, age, gender, religion or experience the therapist may not be able to strike the right balance and observations from the outside may be presented as if they derive from the inside, while inside experiences may be totalised and stereotyped. (Krause 1998, 172)

Writers at every point on this political/apolitical spectrum have offered their own versions of what different cultural groups require from practitioners for successful therapy or counselling to take place. For example, Comas-Diaz (1988, 51) argues that Hispanic/Latin culture 'does not differentiate between physical and emotional concerns ... strong emotions are believed to cause physical illness.' This 'is consistent with Hispanic women's indirect style of communication'. Similarly, Krause (1998, 151–2) discusses the different approach required for working with a couple from a South Asian culture which shows an 'absence of mind – body dualism'. Ridley (1984) and Pedersen (1976) claim that African-American and Native American clients respectively do not self-disclose verbally, and should not be expected to do so. Writing as a family therapist who is also an anthropologist, Krause complains that 'very few, if any, psychotherapy trainings offer courses in kinship' (1998, 173).

All these examples respond to and in turn support the basic axiom that 'each cultural group requires a different set of skills, unique areas of emphasis, and specific insights for effective counseling to occur' (Pedersen 1976, 26). Some of the often-cited preferences of ethnic minority groups go directly against what is widely regarded as good therapeutic practice – for example, some groups are said to prefer a therapist who leads actively, offers structure, and self-discloses (Patterson 1995). How much sense does it make for therapy and counselling to reconstruct themselves in order to meet the needs of specific groups?

This question itself is a subtle political one. If the primary goal is to meet people's needs for psychological support, then it makes sense to offer support that is in fact welcome and usable – in fact, not to do so is unjust. It may be, though, that therapy and counselling are activities which only certain people find useful – perhaps only a minority of the population, perhaps including some members of every ethnic group. In that case it is only the false assumption that therapy is a universal good which creates a circular argument that therapy *has to be* a universal good. The arguments here are closely tied to the question of whether psychotherapy is appropriately a public service – and hence should be tailored to the range of public needs. The difference is between expecting a restaurant to serve every kind of food, or every kind of customer.

More experience of transcultural work is leading towards a new view that 'recommendations that admonish therapists to be culturally sensitive and to know the culture of the client have not been very helpful' (Sue and Zane 1987, 37). The same authors continue: 'The major problem with approaches emphasizing either cultural knowledge or culture-specific techniques is that neither is linked to particular processes that result in effective psychotherapy' (ibid., 39). Two realizations have come together to change the general view of

cross-cultural therapy. One is that each human being is a member of a large
number of different groups; to develop specific theories and techniques with
which to approach each definable permutation of cultures and sub-groups is
both impossible and ridiculous (Patterson 1995). Since each of us constitutes a
unique 'culture', all communication, let alone all therapy and counselling, is
'cross-cultural' (Owen 1990; cf. Pedersen 1990, 94; Speight et al. 1991). As
Krause puts it (1998, 165) 'we are always interpreting each other'.

The other realization, coming from the other direction, is that although we
are all different we are also all quite similar. Thus Richardson (1981) suggests
that Native American clients prefer counsellors who listen, accept, respect their
culture, are natural, honest, honour their presence, and are not condescending –
scarcely an exotic collection of values. Vontress similarly demystifies the issue of
racism in counselling:

> what is needed most are affective experiences designed to humanize counselors.
> ... Few counselors ever ask what they can do to change themselves; few want to know
> how they can become better human beings in order to relate more effectually with
> other human beings who, through the accident of birth, are racially and ethnically dif-
> ferent. (Vontress 1976, 62)

From this perspective, the problems experienced by ethnic minorities in using
the space offered by therapy can be differently understood.

> On the whole, disadvantaged minority group members have had limited experiences
> with counselors and related therapeutic professionals. Their contacts have been
> mainly with people who tell them what they must and should do....Therefore, the
> counselor working within such a context should structure and define his [*sic*] role to
> clients; that is he should indicate what, how, and why he intends to do what he will
> do.... (Vontress 1976, 47)

Here structure is recommended as a way of making unstructuredness compre-
hensible and useful.

But this sort of viewpoint, although less mystifying and more flexible and
realistic, does not dissolve the issue of power in cross-cultural therapy and counselling. Krause rightly insists that 'in Euro-American countries power lies with
the white therapist and, to a lesser extent, also with the black therapist trained in
the disciplines and theories dominated by white professionals and Euro-
American philosophy' (Krause 1998, 153). The issues of cross-cultural therapy
thus lead directly on to the whole question of the power of the therapist.

THE POWER OF THE THERAPIST

> At the end of the dream her head was kicked in, possibly a reference to her feeling she
> had not been allowed to think for herself. (Casement 1985, 116)

All of the above critiques touch on the core issue of the therapist's power; or
put slightly differently, the perceived imbalance of power between therapist and
client. At the start of the relationship, '[t]he counsellor holds nearly all the cards
in a game of which the client does not even know the rules' (Mearns and
Thorne 1988, 98). And even when the client learns the rules, they are not *her*
rules, but those of the therapist, or of the therapy 'game' itself. This situation is
open to massive exploitation, as Claude Steiner confesses:

As a successful psychotherapist ... I used my power to the hilt – and not always to my client's advantage. ... I interrupted, overrode, ignored, judged, evaluated, insulted, attacked, patronized, discounted, and lied to the people I worked for. I justified this by assuming that they needed my gentle, authoritative, sometimes devious, parental attitude, in order to get better. (Steiner 1981, 214)

Krause applies this situation of power imbalance particularly to transcultural therapy:

[T]here is always the possibility of conflict in communication. There is therefore also always the possibility that the most powerful will persuade, command, or even terrorise the less powerful. And in cross-cultural communication this process always involves a kind of violence. (Krause 1998, 153)

Her point is of course valid for the 'transcultural' element of *all* psychotherapy, the points at which differences of experience and value judgement appear between therapist and client. This is where the therapist may decide to impose her own 'healthy' attitude on the client's 'unhealthy' one – as Cecchin puts it in the context of family therapy, the therapist tries 'to instruct the family in his own pattern' (Cecchin 1987, 411). Mindell makes a similar point about the pathologization of social nonconformity:

Some therapists categorize an inclination towards terrorism as a 'narcissistic disorder'. Rebellion is often seen as evidence of 'paranoia'. By diagnosing terrorist behavior as inappropriate, deviant, sociopathic or psychopathic, psychology and psychiatry lull the mainstream into deeper complacency. ... Insisting that psychological work take precedence over social change is abusive and undemocratic. (Mindell 1995, 91–2)

And Felix Guattari describes Lacanian psychoanalysis as 'despotic' and 'rigid' in its 'semiotic subjection' of its analysands (Guattari 1984, 49; cf. Roustang 1986).

It is wonderful to succeed in totally subjecting another person, to hold him bound hand and foot, financially, emotionally, without even having the trouble of making any attempt at suggestion, interpretation, or apparent domination. The psychoanalyst of today doesn't say a word to his [*sic*] patient. Such a system of channelling the libido has been achieved that silence is all that is needed. (Guattari 1984, 50)

The abuse of therapeutic power can take very practical forms, including financial and sexual exploitation. Prozan (1993, 354–6) surveys American research on sexual abuse in therapy, and concludes that something like 5–7 per cent of therapists admit anonymously to sexual contact with clients, while 65–70 per cent report hearing this from a client about a previous therapist. Critics often argue that these abuses should be related to the way in which therapy is structured, and the feelings this fosters; and we shall examine in the next chapter some attempts to alter the dynamics of the situation.

Most of the writers we have quoted are criticizing specific abuses of psychotherapy, and often campaign for a reformed or revised practice to eliminate the problem. Jeffrey Masson, however, argues that all of these separate critiques point to a structural fault in psychotherapy as a whole.

Psychotherapy cannot be reformed in its parts, because the activity, by its nature, is harmful. Recognizing the lies, the flaws, the harm, the potential for harm, the imbalance in power, the arrogance, the condescension, the pretensions may be the first step in the eventual abolition of psychotherapy that I believe is, one day in the future, inevitable and desirable. (Masson 1990, 297)

Is Masson right or wrong? I believe that he is wrong, and will address the point again later. But I think he is right to suggest that it is not only the 'bad' therapist (in terms of either ethics or competence) who imposes her own judgements and understandings on her clients. For example, Patrick Casement's book *On Learning from the Patient* (1985) is a humane, intelligent and influential attempt to question orthodox thinking about the role of interpretation in psychotherapy, and to offer a model which is more open to the client's feedback.

But Casement's own work is vulnerable to the same criticisms he himself makes of others. In Chapter 5, he tells us of 'Mrs B.', who in her third year of analysis was faced with the prospect of tapering off the number of weekly sessions. Casement has suggested what he calls 'flexible weaning' (1985, 104): he will keep her Friday slot open for a few months, while Mrs B. explores how it feels to come four times a week instead of five. When she expresses concern that he may want the space for another client, he tells her that he will use the time for his own reading.

We should note that 'flexible weaning' is already an interpretation, and a major one. Casement has himself introduced both the material (the idea of the flexible session) and its interpretation. When Mrs B. expresses worry about the arrangement, he tells her she can have the Friday session as and when she needs it – calling this 'demand-feeding' (ibid., 105–6). He also suggests that there is something striking in her not bringing him her new baby to meet, or a photograph of the baby.[39] Not surprisingly, Mrs B. is getting anxious.

> Mrs B. continued by telling me a dream: She was holding a container with something valuable in it. There were other people around and they seemed to want their share of what was in the container. She felt as if they had robbed a bank, or something, and she was now carrying the loot for all of them. They were sent to prison, but there was a friendly prison officer who saw to it that she was put into a cell on her own for her protection. She finished her sentence before the others. She was being conducted across the yard towards the gate to freedom when the others set upon her and kicked her head in. She lay dead on the ground. (Ibid., 111–12)

Casement cannot afterwards remember Mrs B.'s associations to the dream – as he acknowledges, this 'indicates a difficulty in following, rather than leading'. He does remember his interpretation:

> I said the patient was trying to preserve her analysis, as the container with something valuable in it, from whoever was threatening to take it from her. She needed me to be a protector of it. (Ibid., 112)

In other words, 'Let's talk about *me*!' The interpretation performs what it describes, and what the dream describes: invasion. In the dream, Mrs B. is the holder; but Casement wants to substitute himself. She is being released; but with a flying tackle the analyst recaptures her.

Mrs B. has already told Casement that he is too controlling:

> Her niece had been away for the weekend. She had a favourite cookery book that she had brought with her for her stay; and she had also taken this with her for the weekend, so her brother would not use it while she was away. Mrs B had let her nephew … cook with her. … Halfway through making something in the kitchen with her, he complained that she was not really letting him do the cooking. She was doing too much of it for him. (Ibid., 110)

(Something very bad, we know, happened to Mrs B. in a kitchen when she was small.) Casement can hardly miss the point: 'I reflect on this and feel she is alerting me to my having done too much for her.' But his interpretation is again shrivelling: 'I said I felt she needed to confirm that she was being allowed enough freedom for her decision about the Friday sessions to be really her own' (ibid., 110–11). Nested within an enormous set of contextualizations – 'I said I felt she needed to confirm' – is the assumption that Mrs B.'s freedom needs to be *allowed* by Casement. 'Mrs B. replied to this by saying she didn't feel I was interfering in any way with that. There was then a silence' (ibid., 111).

Not interfering with that; but interfering, perhaps, by defining 'that' as the agenda. What emerges is the extent to which Casement decides not only what Mrs B. means, but what it is *possible* for her to mean: shifting between past and present, 'reality' and 'transference', as it suits him. Surely the first thing to acknowledge about a dream like Mrs B.'s is the enormous range of meanings which it condenses. One of those ignored by Casement gains its context from the fact that he is planning to present the week's sessions with Mrs B. to a supervision group, whose criticism he fears (ibid., 123). Is this not the group of 'others' who want to share what is in the container? But of course Mrs B. can't know about them! (And Casement can't tell her.) However, most experienced therapists will agree that clients do in some sense 'know' things that we haven't told them, that they pick up the subliminal effects on the therapist.

I am not trying to substitute one interpretation for another here; but rather to point out several things about Casement's use of interpretation. The biggest of these is perhaps that he consistently tells Mrs B., not what she has *said*, but what she *means*.

'I know what you're thinking' can be seen as the basic platform of psycho-therapy; but it lays therapists open to the profound and valid criticism made by Fliess to Freud before psychoanalysis even officially existed: 'The reader of thoughts merely reads his own thoughts into other people' (Masson 1985, 447). Casement's position, however – typically for many therapists – is that it is his *job* to know what his clients are thinking and feeling, so as to help them to feel 'held'. In other words, he has a major counter-transference burden built into his version of the therapeutic project. He must do the impossible in order to do his job properly. The truth is that, being human, we cannot *know* what our clients are thinking. All we can do, if we insist that thought and knowledge must come together, is to *persuade them to think what we know*.

There is a good example of this dangerous procedure in the Casement case history. No fewer than four times in the week's sessions, Mrs B. talks about parents who are making mistakes in their parenting, or managing to avert potential mistakes: abrupt weaning, separation, over-careful behaviour, and so on. It's clear enough that these remarks refer both to her childhood experience, *and* to her criticisms of the way in which Casement is relating to her; he more or less recognizes all this, and interprets it back to Mrs B.

My main question is not about his grasp of the material – although he does seem oddly blind to the analysand's worries about whether he is all right, or 'ill and helpless' (Casement 1985, 118). My main question is rather: whose language is this that is being spoken? Is Casement actually interpreting the language of the unconscious; or has he put Mrs B. in the position where, in order to be understood by him, she has to learn *his* language? It was Casement who introduced the vocabulary of 'demand-feeding'; and clearly he will have done the same thing over and over again, coaxing and gently guiding the analysand until she settles into the 'right' way of speaking. It is not so much a matter, perhaps, of the analysand feeling 'held', as of the analyst feeling 'holding'.

My argument, I feel, is strengthened rather than weakened by the fact that Casement himself makes the same point about 'patients being taught to speak the language of the analyst; and not only language. Parallels may be found ... with mothers who assume they know best what their baby needs' (ibid., 25). There he goes again, in fact: nothing can be about anything other than parenting.

In this lengthy critique, I am not trying to suggest that Casement is a particularly bad practitioner; in many ways he comes across as a good and honourable one. I am seeking rather to do something parallel to Masson's discussion of Carl Rogers (Masson 1990, 229ff.): to ask whether something about *the practice itself*, rather than about particular practitioners, is questionable on grounds of power. Felix Guattari argues in a parallel way that even a radical analyst is still repressive through the nature of her work:

> his [*sic*] whole way of working reproduces the essence of bourgeois subjectivity. A man who sits on his chair listening to what you say, but systematically distances himself from what it is all about, does not even have to try to impose his ideas on you: he is creating a relationship of power which leads you to concentrate your desiring energy outside the social territory. (Guattari 1984, 69)

This is another version of the argument we have already encountered about the hermetically sealed atmosphere of the consulting room. '[T]he construction of a socially, culturally, and politically neutral analytic setting may be a fantasy, one that embodies the wish that the outside can be ignored, denied, or wished away' (Laufer et al. quoted in Samuels 1993, 52). Beyond that, it is a fantasy which is actually destructive of some of the client's most important impulses – the impulses to *change the world*, which Andrew Samuels suggests may be an irreducible 'political drive' (1993, 57), but which psychotherapy in general can treat, almost like Soviet psychiatry, as evidence of mental dysfunction.

As we have repeatedly said, there *is* no political neutrality. Psychotherapy which advocates dealing exclusively with 'the world as it is' damages the client's capacity to tolerate a *difference* between their desire and reality – and do something about it. As Joel Kovel points out:

> Many anxieties can be stilled by fostering acceptance of the established order of things. The therapist, then, who subtly or not-so-subtly suggests to his female patient that she would feel better if she accepted her submissive role is, at least in the short run, not necessarily being non-therapeutic, though he *is* being reactionary. (Kovel 1978, 316)

But the sense in which Kovel is here using the term 'therapeutic' – as roughly equivalent to 'soothing' – is not the only one available. If therapy is also to do with *change*, then what he describes is its antithesis.

The therapist in his example is using his power to create a political effect in his client. But is this not just as much true of a feminist therapist who, faced with the same client, 'subtly or not-so-subtly suggests' that she would feel better if she got angry and joined a consciousness-raising group? Does it make a difference to our judgement of the therapeutic power relationship *which* position the therapist is inculcating in their client? I do not see how it can; which means that therapy is faced with a fundamental political problem at its heart.

The only way to tackle this adequately, I suggest, is that instead of trying hopelessly to *eliminate* power struggle from the therapeutic relationship, we place it dead centre: we highlight the battle between therapist and client over the definition of reality, bare it to the naked gaze and make it a core theme of our work. This is one style of working with transference and counter-transference. It means that, faced with conflicting demands, we do what is best done in every such situation: we *negotiate*. This negotiation of realities (where 'negotiation' also has the meaning of crossing tricky and dangerous terrain), I would argue, constitutes an authentic and viable psycho-political practice.

17

Challenging the Therapeutic Relationship

In this chapter, we will look at some attempts to alter the dynamics of the therapeutic relationship, so as to meet the sorts of criticisms which we have just been discussing. As we shall see, these attempts have been many and varied.

MUTUAL ANALYSIS

Sandor Ferenczi (1873–1933) was a leading figure in early psychoanalytic history, a close friend and confidant of Freud. In his last years, Ferenczi became increasingly critical of some of the central tenets of psychoanalysis, including infantile sexuality and the emphasis on fantasy rather than actual trauma; this led him to accuse psychoanalysis of retraumatizing its clients rather than helping them (Ferenczi 1949; Stanton 1991; Totton 1998, 67–8). Freud and the analytic movement were unable to hear what Ferenczi had to say; instead he was silenced and excluded.

Ferenczi's tremendous – perhaps neurotically exaggerated – dedication to helping his patients led him to work with people who would now be seen as massively traumatized and 'borderline'. Sometimes he would see patients twice a day, for several hours; and he allowed certain patients to follow him on holiday, stay in the same hotel and continue their daily work. With at least one patient, 'R.N.' (identified as Elizabeth Severn: Fortune 1993), Ferenczi undertook a radical experiment in what he termed 'mutual analysis' – allowing his patient to analyse *him*.

This experiment arose out of Ferenczi's increasing concern with issues of trust in therapy. Ferenczi argues that in order to turn the patient's intellectual acceptance of a reconstructed trauma into felt reality, the analyst must transcend her stance of neutrality and uninvolvement, which simply cannot be trusted in relation to such enormously painful material.

> It appears that patients cannot believe that an event really took place, or cannot fully believe it, if the analyst ... persists in his [*sic*] cool, unemotional, and, as patients are fond of stating, purely intellectual attitude, while the events are of a kind that must evoke, in anyone present, emotions of revulsion, anxiety, terror, vengeance, grief, and the urge to render immediate help. ... (Ferenczi 1995, 24)

Ferenczi suggests that the traumatized child often had to face the 'deadly silence' of those around her (ibid., 25); this experience can be renewed through the analyst's uninvolved stance, leading the patient to re-experience the self-doubt and loss of reality they felt in the original situation.

> The only course left … is to be honest with the patient about his own real feelings and to confess, for example, that burdened with his own personal troubles he often has to struggle to summon up sufficient interest to listen to the patient. Further confessions: the doctor exaggerates the friendliness of his feelings, smiles amiably, and thinks 'To hell with you, you have disturbed my afternoon sleep'. … (Ibid.)

Ferenczi found that certain of his patients – in particular, 'R.N.' – needed to check out very thoroughly their suspicions that his uninvolvement and distance 'stems from the continued existence in the analyst of complexes of his own, which may be as yet unresolved, uncontrolled, or even quite unconscious' (ibid., 26). In other words, not content with his assurances, they wanted to explore the real contents of his psyche.

He describes some fragments of the 'rather systematically conducted analysis of the analyst' by 'R.N.', revealing 'proof of affective exaggeration and an almost unbearable superperformance … with corresponding feelings of hate towards the patient' (ibid.): in other words, Ferenczi was compelled to face the fact that he tried too hard, pretended to care, and secretly hated 'R.N.', perhaps for not getting better. This leads to a therapeutic breakthrough:

> The disinclination for any kind of role-playing that is so characteristic of the analyst, rejection of affects as 'affectation', is soon followed by appearance of 'weak' emotional outbursts (grief, shock, regret, breaking down with tears in the eyes) in contrast to the previous coldness. *At the same moment* the patient opens up, is permeated by feeling that I have at last understood (that is, felt) her suffering, consequently with an increased sense of certainty about … the reality of her own experiences. (Ibid., 26–7, original italics)

This heroic self-revelation on Ferenczi's part would be criticized by many other therapists and analysts; certainly it led to problems with 'R.N.' herself, who demanded more and more uninhibited free association from Ferenczi until eventually she was deeply wounded to learn some of his feelings about her. There are also problems of a general nature: 'Obvious objection: one cannot allow oneself to be analyzed by every patient! What I can answer to this objection, if I can answer it, remains to be seen' (ibid., 27).

It is surely right to relate the experiment to the fact that, like many other prominent analysts at the time, Ferenczi had himself been analysed (by Freud) only for a matter of weeks, and on what now appears a bizarrely informal basis. Had Ferenczi known himself more deeply and securely, his response to 'R.N.' might have been different. We may believe, though, that further analysis would not have deprived Ferenczi of the extraordinary humility and commitment to the therapeutic relationship which he showed in his 'mutual analysis' experiment. As he indicates, the question really is: on what basis can therapists justify a *refusal* to self-disclose? Perhaps it is not enough simply to treat the rightness of this refusal as self-evident.

No later analyst has admitted to exploring 'mutual analysis'. We should be clear that this procedure is significantly different from that of two partners exchanging therapy sessions, for example in co-counselling (see Chapter 18): in Ferenczi's work, the clear goal is to facilitate the process of *one* of the participants – the 'analysis of the analyst' in no way changes the fact that she *is* the analyst. It is important as well to notice that Ferenczi explicitly connects mutual analysis, not just with a technical problem of therapy with particular clients, but also with a structural critique of the analytic stance itself.

Interestingly, this critique, together with the use of the term 'mutuality' (apparently without any knowledge of Ferenczi's work), recurs in the American Radical Therapy movement of the 1970s:

> For us a democratic framework means a system which is explicit, teachable, mutual and negotiable. ... by [mutuality] we mean simply that the therapist allows herself to be explored[40] – that a large part of her role involves self-disclosing and helping the client relate to those disclosures. (de Chenne 1974, 74)

De Chenne is describing the work of a radical therapy collective ('Changes', around the University of Chicago) which operated within the person-centred model of Carl Rogers'; but he suggests that other therapy techniques could be employed within the same framework.

> I suppose that even the unconscious/interpretative orientation of the analyst *could* find a place here; but I dare say that no analyst alive *would* ever opt for a truly explicit, teachable, mutual and negotiable system. (Ibid., 75, original italics)

He may be right; but at least one dead analyst felt differently!

PERSON-CENTRED THERAPY

Person-centred (or client-centred, or Rogerian) therapy and counselling claim to have solved the problem of power in the therapeutic relationship – by never entering into it in the first place. 'The politics of the client-centered approach is a conscious renunciation and avoidance by the therapist of all control over, or decision-making for, the client' (Rogers 1978, 14). As Bozarth puts it, 'the revolutionary crux of Rogers' theory is that the therapist does not intervene and has no intention of intervening' (Bozarth 1998, 4).

This stance is not an *absence* of involvement, but a very particular *kind* of involvement, 'built on a basic trust in the person ... on the actualizing tendency present in every living organism's tendency to grow, to develop, to realize its full potential' (Rogers 1986, 198). Hence the therapist 'truly believes that the client who experiences the freedom of a fostering psychological climate will resolve his or her own problems' (Bozarth 1998, 4). This stance is known as 'unconditional positive regard', and is seen as a 'core condition' for therapeutic success: 'it is creating an atmosphere of unconditional positive regard that enables the person to develop unconditional positive self-regard and, subsequently, to resolve his or her specific problems' (Bozarth 1998, 5). This is surprisingly similar to the concept of a reparative, re-mothering relationship held by some psychoanalysts – for example, Phyllis Greenacre:

> the analytic situation is an artificial, tilted one; ... there is none other in life that it really reproduces. In this very fact is its enormous force and capacity for utilization as a medium of establishing new integration. It is one which more nearly reproduces the demand of the child for a perfectly understanding parent, than any parent–child relationship can possibly approach, and it is the only one in life in which no emotional counterdemand is to be expected. (Greenacre 1954, 684)

Unlike the analyst, however, the person-centred therapist believes that she can offer this enormous gift to a client *without* producing powerful and intractable transference feelings.

Cleaving to this fundamental attitude, the person-centred therapist necessarily eschews all techniques and strategies: 'when the therapist has intentions of treatment plans, of treatment goals, of interventive strategies to get the client somewhere or for the client to do a certain thing, the therapist violates the essence of person-centered therapy' (Bozarth 1998, 11–12). Bozarth is therefore scathing about all attempts to combine unconditional positive regard with other therapeutic methods (ibid., 4–5; cf. Merry 1990).

However, there are real questions about this quality; not least – how does the therapist achieve it? A powerful section of Masson's *Against Therapy* is his critique of Carl Rogers, whom Masson accepts to be essentially benevolent and not intentionally abusive – but whose work he characterizes as 'benevolent despotism' (229). Masson asks:

> What guarantee is there, what guarantee could there possibly be, that any given therapist is this genuine person Rogers posits him to be? The unconditional positive regard that Rogers wants the therapist to feel is something that cannot be legislated into existence any more than can love. ... 'Unconditional regard' is not something that seems either likely or desirable. (Masson 1990, 234)

Rogers addresses this specific question, and stresses that unconditional positive regard is not something guaranteed, or even demanded – it is simply that 'constructive client change is less likely' without it (Rogers 1978, 10). However, a problem still remains: if unconditional positive regard is in effect the trademark of person-centred work, the fundamental activity of the therapist, then what does one do in its absence?

Some person-centred therapists have struggled with this. Lietaer concludes that 'unconditionality' is a receding ideal: 'it is a rare person and a rare time in which the constancy of acceptance can be provided by any therapist for any client. Thus, while unconditionality is not impossible, it is improbable' (Lietaer 1984, 41).

Bozarth responds loftily that 'it is not difficult for many of my personal acquaintances who are seasoned client-centered therapists' (Bozarth 1998, 84–5). And certainly Bozarth is very definite that unconditional positive regard is the norm rather than an exceptional achievement; as are, for example, Mearns and Thorne:

> The counsellor who holds this attitude deeply values the humanity of her client and is not deflected in that value by any particular client behaviours. The attitude manifests itself in the counsellor's consistent acceptance of and enduring warmth towards her client. (Mearns and Thorne 1988, 59)

A second core condition for effective person-centred therapy is known as 'congruence': the practitioner's ability to show him or herself authentically in the therapeutic relationship.

> It is only as the therapist provides the genuine reality which is in him/her, that the other person can successfully seek the reality in him/herself. The therapist is nondefensive about the reality in him/herself, and this helps the client to become nondefensive. (Rogers 1956, 200)

Many people have questioned whether congruence and unconditional positive regard are compatible (cf. Bozarth 1998, 84–6). The bottom line seems to be that the practitioner can only employ unconditional positive regard if this is genuinely felt. Mearns and Thorne suggest that person-centred training enables the practitioner reliably to attain this position through personal work on her own issues (Mearns and Thorne 1988, 65–6, 70–4). However, this makes the assumption that unconditional positive regard is a natural and basic human attitude, which only needs to be uncovered in order to shine through. Many other forms of therapy would disagree.

Masson makes a subtle point about how the belief system of person-centred therapy could be misused.

> One of the signs, for Rogers, of a client's making progress was that 'he becomes increasingly able to *experience*, without a feeling of *threat*, the therapist's *unconditional positive regard*.' Note the dilemma: if the client does *not* feel this, if the client feels the opposite, that the therapist is filled not with liking, but with loathing, then this is a sign that the patient is not yet well, still 'defensive', still 'resisting'. ... But what if, in fact, the therapist does not feel such positive regard? (Masson 1990, 234, original italics)

Granted, Rogers would never have used terms like 'defensive' or 'resisting' which were not part of his system. However, the point is still valid: the sole guarantor of the therapist's supposed acceptance and non-judgemental stance is – the therapist's own honest self-report. The problem of power and abuse still remains.

LEADERLESS GROUPS

We have repeatedly encountered the crucial role of group therapy in politically conscious styles of working. This is for several reasons: for example, the group makes therapy available to more people, it enables 'clients' to support and challenge each other rather than everything coming from the therapist, and it reflects social rather than just dyadic interaction in the world at large. We have also seen how the role of leader has often been opened up and democratized, for example in encounter groups. There is a further step that can be taken, however: to eliminate the leader altogether.

An influential account of this approach is *In Our Own Hands: A Book of Self-Help Therapy* (Ernst and Goodison 1981), a manual for those interested in starting leaderless therapy groups which emerged from the experience of the Red Therapy group in London in the 1970s (see also Kent Rush 1974). Red Therapy was started in 1973 by women and men involved in libertarian socialist political action. It drew very strongly on the women's movement, and the experience of small, informal 'consciousness raising groups' which often benefited from their members' experience of psychotherapy (Ernst and Goodison 1981, 4).

The people who started Red Therapy felt that 'therapy is often used in mindless and reactionary ways' (ibid., 1); they wanted 'a therapy which we can control ourselves' (ibid., 4). They at first 'encountered fierce criticism both from within the women's movement and from others active in left politics' (ibid., 6); writing at the start of the 1980s, Ernst and Goodison suggest that therapy was now more acceptable and integrated into radical political perspectives. In 1975 Red Therapy split into separate men's and women's groups; the women's group ceased to function in 1979, but the authors stress that the energy of Red Therapy simply took new directions. Interestingly, Sheila Ernst became a leading British practitioner of feminist psychodynamic therapy, whose work is quoted elsewhere in this book.

According to Ernst and Goodison, 'we found it possible to use therapy as part of a rich and inclusive political practice' (ibid., 303). The style of therapy used in the group was eclectic, drawing on, for example, Gestalt, bodywork, encounter, Transactional Analysis and psychodrama; they were strongly influenced by co-counselling (ibid., 50; see Chapter 18 below), but criticize it for political naïveté and an emphasis on discharge rather than on exploring the relationship of the counselling dyad (ibid., 52).

Red Therapy developed partly to counter what was experienced as a poor style of leadership in humanistic therapy, rather than in complete opposition to the idea of leadership.

> In spite of the more egalitarian style of the groups … the issue of leadership itself is rarely challenged within the growth movement therapies. There is still a great tendency to defer to the expert. … This lack of respect for, or understanding of, the significance of the group process is reflected in some leaders' lack of respect for the group as an entity. They see the group as a series of individuals without recognising the significance of their relationships with each other. (Ibid., 313)

Hence it is not inappropriate that several Red Therapy members have gone on to become group leaders – presumably, respectful ones.

FEMINIST THERAPY: 'SAFE HOUSES FOR THE UNDERGROUND'

> 'What is feminist therapy?' is … a part of a debate in progress. (Ernst and Maguire 1987, 1)

As we have already seen, there are many different views about what constitutes a feminist form of psychotherapy; but one frequently emphasized component is a different attitude towards the therapeutic relationship. In its more clearly political form, this view argues that the feminist therapist has a responsibility directly to support her clients *as women*. Phyllis Chesler suggests that

> [t]raditionally the psychotherapist has ignored the objective facts of female oppression. Thus, in every sense, the female patient is still not having a 'real' conversation. … But how is it possible to have a real 'conversation' with those who directly profit from her oppression? (Chesler 1973, 169)

The antithesis is succinctly stated by Walker: 'The goal of feminist therapy is the *empowerment of the woman*' (Walker 1990, 93, original italics).

The papers collected in Gilligan et al. 1991, constitute a series of versions of this project of empowerment.

> Because women and girls who resist disconnections are likely to find themselves in therapy – for having gotten themselves into some combination of political and psychological trouble – therapists are in a key position to strengthen healthy resistance and courage, to help women recover lost voices and lost stories, and to provide safe houses for the underground. (Gilligan et al. 1991, 27)

In her contribution to this collection, 'A Feminist Poetics of Psychotherapy', Annie Rogers (1991) describes 'the Angel in the Consulting Room', analogous to Virginia Woolf's self-sacrificing 'Angel in the House' who undermines women's career struggles. Rogers unflinchingly uncovers her own failures to support girl clients, and how they have rebelled against her failure.

> In fighting with their therapists, girls may be able to disrupt radically an inauthentic relationship and to heal their women therapist, so that women may in turn heal girls. This resistance on the part of girls, however, depends upon their potential to be taken seriously in such a struggle. (Rogers 1991, 50)

She emphasizes another key aspect of liberation therapy, the need for *the practitioner to learn from the client.*

> In my own tentative and raw new practice with girls, my resistance to the language and rules of traditional psychotherapy, the very way that I learn a different practice, deeply depends upon the resistance of girls. (Ibid., 52)

Thus a number of feminist therapists argue for a reassessment of therapy's parameters. According to Walker, the tenets of feminist therapy are as follows: an egalitarian therapeutic relationship; encouraging women to take power and control; enhancement of strengths 'rather than remediation of weaknesses'; a non-pathologizing and non-victim-blaming orientation; an educative 'rather than ameliorative and reparative' emphasis; and the acceptance and validation of feeling (Walker 1990, 81–2). Walker also quietly suggests that 'feminist therapy', on this definition, can be and is being offered to men, children, racial minorities and the elderly (ibid., 83).

Hammond (1988), an African-American feminist therapist, argues for 'conscious subjectivity', the active 'use of self' in therapy. Her examples include self-disclosure to build solidarity and offer a role model; validating the client's strength; offering practical help in dealing with state agencies, landlords and so on; and even skill-sharing. This approach follows on directly from 1970s Radical Therapy:

> As women working for the mental health of women, we have an important job – to heal our battered sisters and strengthen each other for the fray. But we must remember that therapy only helps individuals, it doesn't change the system. In order to do that we must work together – collectively and politically. (Wolman 1975, 5).

Marie Langer, the Argentinian analyst whose career I have discussed, also 'critiqued the idea of therapeutic neutrality' specifically in relation to work with women and argued that 'oedipal interpretation' can disempower women, since it plugs directly into a 'husband–father' model rather than a potential 'husband – brother' one (in using these terms she is referring to Freud's work *Totem and Taboo* – Freud 1912). She gives examples of interpretations which *support* the desire, for example, to go further than one's mother or have equal opportunities with one's husband, instead of using phrases commonly heard in analytic sessions such as 'surpass' or 'compete with' which are inevitably heard as critical. Her own interpretations also encourage women to consider the option of collective social struggle (Hollander 1988, 102–4).

FEMINIST THERAPY: 'PSYCHIC RESTRUCTURING'

An equally radical approach on a less concrete level is taken by the well-known feminist analytic therapists Luise Eichenbaum and Susie Orbach. Feminist psychotherapy, for them, is concerned ... with psychic restructuring so that the very parameters of femininity (and masculinity) are expanded and changed. ... just as feminism fights on the political front to restructure public life, feminist psychotherapy focuses on the individual psyche and the restructuring in the here and now of aspects of private life. (Eichenbaum and Orbach 1987, 51–2)

They question the orthodox emphasis on helping women to separate as 'too uncomfortably reflect[ing] the social realities of women's subordination' (ibid., 61) – why *shouldn't* women receive ongoing nurturance?' 'In so far as it is manifest as a present wanting for authentic relating, then this desire needs to be *and can be* met in the therapeutic relationship' (ibid., 62). Hence they place emphasis on the issue of intimacy in therapy; arguing that feminist therapy offers '*a real relationship* between the two people doing therapy together which ... is central to the reparative work' (Eichenbaum and Orbach 1982, 50).

This concept of a 'real relationship' at the heart of feminist therapy – or indeed of any therapy[41] – is more than problematic (see the critique in Bar 1987, 224–31, and Orbach's response in an addendum to Bar's chapter). Other work by close associates of Orbach and Eichenbaum outlines the difficulties.

> How will the therapist address social power and social difference so that she does not mistake personal responses for objectivity and abuse her power? How will the therapist ensure that she maintains an appropriate balance between the reality of the client's current and past experience ... and the importance of what transpires between therapist and client within their relationship? (Ernst 1997, 11)

The conclusion, unfortunately but accurately, is that '[t]here are no simple or straightforward answers to these questions' (ibid., 12).

Ernst does argue, though, that 'important psychic change does not only take place in early infancy' (ibid., 19); hence 'we must be able to make interpretations based on the transference of other social, political or historical material' (ibid.). In other words – another important theme for feminist therapy – it is legitimate, or as many would argue essential, to refer to the political circumstances *surrounding* the therapy, the objective oppression of women.

> The cornerstone of [feminist therapy's] development has been to locate the origins of widespread emotional suffering amongst women, in the gendered nature of social relations. As a mode of intervention, it has created forms of interaction in therapy, counselling, groupwork and resource centres aimed at more genuinely meeting women's emotional needs. (McLeod 1994, 1)

McLeod suggests that feminist therapy carries on the feminist 'tradition' of treating feelings as 'a permeable membrane, i.e. as being the site of interaction between various "emotional" and "non-emotional" factors' (McLeod 1994, 7). Hence therapy can move fluently between the 'inside' and the 'outside' of the client, pulling together objective and subjective issues. McLeod also stresses the importance, but great difficulty, of creating new structures and methodologies:

> [F]eminist therapy ... faces pulling off a tricky dual requirement – enhancing existing cooperative working strategies, while negotiating support from and within central and local state institutions. Thus ... the egalitarian nature of the organization of feminist therapy largely remains to be constructed. (Ibid., 143)

What also, perhaps, largely remains to be constructed is the appropriate nature of a 'gendered therapy'. Do women need different things from men in therapy, beyond acknowledgement of their social oppression? Ernst suggests that through experience of feminists working with women clients 'we become more aware not only that the gender of client and therapist may be significant but also that the client's fantasies are gendered' (Ernst 1997, 25); she argues that it is vital to think about how gender affects counter-transference, for example – how a woman client feels differently about a women therapist from the classic model which is largely based on a woman client and a male therapist. 'When a woman chooses a woman therapist she is asking for someone who is the same as her' (ibid.).

Taking the argument one step further, Lester claims that

> gender, being a major organizer in early years, remains a crucial modifier, a key element of patterned form in the continuous processing of perception throughout life. Besides body schema configurations, gender ... continues to qualify, largely unconsciously, the psychic reality of everyday life. Gender inevitably qualifies the particular realities of analyst and patient during the session. (Lester 1990, 435–6)

The clear difficulty here is find a way of working with gender difference without smuggling in essentialism, an assumption of *absolute* difference between women and men which in the view of many feminists is ultimately undermining.

Although tending to agree on many issues, feminist therapy has by no means transcended the distinctions between different schools of psychotherapy: there continue to be feminist analytic therapists, feminist humanistic therapists, feminist Jungians, and so on. (Exactly the same is true of gay-affirmative therapists.) Among the Jungian group are Young-Eisendrath and Wiedemann, who develop a therapeutic approach to the empowerment of women through restoring the missing possibility of 'female authority':

> [t]he ability of a woman to validate her own convictions of truth, beauty and goodness in regard to her self-concept and self-interest. ... Body image, self-confidence, personal agency, social functioning, occupational functioning, sexual pleasure, and subjective self-assessment are all related to female authority. (1987, 8)

Although not wholly dependent on Jung (and highly critical of some aspects of his work), Young-Eisendrath and Wiedemann use

> Jung's concept of animus and some of his psychology of individuation to understand the excluded masculine complex of authority and competence in a woman's personality. Women who grow up and are socialized in a patriarchal culture are forced to exclude authority from their self-concepts. They must retrieve it from experiences in the masculine world of culture and then convert these experiences to confidence in themselves. (Ibid., 9)

This is a creative *détournement* of Jung's sexist conceptualization of the animus, and a useful general approach to helping clients retrieve denied parts of their own capacities from where they have projected them out into the world. But it does not go so far as to question the division of reality into 'masculine' and 'feminine': the essentialism to which I have just referred, which in a patriarchal society will surely always end up supporting patriarchy.

18

Beyond Therapy?

Here I want to offer some examples of initiatives which have begun within or been inspired by therapy, but which have aimed to leave the therapeutic arena entirely and develop a new sort of political practice. They are a mixed bunch, including co-counselling, which is often considered a form of psychotherapy but has dropped some of therapy's key features; Hillman's and Ventura's stab at a re-foundation of therapy on new lines; the AAO's practical application of Wilhelm Reich's psycho-political vision; and David Smail's argument that therapy needs to be replaced with a moral and ethical framework of 'taking care'.

CO-COUNSELLING

Co-counselling makes a simple and profound challenge to psychotherapy: it disputes the role of the therapist as expert. In place of the specialist practitioner, it offers the skilled amateur, who alternates between the roles of facilitator and of client.

> The peer relationship is crucial. … Co-counseling is two-way, the co-counselors taking turns. If A is client and B is counselor at this session, at the next session A is counselor and B is client. … No one acts as counselor without being counseled. (Jackins 1973, 15)

Co-counselling was originally developed by Harvey Jackins in the Seattle area of the USA in the early 1950s (for a brief history, see Heron 1980). According to Heron, Jackins was influenced by Ron Hubbard's Dianetics (later Scientology); theoretical knowledge of traditional verbal therapies; self-help recovery groups like Alcoholics Anonymous; the atmosphere of old-time fundamentalist religion; and the democratic centralist principles of the Communist Party – Jackins had been a member and labour organizer. Oddly, Jackins used business methods to control his new creation: he set up a limited company and registered 'Re-evaluation Co-Counseling' as a service mark which others could use only as 'authorized' by Harvey (co-counselling traditionally uses the founder's first name).

At the heart of co-counselling is the client's control over what happens.

> [T]he client is in charge of the process of counseling and … the counselor is a necessary but precisely limited helper. …Any diagnoses are made by the client. …The counselor draws no conclusions for the client. It is expected that the client will do his or her own thinking. (Jackins 1973, 13–14)

The alternation of roles in each session between counselor and client is there partly to reinforce this equality of power.

Clearly, for such a method to work, both technique and theory have to be kept simple enough for everyone to learn and use effectively. The style of co-counselling writing and teaching is clear, pithy and slogan-based; and the style of the work is fairly stereotyped, a set of robust but unsubtle methods for steering the client towards 'emotional discharge': a term popularized by co-counselling, and encapsulating the cathartic theory which has been around since well before Freud's time. Discharge of held emotion is seen as the key to releasing stuck patterns of behaviour and restoring clear intellectual functioning in any individual (Heron 1977; Jackins 1973). The fundamental social criticism made by co-counselling, therefore, is that 'our culture doesn't recognize the usefulness of Discharge. We are told as children that showing emotions is weakness, a sign of childishness, of being out of control. ... Thus as children we are punished for Discharging' (Evison 1980, 92). Co-counsellors believe – like Ferenczi – that the essential condition for discharge is 'balance of attention' between 'a distressed feeling arising from the past and a safe present' (Evison 1980, 93). With some validity, they suggest that all therapies which value and focus on feelings have ways to induce this state. Among the other tools for facilitating discharge are bringing memories into the 'present tense'; verbal repetition of key phrases; 'acting into' emotions by consciously imitating them; 'going against', i.e. repeating phrases which prohibit discharge, so that the client can fight back (ibid., 94–5).

A crucial aspect of co-counselling theory is the belief in the inherent intelligence, lovingness and vitality of human beings (Evison 1980, 90; Jackins 1973). In the tradition of Reich and Berne, co-counsellors believe that we are naturally kind, decent and rational; it is only circumstances that distort our perception and behaviour. Unsurprisingly, therefore, co-counselling has become militantly anti-oppression, not just in words but in method. Also unsurprisingly, it took direct action on the part of minority group members to make this happen!

> Co-counselors who considered themselves highly liberal were told by blacks and third-worlders that their unaware racism stuck out for miles. Efforts to raise consciousness on this and [sexism and class oppression] gave rise to the practice of scanning all incidents where a perceived difference between people had been used to justify mistreatment. There emerged techniques for linking work on one's own hurts with efforts to change the ways in which each of us either directly perpetuates or colludes in the oppression of others. (Winkler 1980, 108)

In line with Harvey's original Communist Party background, however, it was concluded that 'the basis of all oppression is an economic system where wageworkers are dispossessed. ...This fundamental mechanism of classism is analogously expressed in the situations of all oppressed groups' (ibid.). As a result of these new understandings, 'the practice of co-counselling has become more complex than it was once understood to be ... the counsellor now tries to distinguish in [the person's story] the hidden history of her race, class, sex and culture' (ibid., 109).

Unfortunately, Re-evaluation Co-counselling (RC) has been unable to process major criticisms of Harvey Jackins' own authoritarian style. Despite the egalitarianism of its method, the organization is centralist: all teachers must be 'authorized' by Harvey, while local 'communities' are administered by 'Area

Reference Persons' who draw all policy and theory from the 'International Reference Person' – Harvey, who essentially owns the whole thing. This authoritarianism, as John Heron says, is 'curiously discordant with ... the core theory and practice' of RC (Heron 1980, 103). There have also been repeated allegations of sexual abuse by Harvey. Heron, originally an authorized teacher, was instrumental in the creation of 'Co-Counselling International' (CCI), a forum and common platform for all the various offshoots of RC – including in theory RC itself, which of course doesn't participate.

CCI, according to Heron, is not only more libertarian in its structures, but also more creative in its explorations of new areas of theory and practice – since there is no one authority figure at the centre. He emphasizes the key importance of community organization, peer assessment and accreditation, and developing 'methods of confrontation and conflict resolution that deal realistically with the inescapable tensions of human interaction in a community' (1980, 105). Heron has been an inspiring force in several projects for peer organization in psychotherapy and counselling.

Re-evaluation Co-counselling, the original system created by Harvey Jackins, suffers from limits to the complexity of both its theory and its practice; limits which may be imposed by its anti-expert peer structure. Heron argues that it is 'a movement devoid of any theory of a method of enquiry into the ideas on which it rests' (Heron 1980, 101). The same criticism of limited complexity could to some extent be applied to CCI. As a result, co-counselling individuals and communities have repeatedly found their way to some more complex therapeutic system – Reichian work, Gestalt, Transactional Analysis – to supplement their practice. Many co-counsellors have discovered a gift, found themselves in demand as peer counsellors, and ended up training as 'expert' one-way therapists. Partly as a result of this process, co-counselling has had an enormous effect upon the whole field of humanistic psychotherapy and counselling.

TRANSCENDING THE NUCLEAR FAMILY

Co-counselling frequently creates the feeling that emotional discharge work is *the* way to solve both individual and social problems – that there is no limit to its effectiveness in changing human beings into what they would like to be. Another practice with similar aspiration evolved gradually in the 1970s out of a collective household in Vienna, becoming a network of organized communes known as 'Actions-Analytical Organization for Conscious Life Praxis' (AAO), running several businesses and farms on a basis of 'direct democracy', which it argued depended on the collective therapeutic work of the organization.

> Direct democracy and a structure of responsibility for the organization of the material; and emotional consciousness work is only possible among humans who have become free of their fear of authority. In groups that have not been able to develop the consciousness of free sexuality and collective work organization, there is often an unspoken hierarchy hidden under the surface which ... exposes itself in hidden competition (AAO 1977, 14)[42]

The AAO's main tool to 'remove the damage from our upbringing that causes this belief in and fear of authority' (ibid.) is the technique of '*selbstdarstellung*' (SD), 'self-presentation', developed collectively over a period of years from the work of Wilhelm Reich and from 'various expressive elements of Viennese actionism' (ibid., 28). Beginning as intensive bodywork and regression to birth and infancy, SD became a unique intensive primal performance in front of the group, using breath and body work to generate emotional and biographical material that is turned directly into performance. 'The selbstdarstellung culminates in emotional ecstasy, ecstasy as perception and consciousness-expanding principle' (ibid., 32). The experience of exposing oneself so profoundly and spontaneously in front of a supportive group clearly acts as a rite of passage, an initiation. 'Once the selbstdarsteller has overcome his [*sic*] initial fear of stepping into the middle and has experienced the emotional ecstacy of SD, it becomes more and more a daily existential need' (ibid., 90).

SD played a central role in the theory and practice of the AAO.

> The selbstdarsteller is an actor without a preconceived role, he finds his role spontaneously within himself. In the selbstdarstellung he exposes the role as one which has been forced on him from the outside. He exposes the role as an acquired damage. The selbstdarstellung begins when he forgets himself as an actor. He acts out his damage back to birth. ... He wanders through childhood again from the bottom up and corrects his damages at the same time. (Ibid., 40)

What began as therapy took on elements of theatre, using props, music, voice, etc. Life, therapy and art came together: 'The selbstdarstellungs artist is capable of realizing himself socially and genitally in life. He has become a "life artist"' (ibid.).

The political theory of the AAO is a rigorous following through of the ideas of Wilhelm Reich. 'Sexuality is in fact the most important and primary life energy in nature' (ibid., 285); the repression of sexuality in the nuclear family is the cause of all individual and social evil.

> The prevention and blocking of the streaming of sexual energy is produced from the first day on every minute by the atmosphere of the surroundings and the cold stereotyped behavior of the mother and father ... even [the various forms of childhood trauma] are only the external symptoms of a much deeper emotional sickness and crippling of the parents in nuclear family society. (Ibid., 284)

The AAO believes, with Reich, that the simple though difficult solution to human problems is to 'overcome our sexual damage and restore our ability to fuck without defense and fear and restore our orgastic streaming'. They argued that this makes it possible for people to be emotionally open enough to live communally, which Reich might well have welcomed. However, instead of Reich's belief in serial monogamy, they were strongly committed to 'free sexuality' – 'a revolutionary act in every respect' (ibid., 273): 'the couple relationship proved to be a barrier for every further development of society' (ibid., 274).

> Commune society can only be realized when the majority of nuclear family humans have reached the level of consciousness which enables them to give up their inbred egoism, which is nothing other than fear, and to burst the asocial framework of the family and enlarge it into living together in groups, with free sexuality and common property. (Ibid., 38)

Jealousy and possessiveness ('a sickness which originates from the Oedipal situation' – ibid., 271) can, they believed, be dissolved through sufficient SD. Unfortunately, then, the AAO was committed to the most simplified and utopian elements in Reich's thinking; and also to some of his bigotries, for example the condemnation of 'mysticism' (ibid., 265ff.) and the rejection of homosexuality as a form of 'sexual damage': 'the homosexual rejects his mother and all women' (ibid., 282); 'homosexuality ... hide[s] the hate against the mother' (ibid., 256).

The AAO survived for some years, and expanded into a European network of centres. Many people who were part of it seem still to be living productive and satisfying lives. It collapsed in the late 1980s after its founder was jailed for sexual abuse involving pubescent girls. The AAO has been characterized as a cult, and as a 'fascist' organization. Without personal experience, I cannot judge (though accusations of fascism seem wild); except that the numerous photographs in the book I have been quoting reveal a tremendous amount of what in Reichian terms one would call 'ocular armouring' – tension in the neck and base of the skull, which could be interpreted as a consequence of constantly being *seen*, acting out a role which, however wonderful in theory, it may not be possible genuinely to sustain. As the AAO itself says, SD 'becomes more and more a daily existential need' (ibid., 90); is that because there is a constant need to discharge the distress created by living in this style?

TAKING CARE

The AAO is an example of a group of people carrying the theories of a certain form of psychotherapy to its logical conclusion, and generalizing it into a life-style: their point of view (shared by many co-counsellors) could be summarized as 'therapy can solve everything'. The British clinical psychologist David Smail takes the opposite point of view. He has for some years been arguing that

> psychological distress occurs for reasons which make it incurable by therapy, but which are certainly not beyond the powers of human beings to influence. We suffer pain because we do damage to each other, and we shall continue to suffer pain as long as we continue to do the damage. The way to alleviate and mitigate distress is for us to *take care of* the world and the other people in it, not to *treat* them. (Smail 1987, 1)

Smail attacks (ibid., 3) the increasing self-presentation of therapy as 'a *technical* procedure of the cure and adjustment of emotional or psychological "disorder" in individual people' – a task which he believes to be basically impossible; and suggests that 'what most often psychotherapists actually do is to *negotiate* a view of what the patient's predicament is about which both patient and therapist can agree ... and then to *encourage* the patient' to do what they can to change what is changeable (ibid., 4).

> This almost inevitably means that patients begin to criticize elements of a social 'reality' which before they had always taken for granted, and ... to learn actively to dissent from and oppose the constraints it had placed upon them. (Ibid.)

Smail believes psychotherapy to be incapable of carrying out its official goals of cure and adjustment, for two reasons. Firstly, people cannot easily be changed, nor damage repaired. This is in some ways positive:

If we really were as alterable as many therapeutic systems ... would have us believe, there can be little doubt that a politically dominant power group would quickly establish those norms of 'personality' and 'behaviour' which best served its interests. (Ibid., 87)

The other reason why psychotherapy is ineffective has been often pointed out: our pain and suffering is largely caused by external rather than internal factors. To a considerable extent, tragedy is an inbuilt part of life (Smail 1997). If human existence can be improved, it is through social change, through 'the creation of a social structure which encourages us to take care of each other' (Smail 1987, 142).

Smail indicates two qualities he sees as essential to progress in the title of one of his chapters: 'Growing up and Taking Care' (ibid., 122). They are very much bound up with each other: 'in order to grow up, we have perhaps above all to learn renunciation rather than longing' (ibid., 128), and having done so we become able to act in the public sphere and for the public good, rather than living wholly private lives. He sees this as a potentially enormous shift: 'a society ... which permitted or encouraged all its members to turn their lives towards some public function' is currently unimaginable (ibid., 130). In the very traditional language which Smail favours, '[o]urs ... is no longer an ethical community' (ibid., 143).

What, then is left for the psychotherapist or counsellor to do? As Smail sees it, the possibilities are limited: 'our principal and most potent function lies in accepting people as they really are and providing solidarity in the face of tragedy' (Smail 1997, 169). This is, he says, 'a modest aim indeed' (ibid.). But is it really so modest? It amounts to the entire project of person-centred therapy, which Smail oddly never mentions. 'Accepting people as they really are' is certainly not easy, nor is it a common experience. And if, as Smail says, this function leads clients to question and contest social arrangements (Smail 1987, 4), then it is hardly modest at all; in fact, it is difficult to see how it can be true that it 'certainly wouldn't change the world' (Smail 1997, 169).

THE WONDERFUL AVIARY

In their well-known book *We've Had a Hundred Years of Psychotherapy – and the World's Getting Worse*, James Hillman and Michael Ventura take positions which are often quite similar to Smail's – especially in the emphasis on the importance of public life and the belief that psychotherapy can be privatizing in its effects. 'There is a decline in political sense. No sensitivity to the real issues. Why are the intelligent people – at least among the white middle class – so passive now? Why? Because the sensitive, intelligent people are in therapy!' (Hillman and Ventura 1992, 5). Like Smail, they suggest that the real and appropriate function of therapy is 'the six months, or six years, of grief. The mourning. The long ritual of therapy' which offers support until 'your body has absorbed the punch' of painful experience (ibid., 32). They claim that 'the different schools of therapy have different processing systems, but *all* of them are fixers' (ibid., 31, original italics); however, in their view pain and difficulty are not there to be fixed, but to be lived through.

Hillman, an eminent Jungian analyst, now describes himself as a 'dysfunctional therapist' (ibid., 156) who has rebelled against his assigned function of encouraging

> counterphobic attitudes to chaos, marginality, extremes. Therapy as sedation, benumbing, an-aesthesia ... for me the job of psychotherapy is to open up and deal with – no, not deal with, encourage, maybe even inflame - the rich and crazy mind, that wonderful aviary ... of wild flying thoughts, the sex-charged fantasies, the incredible longings, bloody wounds, and the museums of archaic shards that constitute the psyche. (Ibid., 151)

Here Hillman believes himself to be breaking radically with traditional psychotherapies. But he is only rediscovering a powerful tradition *within* psychotherapy when he complains that

> the psyche, the soul, is still only within and between people. We're working on our relationships constantly, and our feelings and our reflections, but look what's left out of that. ...What's left out is a deteriorating world. (Ibid., 3)

Hillman asks

> could analysis have new fantasies of itself, so that the consulting room is a cell in which revolution is prepared?... Therapy might imagine itself investigating the immediate social causes, even while keeping its vocabulary of abuse and victimization. (Ibid., 38)

It is hard to locate Hillman and Ventura on the political spectrum. Often they come across as a pair of reactionary old curmudgeons who think that everyone should just pull themselves together and stop moaning – or at any rate, focus their complaint outwards rather than inwards. 'Every time we try to deal with our outrage over [the deteriorating environment] by going to therapy with our rage and fear, we're depriving the political world of something' (ibid., 5). Their critique of the child-centredness of much psychotherapy also draws on a traditionally right-wing rhetoric. 'By emphasizing the child archetype, by making our therapeutic hours rituals of evoking childhood and reconstructing childhood, we're blocking ourselves from political life' (ibid., 6).

For a book which criticizes self-indulgence so strenuously, there is a tremendous amount of self-indulgence on display, a continuous criticism of everyone else and congratulation of themselves and each other for their profound perceptions. Despite this, though, there are the germs of a genuinely radical reappraisal of our practice, hints towards

> a completely different method of psychotherapy. Instead of starting with the small (childhood) and going towards the large (maturity), instead of starting with causal traumas and external blames that determine what is to come, we start with the fullness of maturity, who and where you are in your communal world now. (Ibid., 67)

In other words, Hillman and Ventura are arguing for a break with two prominent features of psychotherapy: the assumptions that something is *wrong*, and that we need to look for childhood causes. Instead, like Jung, they highlight the search for meaning and purpose: 'the puzzle in therapy is not how did I get this way, but what does my angel want with me?' (ibid., 70). And in a similar way to Mindell, they seek to reinsert the individual into the social field.

> Drunkenness, absenteeism, illiteracy and quitting school, fraud, defacing public property, noncompliance with regulations, cheating institutions – these are symptoms too.

...We need to read these symptoms as belonging to the body politic, and not only to the individual patient. (Ibid., 154)

Hillman and Ventura, then, seek to shock psychotherapy out of its trance by facing it with other realms of human experience – the political, the spiritual, the ethical. However irritating, one-sided, and at times just plain wrong, their book offers some important signposts for a psycho-political refoundation which clears away the tired clichés of trauma and adjustment and offers an exciting vision of self-creation. But the 20th century has taught us to be cautious about political clearance programmes.

Conclusions to Part IV

The material we have been looking at establishes clearly that, whatever the degree of complacency and conformism in mainstream psychotherapy, the field is by no means without self-criticism and efforts at reform and revolution. The various critiques of psychotherapy and counselling seem to boil down to two main issues and three proposed solutions.

The first of the two issues is that therapy is accused of narrow vision: of taking for universal truth a picture of human beings in the world which is highly specific – to the West, to the middle class, to whites, to men, to heterosexuals, or to all of these. Therapy, according to this view, privileges certain sorts of experience, certain ways of being in the world, at the expense of others; and the style it privileges is exactly that of a politically privileged group. Hence, whatever its pretensions, psychotherapy shores up the status quo by supporting a mainstream world-view.

At least in theory, therapy could reform itself on this issue, as some forms and branches already have done. It could – and this is the first proposed solution – take on a different world-view: for example, one which privileged and supported the experience of marginalized groups, of blacks, gays and women. It could even abandon what many have characterized as its most subtle and powerful bias, its tendency to privilege internal experience over external, the individual psyche over the social world, the past over the future: it could commit itself directly to 'liberation therapy'. It could also, crucially, do something about money.

On a deeper level, though, all this – implausibly radical as it is – could be understood as simply replacing one privileged version of reality with another. As we have already asked: is an activist radical therapy, for example, not in danger of exploiting the practitioner's power just as much as a quietist conservative therapy? This is the second major political criticism of therapy: that it is oppressive *by the structure of the situation*, in that the therapist inevitably has more control and influence than the client – at best, as Masson says, she can be a 'benevolent despot'. Among other things, the therapist, in most forms of practice, is encouraging vulnerability and emotion in the client, while reserving it in herself. This has the positive function of leaving a clear space for the client; but the negative one of keeping the therapist in a safe, 'adult' position in relation to a weak, emotional 'child'. Such a situation can be termed inherently retraumatizing.

However, it is not a simple solution (the second of the three I have mentioned) to speak of the therapist being 'emotionally genuine' in the consulting room, of establishing a 'real relationship' between the two people involved. So long as the therapist is the final arbiter of her own genuineness, the one who decides whether or not the therapeutic relationship is 'real', she is still exercising despotic power. To draw on Gertrude Stein, transference is transference is transference; and therapy takes place *within* it, within a situation structured by the fact that one person, however misguidedly, is seeking help from the other.

This leads on to the third proposed solution: to take therapy out of the dyad of the consulting room, and in various ways collectivize it, by doing it in groups, either with or without leaders, and/or by making it an integral part of community life. There are great strengths to this idea from a political point of view, which is why it constantly recurs in different forms of psycho-politics. The major weakness, however, is that in any form of group it becomes exponentially more difficult to keep track of what is going on, to bring awareness to the emotional interactions, the fantasies, the misunderstandings, the attempted manipulations. The more spontaneous and free-form the group, the greater the likelihood that the sheer emotional power of therapy techniques will set up a cult-like situation, an *acting-out* of psychological material as opposed to its understanding and dissolution – the 'basic assumption groups' described by Bion (Bion 1961; Menzies Lyth 1970).

This scenario brings in a psycho-political position which has probably been under-represented in this book so far: a conscious conservatism, which stresses the dark side of human psychology, our capacity for malice (Berke 1989), distortion and corruption; and insists that containment and management are essential and positive qualities of therapeutic work. This position can be found in all forms of therapy, from psychoanalysis (e.g. Chasseguet-Smirguel and Grunberger 1986; Hartmann 1939a) through bodywork (e.g. Baker 1967) and even including humanistic psychotherapy, which as we have seen generally takes a very positive view of 'human nature'.

I have already suggested an approach to the psycho-politics of the therapeutic relationship which I believe recognizes both its creative and its oppressive aspects. This is to focus directly on the differences in the experience of the two participants, and the ways in which each tries to manoeuvre, manipulate or force the other into accepting their reality; with the aim of eventually reaching a point of mutual recognition where real negotiation - including agreement to differ - can take place.

Another key theme of this book, then, is that of *difference*. Many of the critics from whom we have heard are in one way or another insisting on people's right and need to be different from each other without being pathologized. This strikes a note which reverberates right through Western culture at the turn of the millennium: the note of pluralism, which is increasingly emerging as our last, best hope of a path through global crisis.[43] The therapies which are responding to this may well be the ones which have a future.

Notes

1   Although one can discern precursors to psychotherapy virtually throughout human history (Ellenberger 1994, 3ff.), the specific activity clearly originated with Freud's invention of psychoanalysis in Vienna around the turn of the 19th and 20th centuries.

2   Foucault portrays power not as a top-down phenomenon of control, but as 'the multiplicity of force relations immanent in the sphere in which they operate and which constitute their own organization ... relations of power ... have a directly productive role' (Foucault 1979, 93–4).

3   As I proceed, I will sometimes spell out the phrase 'psychotherapy and counselling', sometimes distinguish between the two, and sometimes use 'psychotherapy', or just 'therapy', to stand for the whole field. Context should make clear which is meant.

4   Rice and Greenberg (1992, 198–9) identify four themes of humanistic therapy: a phenomenological approach based in individual experience; emphasis on an actualizing or growth tendency in human beings 'guided by awareness of the future and the immediate present rather than only by the past'; belief in a capacity for self-determination – 'individuals ... are agents in the construction of their world'; and person-centredness – 'each person's subjective experience is of central importance'.

5   David Cooper calls this 'psycho-technology', and concedes cuttingly that 'I've no doubt that after some of these experiences some people feel better, or begin to "feel", or feel more "real" – or whatever the ideals of capitalism prescribe for them' (Cooper 1980, 118–19).

6   Cost-effectiveness is not a simple concept, as the environmental movement has long argued: we have to decide which costs to include, and in what terms to define effectiveness. These are political decisions.

7   In 1927, Jung wrote: 'it is a quite unpardonable mistake to accept the conclusions of Jewish psychology as generally valid. ... The cheap accusation of anti-semitism that has been levelled at me on the ground of this criticism is about as intelligent as accusing me of anti-Chinese prejudice' (Jung 1928, 149n.). In other words, some of his best friends are Jewish (or Chinese); which of course does not acquit anyone of intellectual racism.

8   Jung also explicitly states that a European is *born with* a brain that works differently from the brain of 'an Australian black fellow' – quoted Dalal 1988, 10–11.

9   A T-Group is a form of largely unstructured group work developed by Kurt Lewin in the late 1940s.

10   A number of important articles from *IRT* are more easily available in Wyckoff 1976.

11   We should perhaps also consider that it is a time-honoured tactic of cults and cadres to *make it hard to understand what they are about*; so that curiosity acts to draw the enquirer further in.

12   Contact details for these and many other organizations appear in Parker et al. 1995.

13   It is not entirely clear how far the field is regarded as a useful metaphor, and how far as literally real.

14   In the culture of worldwork, however, there does seem to be a strong tendency to triumphalism, to the belief that this technique is what every conflict situation truly needs. 'There wasn't a murder for 25 days following our [Oakland] seminar' (Mindell 1995, 164). Mindell turns aside the idea that the seminar *caused* this very unusual statistic – but if not, why mention it at all?

15   This was the original intention, but on reading the contributions the editors realized that all they could offer was 'something more elusive and evocative – hints and glimpses rather than practical proposals' (Kennard and Small 1997, 5).

16   Wherever possible, page references to Freud are given for the Penguin Freud Library edition.

17   Freud's term '*trieb*' was mistranslated by Strachey in the Standard Edition as 'instinct': see Ornston 1992, 93–5.

18   'Genital achievements' are alarmingly described elsewhere in the article as having 'phallic-intrusive qualities, pleasure in attack and conquest' (Levitt and Rubenstein 1974, 330). This seems to indicate a simple confusion between the phallic and genital stages of development.

19   Academic reactions were equally strong, apparently including refusal of membership of scholarly associations, loss of tenure, refusal of doctoral degrees to students using deMause's work, etc. (deMause 1982, 300). I have myself experienced the enormous difficulty of persuading other people even to look at deMause's ideas.

20   This critique began within the psychoanalytic movement itself in the 1920s, with Freud's views on femininity opposed by figures including Ernest Jones and Karen Horney as 'phallocentric' and ignoring social factors (Wieland 1988, 57n.).

21   Pilgrim (1992, 227) calls this 'an unsupportable stereotyping of complete strangers'; he criticizes the generalization but not, apparently, the pathologization.

22   The anthropologist Melvin Harris offers a powerful statement of the view that both aggression and sexism are wholly the effect of material conditions: 'War and sexism will cease to be practised when their productive, reproductive and ecological functions are fulfilled by less costly alternatives' (Harris 1978, 77).

23   Of course, Freud may here actually *mean* men, as opposed to women; and this is one of the ways in which questions of aggression and sexism interact.

24   Harris (1978), not a psychotherapist but an anthropologist, traces out how this might be the case for war, patriarchy and the state. Other anthropologists like Sahlins (1972), however, have argued equally strongly that life in a hunter-gatherer society can be relatively easy and luxurious; if this changes with the invention of farming, one has to account for why farming was invented. Like

psychotherapeutic material, the anthropological evidence can be interpreted in many ways, depending upon the assumptions of the interpreter.

25   Nowadays, of course, there is also the new category of counselling psychologist to contend with. Much of what I say about counselling and psychotherapy seems to apply here as well, with counselling psychology simply providing another route to qualification for another group of prospective practitioners.

26   Some clearly succeed in doing so, however – for instance, the authors of these criticisms, many of whom are very eminent analysts.

27   Riccardo Steiner has explored how the IPA was shaped by 'the political and cultural strategy of [the British analyst Ernest] Jones in founding and developing the "International Journal of Psycho-Analysis"' so as 'to have administrative and cultural control of psychoanalysis in the English-speaking countries' (Steiner 1994, 883).

28   This has diminished somewhat: in 1982 45 per cent were North American, with 18 per cent from Latin America, and 37 per cent from the rest of the world (Kurzweil 1989, 208).

29   Jacoby points out (1986, 148) that medicalization also had the effect in the USA of excluding women, who constituted only about 7 per cent of physicians in the 1960s.

30   For details of some of these, see Kurzweil 1989, 55.

31   Although the IPA has frequently compromised, it has of course also frequently expelled and suppressed. A famous and fascinating example of compromise is the 'gentlemen's agreement' whereby three different trainings coexist in the British Institute of Psychoanalysis (Kurzweil 1989, 202–3).

32   For documentation of the Lacanian side of all this, see Lacan 1990.

33   Kurzweil, in a strongly anti-Lacanian account, mentions both personal tensions between Lacan and the SPP president Sacha Nacht, and the claim that 'Lacan was supervising about forty of the candidates [for SPP analytic training] and therefore was unable to give any of them more than twenty to thirty minutes a week' (Kurzweil 1989, 221).

34   By 1986, according to Kurzweil (1989, 224) 'there were fourteen Lacanian groups, each claiming to be the "true" successor'.

35   A second group, the 'Documento' group, also split away from the Argentinian Psychoanalytic Association at the same time, and for reasons which from the outside are hard to distinguish from those of the Plataforma group: see Langer 1989, 119–20, 247–9.

36   I am sure that I am not the only practitioner whose clients constantly distinguish between what happens in therapy and what happens in 'the real world'; which tends to create a rather spectral sense of oneself!

37   The nature of this registration is not specified, but the authors probably refer to the United Kingdom Council for Psychotherapy register.

38   In some ways this is not an argument specifically about therapy, but one about society in general. Many things are reserved for the rich. However, it might be chastening for therapists to think of themselves as purveyors of luxury trinkets.

39   I should emphasize that Casement is very aware of his own counter-transference here, and critical of his own remarks. However, I don't believe that his self-critique goes deep enough.

40   The use of the word 'explore' here connects with one of the analytic critiques of mutuality, that it constitutes simply an acting out of the client's fantasies – in this case, perhaps, of exploring the mother's body.

41   Writing from an analytic perspective, the authors make no reference to the fact that humanistic therapies have, rightly or wrongly, long insisted on the crucial importance of such a 'real relationship'.

42   For ease of reading, in all quotations in this section I have restored capital letters to a text that has none.

43   For therapy-linked accounts of these matters, see Heron 1997, Samuels 1997a.

Bibliography

AAO (1977) *The AA Model*, Volume 1 (Nuremberg: AA Verlag).

Alford, C.F. (1990) 'Reparation and Civilization: A Kleinian Account of the Large Group', *Free Associations* 19, 7–30.

Althusser, L. (1971) 'Ideology and Ideological State Apparatuses (Notes towards an Investigation)'. In L. Althusser (1971), *Lenin and Philosophy and Other Essays* (London: New Left Books), 123–73.

American Psychiatric Association (1994) *Diagnostic and Statistical Manual of Mental Disorders*, 4th edition (Washington, DC: American Psychiatric Association).

Appignanesi, L. and Forrester, J. (1992) *Freud's Women* (London: Weidenfeld and Nicolson).

Arden, M. (1998) *Midwifery of the Soul: A Holistic Perspective on Psychoanalysis* (London: Free Association Books).

Arlow, J.A. (1972) 'Some Dilemmas in Psychoanalytic Education', *Journal of the American Psychoanalytic Association* 20, 556–66.

Baker, E.F. (1967) *Man in the Trap: The Causes of Blocked Sexual Energy* (London: Collier Macmillan).

Balint, M. (1952) 'Soviet Psychiatry', *International Journal of Psycho-Analysis* 33, 63–4.

Bar, V. (1987) 'Change in Women'. In Ernst and Maguire, eds (1987), 214–58.

Barnes, M. and Berke, J. (1982) *Mary Barnes: Two Accounts of a Journey Through Madness* (Harmondsworth: Penguin).

Basaglia, F. (1987) *Psychiatry Inside Out: Selected Writings* (New York: Columbia University Press).

Bateson, G., Jackson, D., Haley, J. and Weakland, J.H. (1956) 'Toward a Theory of Schizophrenia'. In G. Bateson (1973) *Steps to an Ecology of Mind* (St Albans: Paladin), 173–98.

Benjamin, J. (1996) *Like Subjects, Love Objects: Essays on Recognition and Sexual Difference* (Yale: Yale University Press).

Bentall, R.P., ed. (1990) *Reconstructing Schizophrenia* (London: Routledge).

Berenstein, I. (1987) 'Analysis Terminable and Interminable Fifty Years On', *International Journal of Psycho-Analysis* 68, 21–35.

Berke, J. (1989) *The Tyranny of Malice* (London: Simon and Schuster).

Berne, E. (1967) *Games People Play* (Harmondsworth: Penguin).

Bernfeld, S. (1962) 'On Psychoanalytic Training', *Psychoanalytic Quarterly* 31 (4), 453–62.

Bernstein, B. (1971) *Class, Codes and Control*, Vol. I (Routledge).

Berry, T. (1988) *The Dream of the Earth* (San Francisco: Sierra Club).

Bion, W.R. (1961) *Experiences in Groups and Other Papers* (London: Tavistock).

Bloch, S. and Reddaway, P. (1977) *Russia's Political Hospitals: The Abuse of Psychiatry in the Soviet Union* (London: Gollancz).

Boadella, D. (1991) 'Organism and Organisation: The Place of Somatic Therapy in Society', *Energy and Character* 22.

Bornstein, K. (1994) *Gender Outlaw: On Men, Women and the Rest of us* (London: Routledge).

Bozarth, J. (1998) *Person-centered Therapy: A Revolutionary Paradigm* (Ross-on-Wye: PCCS Books).

Bracken, P.J. (1998) 'Hidden Agendas: Deconstructing Post Traumatic Stress Disorder', in Bracken, P.J. and Petty, C., eds (1998) *Rethinking the Trauma of War* (London: Free Association Books).

Brennan, T., ed. (1989) *Between Feminism and Psychoanalysis* (London: Routledge).

Broverman, I.K., Broverman, D.M., Clarkson, R., Rosencrantz, P. and Vogel, S. (1970) 'Sex Role Stereotypes and Clinical Judgements of Mental Health', *Journal of Consulting and Clinical Psychology* 34 (1), 1–7.

Brown, N.O. (1968 [1959]) *Life Against Death: The Psychoanalytic Meaning of History* (London: Sphere).

Brown, P. (1974) 'Civilization and its Dispossessed: Wilhelm Reich's Correlation of Sexual and Political Repression'. In *Radical Therapist/Rough Times* Collective, eds (1974), 45–53.

Cant, S. and Sharma, U. (1996) *Complementary and Alternative Medicines: Knowledge in Practice* (London: Free Association Books).

Casement, P. (1985) *On Learning from the Patient* (London: Routledge).

Cecchin, G. (1987) 'Hypothesizing, Circularity and Neutrality Revisited: An Invitation to Curiosity', *Family Process* 26, 405–13.

Chaplin, J. (1988) *Feminist Counselling in Action* (London: Sage).

Chasseguet-Smirguel, J. (1983) 'Perversion and the Universal Law', *International Review of Psycho-Analysis* 10, 293–301.

Chasseguet-Smirguel, J. (1988) 'Review: *Les Années Brunes: Psychoanalysis under the Third Reich*, ed. and trans. Jean-Luc Evard', *Journal of the American Psychoanalytic Association* 36, 1059.

Chasseguet-Smirguel, J. and Grunberger, B. (1986) *Freud or Reich? Psychoanalysis and Illusion* (London: Free Association Books).

de Chenne, T. (1974) 'In Defence of Individual Therapy'. In *Radical Therapist/Rough Times* Collective, eds (1974), 70–5.

Chesler, P. (1973) *Women and Madness* (New York: Avon).

Chodorow, N. (1978) *The Reproduction of Mothering* (Berkeley: University of California Press).

Chodorow, N. (1989) *Feminism and Psychoanalytic Theory* (New Haven: Yale University Press).

Chodorow, N. (1992) 'Heterosexuality as a Compromise Formation: Reflections on the Psychoanalytic Theory of Sexual Development', *Psychoanalysis and Contemporary Thought* 15, 267–304.

Chrzanowski, G. (1975) 'Psychoanalysis: ideology and Practitioners', *Contemporary Psychoanalysis* 11, 492–9.

Cohen, D. (1989) *Soviet Psychiatry: Politics and Mental Health in the USSR Today* (London: Paladin/Grafton).

Cohen, P. (1989) 'Reason, Racism and the Popular Monster'. In Richards, ed. (1989), 245–53.

Coles, R., Farber, L., Friedenberg, E.Z. and Lux, K. (1971) 'R.D. Laing and Anti-Psychiatry: A Symposium'. In R. Boyers and R. Orrill, eds (1971), *Laing and Anti-Psychiatry* (Harmondsworth: Penguin).

Comas-Diaz, L. (1988) 'Feminist therapy with Hispanic/Latina Women: Myth or Reality?' In Fulani, ed. (1988), 39–61.

Conn, S.A. (1995) 'When the Earth Hurts Who Responds?' In Roszak et al. eds (1995), 156–71.

Cooper, D. (1970) *Psychiatry and Anti-Psychiatry* (London: Paladin).

Cooper, D. (1976) *The Grammar of Living* (Harmondsworth: Penguin).

Cooper, D. (1980) *The Language of Madness* (Harmondsworth: Penguin).

Cornett, C. (1995) *Reclaiming the Authentic Self: Dynamic Psychotherapy with Gay Men* (Northvale, NJ: Jason Aronson).

Coulson, C. (1998) 'A Personal Perspective on the Origin of the AHPP Working Party on Core Beliefs', *Self and Society* 26 (3), 10–14.

Cousens, K. (1974) 'Professionalism: A Reply to Henley and Brown'. In *Radical Therapist/Rough Times* Collective, eds (1974), 65–9.

Cox, G. (1985) *Psychotherapy in the Third Reich: The Goering Institute* (Oxford: Oxford University Press).

Cunningham, R. (1991) 'When is a Pervert not a Pervert?' *British Journal of Psychotherapy* 8 (1), 48–70.

Dalal, F. (1988) 'The Racism of Jung', *Race and Class* 29 (3), 1–21.

Daly, C.D. (1930) 'The Psychology of Revolutionary Tendencies', *International Journal of Psycho-Analysis* 11, 193.

DeMause, L. (1982) *Foundations of Psychohistory* (New York: Creative Roots).

van Deurzen-Smith, E. (1996a) 'Rivalry and Cooperation: Psychotherapy, Counselling Psychology and Counselling', *Self and Society* 24 (5), 10–15.

van Deurzen-Smith, E. (1996b) 'The Future of Psychotherapy in Europe', *International Journal of Psychotherapy* 1, 121–40.

Dinnerstein, D. (1978) *The Rocking of the Cradle and the Ruling of the World* (London: Souvenir).

Dryden, W. (1996) 'A Rose by any Other Name: A Personal View on the Differences Among Professional Titles', *Self and Society* 24 (5), 15–17.

Dutton-Douglas, M.A. and Walker, L.E.A., eds (1988) *Feminist Psychotherapies: Integration of Therapeutic and Feminist Systems* (Norwood, N.J.: Ablex).

Dyne, D. and Figlio, K. (1989) 'A Comment on Jonathan Pedder's "Courses in Psychotherapy": A Future for Training in Psychotherapy', *British Journal of Psychotherapy* 6 (2), 222–6.

Eichenbaum, L. and Orbach, S. (1982) *Outside In … Inside Out* (Harmondsworth: Penguin).

Eichenbaum, L. and Orbach, S. (1987) 'Separation and Intimacy: Crucial Practice Issues in Working with Women in Therapy'. In Ernst and Maguire, eds (1987), 49–67.

Ellenberger, H. (1994) *The Discovery of the Unconscious* (London: Fontana).

Elliot, P. (1991) *From Mastery to Analysis: Theories of Gender in Psychoanalytic Feminism* (Ithaca, NY: Cornell University Press).

Erikson, E. (1980 [1959]) *Identity and the Life Cycle* (New York: Norton).

Ernst, S. (1997) 'The Therapy Relationship'. In M. Lawrence and M. Maguire, eds (1997), *Psychotherapy with Women* (London: Macmillan).

Ernst, S. and Goodison, L. (1981) *In Our Own Hands: A Book of Self-Help Therapy* (London: The Women's Press).

Ernst, S. and Maguire, M., eds (1987) *Living with the Sphinx: Papers from the Women's Therapy Centre* (London: The Women's Press).

Erös, F. (1993) 'Some Social and Political Issues Related to Ferenczi and the Hungarian School'. Paper delivered at the 'Ferenczi Rediscovered' Conference, Institute of Psychoanalysis, London, 15–16 October.

Evison, R. (1980) 'An Introduction to Co-Counselling', *Self and Society* 8 (4), 90–7.

Fanon, F. (1986 [1952]) *Black Skin, White Masks* (London: Pluto Press).

Feltham, C. (1997) 'Challenging the Core Theoretical Model'. In House and Totton, eds (1997), 117–28.

Fenichel, O. (1945) *The Psychoanalytic Theory of Neurosis* (New York: Norton).

Ferenczi, S. (1949 [1932]) 'Confusion of Tongues Between the Adult and the Child – (The Language of Tenderness and of Passion)', *International Journal of Psycho-Analysis* 30, 225–30.

Ferenczi, S. (1995) *The Clinical Diary* (London: Harvard University Press).

Fortune, C. (1993) 'Sandor Ferenczi's analysis of "R.N.": A Critically Important Case in the History of Psychoanalysis', *British Journal of Psychotherapy* 9 (4), 436–43.

Foucault, M. (1979) *The History of Sexuality*, Vol. I (Harmondsworth: Penguin).

Freud, A. (1946) *The Ego and the Mechanisms of Defense* (New York: International University Press).

Freud, S. (1905) *Three Essays on the Theory of Sexuality, Standard Edition of the Works of Sigmund Freud* (London: Hogarth Press) (hereinafter *SE*) VII, 123–245; PenguinFreudLibrary (Harmondsworth: Penguin) (hereinafter PFL) 7, 45–169.

Freud, S. (1908a) '"Civilised" Sexual Morality and Modern Nervous Illness', *SE* IX, 177–204; PFL 12, 33–35.

Freud, S. (1908b) 'Character and Anal Erotism', *SE* IX, 167–75; PFL 7, 209–15.

Freud, S. (1909) 'Five Lectures on Psycho-Analysis', *SE* XI, 3–55.

Freud, S. (1912) *Totem and Taboo, SE* XIII, 1–162; PFL 13, 49–224.

Freud, S (1918) 'Lines of Advance in Psycho-Analytic Therapy', *SE* XVII, 159–68.

Freud, S. (1920) 'Beyond the Pleasure Principle', *SE* XVIII, 1–64; PFL 11, 275–338.

Freud, S. (1925) 'Some Psychical Consequences of the Anatomical Distinction Between the Sexes', *SE* XIX, 241–58; PFL 7, 331–43.

Freud, S. (1927) *The Future of an Illusion, SE* XXI, 1–56; PFL 12, 183–241.

Freud, S. (1930) *Civilisation and its Discontents, SE* XXI, 57–145; PFL 12, 251–340.

Freud, S. (1931) 'Female Sexuality', *SE* XXI, 221–43; PFL 7, 371–92.

Friedman, P. (1963) 'Psychotherapy in the Soviet Union', *Psychoanalytic Quarterly* 32, 274–7.

Friedman, R.C. (1988) *Male Homosexuality: A Contemporary Psychoanalytic Perspective* (New Haven: Yale University Press).

Fromm, E. (1960 [1942]) *The Fear of Freedom* (London: Routledge and Kegan Paul).

Fromm, E. (1970) *The Crisis of Psychoanalysis* (Harmondsworth: Penguin).

Fromm, E. (1973) *The Crisis of Psychoanalysis* (Harmondsworth: Penguin).

Fromm, E. (1980) *The Fear of Freedom* (London: Routledge and Kegan Paul).

Frosh, S. (1987) *The Politics of Psychoanalysis* (New Haven: Yale University Press).

Frosh, S. (1989) *Psychoanalysis and Psychology: Minding the Gap* (London: Macmillan).

Frosh, S. (1997) *For and Against Psychoanalysis* (London: Routledge).

Fulani, L., ed. (1988) *The Psychopathology of Everyday Racism and Sexism* (New York: Harrington Park Press).

Gay, P. (1995 [1989]) *Freud: A Life for Our Time* (London: Papermac).

Giddens, A. (1991) *Modernity and Self Identity* (Oxford: Polity Press).

Gilligan, C. (1991) 'Women's Psychological Development: Implications for Psychotherapy'. In Gilligan et al. eds (1991), 5–31.

Gilligan, C., Rogers, A.G. and Tolman, D.L., eds (1991) *Women, Girls and Psychotherapy: Reframing Resistance* (London: Harrington Park Press).

Glaser, K. (1974) 'Suggestions for Working with Heavy Strangers and Friends'. In *Radical Therapist/Rough Times* Collective, eds (1974), 241–50

Glasser, W. (1965) *Reality Therapy: A New Approach to Psychiatry* (New York: Harper and Row).

Glendinning, C. (1994) *My Name is Chellis and I'm in Recovery from Western Civilization* (Boston: Shambhala).

Glendinning, C. (1995) 'Technology, Trauma, and the Wild'. In Roszak et al. eds (1995), 41–54.

Glenn, M. (1973) 'Radical Therapy and Revolution', *Issues in Radical Therapy* 1 (1), 26–8.

Glenn, M. (1974) 'People's Psychiatry Sheet I: Handling Psychiatric Emergencies'. In *Radical Therapist/Rough Times* Collective, eds (1974), 251–4.

Goleman, D. (1996) *Emotional Intelligence: Why It Can Matter More Than IQ* (London: Bloomsbury).

Greenacre, P. (1954) 'The Role of Transference – Practical Considerations in Relation to Psychoanalytic Therapy', *Journal of the American Psychoanalytic Association* 2, 671–84.

Greenberg, S., ed. (1999), *Mindfield: Therapy on the Couch – A Shrinking Future?* (London: Camden Press).

Griggs, B. (1982) *Green Pharmacy: A History of Herbal Medicine* (London: Jill Norman and Hobhouse).

Grotjahn, M. (1951) 'Historical Notes: A Letter from Freud', *International Journal of Psycho-Analysis* 32, 331.

Guattari, F. (1984) *Molecular Revolution: Psychiatry and Politics* (Hormondsworth: Penguin).

Guntrip, H. (1977) *Schizoid Phenomena, Object Relations and the Self* (London: Hogarth Press).

Hammond, V.W. (1988) '"Conscious Subjectivity" or Use of One's Self in the Therapeutic Process'. In Fulani, ed. (1988), 74–81.

Harmat, P. (1987) 'Psychoanalysis in Hungary since 1933', *International Review of Psycho-Analysis* 14, 503–8.

Harper, S. (1995) 'The Way of Wilderness'. In Roszak et al. eds (1995), 183–200.

Harris, M. (1978) *Cannibals and Kings: The Origins of Cultures* (London: Fontana/Collins).

Hartmann, H. (1939a) *Ego Psychology and the Problem of Adaptation* (New York: International University Press).

Hartmann, H. (1939b) 'Psycho-Analysis and the Concept of Health', *International Journal of Psycho-Analysis* 20, 308–21.

Hartmann, H. (1956) 'Notes on the Reality Principle', *Psychoanalytic Study of the Child* 11, 31–53.

Heizer, L. (1993) 'The Worldwork Seminars: A Personal Overview', *Journal of Process Oriented Psychology* 5 (1), 5–12.

Henley, N. and Brown, P. (1974) 'The Myth of Skill and the Class Nature of Professionalism'. In *Radical Therapist/Rough Times* Collective, eds (1974), 61–4.

Herman, E. (1992) 'The Competition: Psychoanalysis, its Feminist Interpreters, and the Idea of Sexual Freedom 1910–1930', *Free Associations* 3 (3), 391–437.

Heron, J. (1977) *Catharsis in Human Development* (London: British Postgraduate Medical Federation).

Heron, J. (1980) 'History and Development of Co-Counselling', *Self and Society* 8 (4), 99–106.

Heron, J. (1997) 'A Self-Generating Practitioner Community'. In House and Totton, eds (1997), 241–54.

Hillman, J. and Ventura, M. (1992) *We've Had a Hundred Years of Psychotherapy – and the World's Getting Worse* (San Francisco: Harper Collins).

Hinshelwood, R.D. (1985) 'Questions of Training', *Free Associations* 2, 7–18.

Hoggett, P. and Lousada, J. (1985) 'Therapeutic Intervention in Working Class Communities', *Free Associations* 1, 125–52.

Holland, S. (1992) 'From Social Abuse to Social Action: A Neighbourhood Psychotherapy and Social Action Project for Women', *Changes* 10 (2), 146–53.

Hollander, N.C. (1988) 'Marxism, Psychoanalysis and Feminism: A View From Latin America'. In Fulani, ed. (1988), 87–108.

Holmes, J. and Lindley, R. (1991) *The Values of Psychotherapy* (Oxford: Oxford University Press).

Holzman, L. (1995) '"Wrong," Said Fred: A Response to Parker', *Changes* 13 (1), 23–6.

House, R. (1997) '"Audit-Mindedness" in Counselling: Some Underlying Dynamics'. In House and Totton, eds (1997), 63–70.

House, R. and Totton, N., eds (1997) *Implausible Professions: Arguments for Pluralism and Autonomy in Psychotherapy and Counselling* (Manchester: PCCS).

IPN (Independent Practitioners Network) (1996) *Interim Constitution* (Leeds: IPN).

Isay, R.A. (1986) 'The Development of Sexual Identity in Homosexual Men', *Psychoanalytic Study of the Child* 41, 467–89.

Isay, R.A. (1991) 'The Homosexual Analyst – Clinical Considerations', *Psychoanalytic Study of the Child* 46, 199–216.

Isay, R.A. (1993) *Being Homosexual* (Harmondsworth: Penguin).

Issues in Radical Therapy (1973a) 'Editorial', *Issues in Radical Therapy* 1 (1), 3.

Issues in Radical Therapy (1973b) 'Special Issue: Wilhelm Reich and Body Politics, Part I', *Issues in Radical Therapy* 2, 1.

Jackins, H. (1973) *The Human Situation* (Seattle: Rational Island Publishers).

Jacobs, M. (1996) 'Suitable Clients for Counselling and Psychotherapy', *Self and Society* 24 (5) 3–7.

Jacoby, R. (1977) *Social Amnesia: A Critique of Conformist Psychology from Adler to Laing* (Sussex: Harvester).

Jacoby, R. (1986) *The Repression of Psychoanalysis: Otto Fenichel and the Political Freudians* (Chicago: University of Chicago Press).

Jaynes, J. (1976) *The Origins of Consciousness in the Breakdown of the Bicameral Mind* (Boston: Houghton-Mifflin).

Jimenez, J.P. (1989) 'Some Reflections on the Practice of Psychoanalysis in Chile Today – from the Point of View of the Relationship Between Psychoanalysis and Society', *International Review of Psycho-Analysis* 16, 493.

Jones, D. (1996) 'What is the British Association for Counselling?' *Self and Society* 24 (5), 7–9.

Jones, E. (1964) *The Life and Work of Sigmund Freud*, Abridged Edition (Harmondsworth: Penguin).

Joseph, E.D. (1980) 'Presidential Address: Clinical Issues in Psychoanalysis', *International Journal of Psycho-Analysis* 61, 1–9.

Jukes, A. (1993) *Why Men Hate Women* (London: Free Association Books).

Jung, C.G. (1928) *The Relations Between the Ego and the Unconscious* (Collected Works Vol. VII).

Jung, C.G. (1946) 'Epilogue to "Essays on Contemporary Events"', *Collected Works* 10 (London: Routledge and Kegan Paul), 227–53.

Jung, C.G. (1963) *Memories, Dreams, Reflections* (London: Collins and Routledge and Kegan Paul).

Jung, C.G. (1986) *Analytical Psychology: Its Theory and Practice* (London: Ark).

Kanner, A.D. and Gomes, M.E. (1995) 'The All-Consuming Self'. In Roszak et al. eds (1955), 77–91.

Kearney, A. (1996) *Counselling, Class and Politics: Undeclared Influences in Therapy* (Manchester: PCCS Books).

Keleman, S. (1975) *The Human Ground: Sexuality, Self and Survival* (Palo Alto: Science and Behaviour Books).

Kennard, D. and Small, N., eds (1997) *Living Together* (London: Quartet).

Kennedy, R. (1998) *The Elusive Human Subject: A Psychoanalytic Theory of Subject Relations* (London: Free Association Books).

Kent Rush, A. (1974) *Getting Clear: Body Work for Women* (London: Wildwood House).

Kernberg, O. (1986) 'Institutional Problems of Psychoanalytic Education', *Journal of the American Psychoanalytic Association* 34, 799–834.

Kernberg, O. (1996) 'Thirty Methods to Destroy the Creativity of Analytic Candidates', *International Journal of Psycho-Analysis* 77 (5), 1031–40.

Klein, M. (1975) *Envy and Gratitude and Other Works* (New York: Delta).

Kovel, J. (1978) *A Complete Guide to Therapy: From Psychoanalysis to Behaviour Modification* (Harmondsworth: Penguin).

Kovel, J. (1988 [1970]) *White Racism: A Psychohistory* (London: Free Association Books).

Kovel, J. (1995) 'On Racism and Psychoanalysis'. In A. Elliot and S. Frash, eds (1995), *Psychoanalysis in Contexts* (London: Routledge), 205–22.

Krause, I. (1998) *Therapy Across Culture* (London: Sage).

Kurzweil, E. (1989) *The Freudians: A Comparative Perspective* (New Haven: Yale University Press).

Lacan, J. (1977) 'The Signification of the Phallus'. In J. Lacan (1977) *Ecrits* (London: Routledge), 281–91.

Lacan, J. (1990) *Television: A Challenge to the Psychoanalytic Establishment* (New York: Norton).

Lacan, J. (1998) *The Seminar, Book XX: Encore, on Female Sexuality* (New York: Norton).

LaChapelle, D. (1988) *Sacred Land, Sacred Sex, Rapture of the Deep: Concerning Deep Ecology and Celebrating Life* (Silverton, Colorado: Finn Hill Arts).

Laing, R.D. (1965) *The Divided Self: An Existential Study in Sanity and Madness* (Harmondsworth: Penguin).

Laing, R.D. (1967) *The Politics of Experience and The Bird of Paradise* (Harmondsworth: Penguin).

Laing, R.D. (1970) *Knots* (London: Tavistock).

Laing, R.D. (1971) *The Politics of the Family* (London: Tavistock).

Laing, R.D. (1982) *The Voice of Experience: Experience, Science and Psychiatry* (Harmondsworth: Penguin).

Laing, R.D. and Esterson, A. (1964) *Sanity, Madness and the Family: Families of Schizophrenics* (London: Tavistock).

Langer, M. (1989) *From Vienna to Managua: Journey of a Psychoanalyst* (London: Free Association Books).

Laplanche, J. and Pontalis, J.B. (1988) *The Language of Psychoanalysis* (London: Institute of Psycho-Analysis and Karnac Books).

Larkin, G. (1983) *Occupational Monopoly and Modern Medicine* (London: Tavistock).

Larson, M. (1977) *The Rise of Professionalism* (Berkely, CA, University of California Press).

Laufer, M. (1982) 'Report of the 32nd International Psycho-Analytical Congress', *International Journal of Psycho-Analysis* 63, 101.

Lawrence, M. and Maguire, M. eds (1997) *Psychotherapy with Women: Feminist Perspectives* (London: Macmillan).

Lawrence, W.G. (1998) 'Won from the Void and Formless Infinite: Experiences of Social Dreaming' (unpublished; available on the Internet at http://www.human-nature.com/group/chap8.html).

Lester, E.P. (1990) 'Gender and Identity in the Analytic Process', *International Journal of Psycho-Analysis* 71, 435–44.

Levine, H.B. Jacobs, D. and Rubin, L.J. eds (1988) *Psychoanalysis and the Nuclear Threat: Clinical and Theoretical Studies* (Hillsdale, NJ: Analytic Press).

Levitt, M. and Rubenstein, B. (1974) 'The Counter-Culture: Adaptive or Maladaptive?' *International Review of Psycho-Analysis* 1, 325–36.

Lidz, T. (1964) *The Family and Human Adaptation* (London: Hogarth Press).

Lietaer, G. (1984) 'Unconditional Positive Regard: A Controversial Basic Attitude in Client-Centered Therapy'. In R. Levant and J. Shlien, eds (1984), *Client-Centered Therapy and the Person-Centered Approach: New Directions in Theory, Research and Practice* (New York: Praeger), 41–58.

Lifschutz, J.E. (1976) 'A Critique of Reporting and Assessment in the Training Analysis', *Journal of the American Psychoanalytic Association* 24, 43–59.

Limentani, A. (1996) 'Clinical Types of Homosexuality'. In Rosen, ed. (1996), 216–26.

Lomas, P. (1994) *Cultivating Intuition: An Introduction to Psychotherapy* (Harmondsworth: Penguin).

Lomas, P. (1997) 'The Teaching of Psychotherapy'. In House and Totton, eds (1997), 215–24.

Lowen, A. (1965) *Love and Orgasm: A Revolutionary Guide to Sexual Fulfilment* (London: Collier Macmillan).

Macey, J. (1983) *Despair and Personal Power in the Nuclear Age* (Philadelphia: New Society).

Mair, K. (1992) 'The Myth of Therapist Expertise'. In W. Dryden and C. Feltham, eds (1992) *Psychotherapy and Its Discontents* (Buckingham: Open University Press), 135–68.

Marcus, J. (1976) 'I Did It and I'm Glad!' In Wyckoff, ed. (1976), 270–8.

Marcuse, H. (1966 [1955]) *Eros and Civilisation* (Boston: Beacon Press).

Masson, J., ed. (1985) *The Complete Letters of Sigmund Freud to Wilhelm Fliess* (Harvard: Belknap).

Masson, J. (1990) *Against Therapy* (London: Fontana).

Mays, V.M. (1985) 'Black Americans and Psychotherapy: The Dilemma', *Psychotherapy* 22, 379–88.

McDougall, J. (1995) *The Many Faces of Eros* (London: Free Association Books).

McLaughlin, F. (1978) 'Report of the 30th International Psycho-Analytical Congress', *Bulletin of the International Psycho-Analytic Association* 59, 64–130.

McLaughlin, T. (1996) 'Coping with Hearing Voices: An Emancipatory Discourse Analytic Approach' *Changes* 14 (3), 238–43.

McLeod, E. (1994) *Women's Experience of Feminist Therapy and Counselling* (Buckingham: Open University Press).

Mearns, D. and Thorne, B. (1988) *Person-Centred Counselling in Action* (London: Sage).

Mebane-Francescato, D. and Jones, S. (1974) 'Radical Psychiatry in Italy: "Love is Not Enough"'. In *Radical Therapist/Rough Times* Collective, eds (1974), 101–6.

Mendoza, S. (1997) 'Genitality and Genital Homosexuality: Criteria of Selection of Homosexual Candidates', *British Journal of Psychotherapy* 13 (3), 384–94.

Menzies Lyth, I. (1970) *The Functioning of Social Systems as a Defence Against Anxiety* (London: Tavistock).

Merry, T. (1990) 'Client-Centred Therapy: Some Trends and Some Troubles', *Counselling* 1 (1), 17–18.

Metzner, R. (1995) 'The Psychopathology of the Human–Nature Relationship'. In Roszak et al. eds (1995), 55–67.

Miller, A. (1984) *Thou Shalt Not Be Aware* (London: Pluto Press).

Mindell, A. (1989) *The Year I: Global Process Work* (London: Arkana).

Mindell, A. (1992) *The Leader as Martial Artist: An Introduction to Deep Democracy* (San Francisco: Harper San Francisco).

Mindell, A. (1995) *Sitting in the Fire: Large Group Transformation Using Conflict and Diversity* (Portland: Lao Tse Press).

Mitchell, J. (1975) *Psychoanalysis and Feminism* (Harmondsworth: Penguin).

Modena, E. (1986) 'A Chance for Psychoanalysis to Change: the Zurich Psychoanalytical Seminar as an Example', *Free Associations* 5, 7–22.

Mowbray, R. (1995) *The Case Against Psychotherapy Registration: A Conservation Issue for the Human Potential Movement* (London: Trans Marginal Press).

New York Mental Patient's Liberation Front (1974) 'A Mental Patient's Liberation Project: Statement and Bill of Rights'. In *Radical Therapist/Rough Times Collective*, eds (1974), 107–9.

Newman, F. and Holzman, L. (1993) *Lev Vygotsky: Revolutionary Scientist* (London: Routledge).

Nobus, D. (1998a) 'Splitting Images: Lacan, Institutional Politics and the Social Authorisation of Psychoanalysis', *ps: Journal of the Universities Association for Psychoanalytic Studies* 1, 53–67.

Nobus, D. (1998b) 'The Colours of Oedipus: On the Cultural Limits of the Freudian Field'. Paper delivered at the Universities Association for Psychoanalytic Studies Annual Conference, London.

Noel, B. and Watterson, K. (1992) *You Must Be Dreaming* (New York: Poseidon Press).

Oberndorf, C.P. (1964) *History of Psychoanalysis in America* (New York: Harper and Row).

O'Connor, T. (1995) 'Therapy for a Dying Planet'. Roszak et al. eds (1995), 149–55.

O'Connor, N. and Ryan, J. (1993) *Wild Desires and Mistaken Identities: Lesbianism and Psychoanalysis* (London: Virago).

Ofshe, R. and Watters, E. (1994) *Making Monsters: False Memories, Psychotherapy, and Sexual Hysteria* (New York: Scribner's).

O'Hara, M. (1997) 'Emancipatory Therapeutic Practice in a Turbulent Transmodern Era: A Work of Retrieval', *Journal of Humanistic Psychology* 37 (3), 7–33.

Orbach, S. (1997) 'Family Life'. In Kennard and Small, eds (1997), 19–32.

Orbach, S. (1998) 'It's Official: The Personal Will Be the Political', *Guardian*, 12 August, 7.

Ornston, D.G., ed. (1992) *Translating Freud* (London: Yale University Press).

Owen, I. (1990) 'Re-emphasizing a Client-Centred Approach', *Counselling* 1 (4), 92–4.

Palmer, R. and Rogers, L. (1994) 'Fanatical Therapists Train Secretly in UK', *Sunday Times*, 22 May.

Parker, I. (1995) '"Right," said Fred, "I'm Too Sexy for Bourgeois Group Therapy": The Case of the Institute for Social Therapy', *Changes* 13 (1), 1–22.

Parker, I., Georgaca, E., Harper, D., McLaughlin, T. and Stowell-Smith, M. (1995) *Deconstructing Psychopathology* (London: Sage).

Parkin, F. (1974) 'Strategies of Social Closure in Class Formation'. In F. Parkin, ed. (1974), *The Social Analysis of Class Structure* (London: Tavistock).

Parry, D. (1989) *Warriors of the Heart* (Cooperstown, NY: Sunstone Publications).

Patterson, C.H. (1995) 'A Universal System of Psychotherapy', *Person-Centered Journal* 2 (1), 54–62.

PCSR (n.d.) Leaflet: *Psychotherapists and Counsellors for Social Responsibility* (London: PCSR).

Pearse, I.H. and Crocker, L.H. (1943) *The Peckham Experiment: A Study of the Living Structure of Society* (London: George Allen and Unwin).

Pearson, G. (1983) *Hooligan: A History of Respectable Fears* (London: Macmillan).

Peck, M.S. (1987) *The Different Drum* (London: Rider).

Pedder, J.R. (1989) 'Courses in Psychotherapy: Evolution and Current Trends', *British Journal of Psychotherapy* 6 (2), 203–21.

Pedersen, P.B. (1976) 'The Cultural Inclusiveness of Counseling'. In Pedersen et al. eds (1976), 22–58.

Pedersen, P.B., ed. (1985) *Hondbook of Cross-Cultural Counseling and Therapy* (New York: Praeger).

Pedersen, P.B. (1990) 'The Multicultural Perspective as a Fourth Force in Counseling', *Journal of Mental Health Counseling* 12, 93–95.

Pedersen, P.B. and Ivey, A. (1993) *Culture-Centered Counseling and Interviewing Skills* (New York: Praeger).

Pedersen P.B., Dreguns J.G., Lonner W.J. and Trimble J.E., eds (1976) *Counseling Across Cultures* (Hawaii: University of Hawaii Press).

Perls, F. (1955) 'Morality, Ego Boundary and Aggression'. In Stevens, ed. (1975), 27–38.

Perls, F. (1969 [1947]) *Ego, Hunger and Aggression* (New York: Vintage).

Perls, F., Hefferline, R.F. and Goodman, P. (1973 [1951]) *Gestalt Therapy: Excitement and Growth in the Human Personality* (Harmondsworth: Penguin).

Persaud, R. (1996) 'The Wisest Counsel?' *Counselling* 7 (3), 199–201.

Pilgrim, D. (1990) 'British Psychotherapy in Context'. In W. Dryden, ed. (1990), *Individual Therapy: A Handbook* (Milton Keynes: Open University Press).

Pilgrim, D. (1992) 'Psychotherapy and Political Evasions'. In W. Dryden and C. Feltham, eds (1992), *Psychotherapy and Its Discontents* (Milton Keynes: Open University Press), 225–43.

Pokorny, M. (1995) 'History of the United Kingdom Council for Psychotherapy', *British Journal of Psychotherapy* 11 (3), 415–21.

Polster, E. and Polster, M. (1974) *Gestalt Therapy Integrated: Contours of Theory and Practice* (New York: Vintage).

Poster, M. (1978) *Critical Theory of the Family* (London: Pluto Press).

Prozan, C.K. (1993) *The Technique of Feminist Psychoanalytic Psychotherapy* (Northvale, New Jersey: Jason Aronson).

Puget, J. (1988) 'Social Violence and Psychoanalysis in Argentina: The Unthinkable and the Unthought', *Free Associations* 13, 84–140.

Radical Therapist/Rough Times Collective, eds (1974) *The Radical Therapist* (Harmondsworth: Penguin).

Rado, S. (1949) 'An Adaptational View of Sexual Behaviour'. In P.H. Hoch and J. Zubin, eds (1949), *Psychosexual Development in Health and Disease* (New York: Grune and Stratton), 159–89.

Randall, R., Southgate, J. and Tomlinson, F. (1980) *Co-operative and Community Group Dynamics: Or Your Meetings Needn't be so Appalling* (London: Barefoot Books).

Randhawa, N. (1990) 'Around These Parts, It's What You Produce That Matters, What You Give', *Practice: The Magazine of Psychology and Political Economy* 7 (3), 39–43.

Reich, W. (1953) *People in Trouble* (Rangeley, Maine: Orgone Institute Press).

Reich, W. (1967) *Reich Speaks of Freud* (London: Condor).

Reich, W. (1972a [1945]) *Character Analysis* (New York: Farrar, Straus and Giroux).

Reich, W. (1972b [1930]) *The Sexual Revolution: Towards a Self-Governing Character Structure* (London: Vision Press).

Reich, W. (1972c) *Sex-Pol Essays 1929–34* (New York: Farrar, Straus and Giroux).

Reich, W. (1975a [1933]) *The Mass Psychology of Fascism* (Harmondsworth: Penguin).

Reich, W. (1975b [1953]) *The Murder of Christ* (London: Souvenir Press).

Reich, W. (1983 [1942]) *The Function of the Orgasm* (London: Condor).

Rice, L.N. and Greenberg, L.S. (1992) 'Humanistic Approaches to Psychotherapy'. In D.K. Freedheim, ed. (1992), *History of Psychotherapy: A Century of Change* (Washington, DC: American Psychological Association).

Richards, B. (1988) 'The Eupsychian Impulse: Psychoanalysis and Left Politics since 1968', *Radical Philosophy* 48, 3–13.

Richards, B., ed. (1989) *Crises of the Self: Further Essays on Psychoanalysis and Politics* (London: Free Association Books).

Richardson, A. (1997) 'The Significance for the United Kingdom – A View from the Department of Health'. Address to Conference on 'Regulation of Psychotherapy in Europe' organized by the British Confederation of Psychotherapists, 7 June (transcript).

Richardson, E.H. (1981) 'Cultural and Historical Perspectives in Counseling American Indians'. In Sue and Sue (1990), 216–55.

Ridley, C.R. (1984) 'Clinical Treatment of the Non-Disclosing Black Client', *American Psychologist* 39, 1234–44.

Ridley, C.R. (1995) *Overcoming Unintentional Racism in Counseling and Therapy* (London: Sage).

Riley, D. (1983) *War in the Nursery: Theories of the Child and Mother* (London: Virago).

Rivers, W.H.R. (1920) *Instinct and the Unconscious* (Cambridge: Cambridge University Press).

Robinson, P. (1970) *The Sexual Radicals* (London: Paladin).

Rogers, A.G. (1991) 'A Feminist Poetics of Psychotherapy'. In Gilligan et al. eds (1991), 33–53.

Rogers, C. (1956) *Client-Centered Therapy* (Boston: Houghton-Mifflin).

Rogers, C. (1973) *Encounter Groups* (Harmondsworth: Penguin).

Rogers, C. (1978) *Carl Rogers on Personal Power: Inner Strength and its Revolutionary Impact* (London: Constable).

Rogers, C. (1980) *A Way of Being* (Boston: Houghton Mifflin).

Rogers, C. (1986) 'A Client-centered/Person-centered Approach to Therapy'. In I. Kutash and A. Wolfe, eds (1986), *Psychiatrist's Casebook* (New York: Jossey-Bass), 197–208.

Romme, M. and Escher, A. (1993) *Accepting Voices* (London: Mind).

Rose, J. (1986) *Sexuality in the Field of Vision* (London: Verso).

Rose, J. (1993) *Why War?* (Oxford: Blackwell).

Rose, J. (1998) 'The Cult of Celebrity', *London Review Books* 20 (16), 10–13.

Rosen, I., ed. (1996) *Sexual Deviation* 3rd edn (Oxford: Oxford University Press).

Roszak, T., Gomes, M.E. and Kanner, A.D., eds (1995) *Ecopsychology: Restoring the Earth, Healing the Mind* (San Francisco: Sierra Club).

Roudinesco, E. (1990) *Jacques Lacan and Co: A History of Psychoanalysis in France 1925–1985* (London: Free Association Books).

Roustang, F. (1986) *Dire Mastery* (Washington, DC: American Psychiatric Press).

Rowan, J. (1991) 'Accreditation', *Self and Society* 19, 3.

Rustin, M. (1991) *The Good Society and the Inner World* (London: Verso).

Rutter, P. (1989) *Sex in the Forbidden Zone: When Men in Power ... Betray Women's Trust* (Los Angeles: Tarcher).

Rutter, V.B. (1993) *Women Changing Women: Restoring the Mother–Daughter Relationship* (London: Aquarian Press).

Ryan, J. and Samuels, A. (1996) 'Opening the Profession', *Self and Society* 24 (3), 36–8.

Sahlins, M. (1972) *Stone Age Economics* (Chicago and New York: Aldine, Atherton).

Samdasani, S. (1999) 'The Compulsion of Self-control'. In Greenberg, ed. (1999), 61–5.

Samuels, A. (1993) *The Political Psyche* (London: Routledge).

Samuels, A. (1994) 'Citizens as Therapists', *Self and Society* 22 (3), 25–8.

Samuels, A. (1996) 'Therapists with Attitude', *Red Pepper* July, 28–9.

Samuels, A. (1997a) 'Pluralism and Psychotherapy: What is a Good Training?' In House and Totton, eds (1997), 199–214.

Samuels, A. (1997b) 'Responsibility'. Keynote address to the United Kingdom Council for Psychotherapy Conference, Cambridge, September.

Samuels, A. (1999) 'Feelings and Politics'. In Greenberg, ed. (1999), 99–104.

Schafer, R. (1983) *The Analytic Attitude* (London: Hogarth Press).

Schutz, W. (1979) *Profound Simplicity* (London: Turnstone).

Scott, A. (1996) *Real Events Revisited: Fantasy, Memory and Psychoanalysis* (London: Virago).

Seligman, M.E.P. (1995) 'The Effectiveness of Psychotherapy: The Consumer Reports Study', *American Psychologist* 50 (12), 965–74.

Segal, H. (1988) 'Silence is the Real Crime'. In J.B. Levine et al. eds (1988), 35–8.

Shaffer, J.B.P. and Galinsky, M.D. (1974) *Models of Group Therapy and Sensitivity Training* (Englewood Cliffs, NJ: Prentice-Hall).

Sharaf, M. (1984) *Fury on Earth: A Biography of Wilhelm Reich* (London: Hutchinson).

Shepard, P. (1995) 'Nature and Madness'. In Roszak et al. eds (1995), 21–40.

Showalter, E. (1997) *Hystories: Hysterical Epidemics and Modern Culture* (London: Picador).

Sinason, V., ed. (1998) *Memory in Dispute* (London: Karnak).

Sinfield, A. (1994) 'Effeminacy', *Changes* 12 (4), 246–53.

Smail, D. (1987) *Taking Care: An Alternative to Psychotherapy* (London: Dent).

Smail, D. (1997) 'Psychotherapy and Tragedy'. In House and Totton, eds (1997), 159–69.

Socarides, C.W. (1988) *The Preoedipal Origin and Psychoanalytic Therapy of Sexual Perversions* (Madison, CT: International Universities Press).

Socarides, C.W. (1996) 'Major Advances in the Psychoanalytic Theory and Therapy of Male Homosexuality'. In Rosen, ed. (1996), 252–78.

Sosland, A. (1997) 'The State of Psychotherapy in Moscow', *International Journal of Psychotherapy* 2 (2), 229–33.

Soth, M. (1999) 'Relating to and with the Objectified Body', *Self and Society* 27 (1), 32–8.

Speight, S.L., Myers, L.J., Cox, C.L. and Highlen, R.S. (1991) 'A Redefinition of Multicultural Counseling', *Journal of Counseling and Development* 70, 29–36.

Spiegel, R. (1975) 'Survival of Psychoanalysis in Nazi Germany', *Contemporary Psychoanalysis* 11, 479–91.

Spinelli, E. (1998) 'Counselling and the Abuse of Power', *Counselling: The Journal of the British Association for Counselling* 9 (3), 181–4.

Stacey, M. (1992) *Regulating Medicine: The General Medical Council* (London: Wiley).

Stanton, M. (1991) *Sandor Ferenczi: Reconsidering Active Intervention* (London: Free Association Books).

Stehr, N. (1994) *Knowledge Societies* (London: Sage).

Steiner, C. (1974) 'Radical Psychiatry: Principles'. In *Radical Therapist/Rough Times* Collective, eds (1974), 15–19.

Steiner, C. (1976a) 'Inside T.A.' In Wyckoff, ed. (1976), 239–62.

Steiner, C. (1976b) 'Rescue'. In Wyckoff, ed. (1976), 43–63.

Steiner, C. (1981) *The Other Side of Power* (New York: Grove Press).

Steiner, R. (1994) '"The Tower of Babel" or "After Babel in Contemporary Psychoanalysis"? – Some Historical and Theoretical Notes on the Linguistic and Cultural Strategies Implied by the Foundation of the International Journal of Psycho-Analysis, and on its Relevance Today', *International Journal of Psycho-Analysis* 75, 883–901.

Steltzer, J. (1986) 'The Formation and Deformation of Identity During Psychoanalytic Training', *Free Associations* 7, 59–74.

Stevens, J.O. (1977) 'Hypnosis, Intention, and Wakefulness'. In J.O. Stevens, ed. (1977), 258–69.

Stevens, J.O., ed. (1977) *Gestalt Is* (New York: Bantam Books).

Stoller, R. (1968) *Sex and Gender: On the Development of Masculinity and Femininity* (London: Hogarth Press).

Stoller, R. (1985) *Observing the Erotic Imagination* (New Haven: Yale University Press).

Sue, S. (1977) 'Community Mental Health Services to Minority Groups: Some Optimism, Some Pessimism', *American Psychologist* 32, 616–24.

Sue, D.W. and Sue, D. (1990) *Counselling the Culturally Different: Theory and Practice,* 2nd edn (New York: Wiley).

Sue, S. and Zane, N. (1987) 'The Role of Culture and Cultural Techniques in Psychotherapy', *American Psychologist* 42, 37–45.

Szasz, T.S. (1958) 'Psycho-Analytic Training – A Socio-Psychological Analysis of its History and Present Status', *International Journal of Psycho-Analysis* 39, 598–613.

Tantam, D. and van Deurzen, E. (1999) 'The European Citizen's Right to Ethical and Competent Psychotherapeutic Care', *European Journal of Psychotherapy Counselling and Health* 2 (2), 228–35.

Tarsis, V. (1965) *Ward 7* (London: Collins/Harvill).

Temperley, J. (1989) 'Psychoanalysis and the Threat of Nuclear War'. In Richards, ed. (1989), 259–67.

Thomas, P. (1997) *The Dialectics of Schizophrenia* (London: Free Association Books).

Thorne, B. (1997) 'The Accountable Therapist: Standards, Experts and Poisoning the Well'. In House and Totton, eds (1997), 141–50.

Totton, N. (1997a) 'Not Just a Job: Psychotherapy as a Spiritual and political Practice'. In House and Totton, eds (1997), 129–40.

Totton, N. (1997b) 'Inputs and Outcomes: The Medical Model and Professionalisation'. In House and Totton, eds (1997), 109–16.

Totton, N. (1998) *The Water in the Glass: Body and Mind in Psychoanalysis* (London: Rebus Press).

Totton, N. (1999) 'The Baby and the Bathwater. "Professionalisation" in Psychotherapy and Counselling', *British Journal of Guidance and Counselling* 27 (3), 313–24.

Totton, N. and Edmondson, E. (1988) *Reichian Growth Work: Melting the Blocks to Life and Love* (Bridport: Prism Press).

Totton, N. and Edmondson, E. (1994) 'Founding Conference of the Independent Therapists Network' (Leeds: self-published flyer).

Turkle, S. (1979) *Psychoanalytic Politics: Jacques Lacan and Freud's French Revolution* (London: Burnett Books/André Deutsch).

Verhaeghe, P. (1996) *Does the Women Exist? From Freud's Hysteric to Lacan's Feminine* (London: Rebus Press).

Vontress, C.E. (1976) 'Racial and Ethnic Barriers in Counseling'. In Pedersen et al. eds (1976), 42–64.

Voyer, J.-P. (1973 [1971]) *Reich: How To Use* (Berkeley, CA: Bureau of Public Secrets).

Walker, L.E.A. (1990) 'Mary: A Feminist Therapist Views the Case'. In D.W. Cantor, ed. (1990) *Women as Therapists* (Northvale, NJ: Aronson), 78–95.

Wallerstein, R.S. (1993) 'Between Chaos and Petrification: A Summary of the Fifth IPA Conference of Training Analysts', *International Journal of Psycho-Analysis* 74, 165–78.

Wallerstein, R.S. and Weinshel, E.M. (1989) 'The Future of Psychoanalysis', *Psychoanalytic Quarterly* 58, 341–73.

Waterhouse, R. (1993) 'Wild Women Don't Have the Blues', *Feminism and Psychology* 3 (1), 57–71.

Wehr, D.S. (1988) *Jung and Feminism: Liberating Archetypes* (London: Routledge).

Wieland, C. (1988) 'Femininity as Neurosis', *Free Associations* 13, 48–58.

Winkler, G. (1980) 'Co-counselling, Liberation, and Personal Change', *Self and Society* 8 (4), 106–10.

Wolfenstein, E.V. (1993) *Psychoanalytic-marxism: Groundwork* (London: Free Association Books).

Wolman, C. (1975) 'Therapy and Capitalism', *Issues in Radical Therapy* 3 (1), 3–5.

Woodrow, P. (1976) *Clearness: Processes for Supporting Individual and Groups in Decision-Making* (Philadelphia: Movement for a New Society).

Wortis, J. (1951) *Soviet Psychiatry* (London: Baillière, Tindall and Cox).

Wyckoff, H. (1976) 'Problem-Solving Groups for Women'. In Wyckoff, H., ed. (1976) 3–27.

Wyckoff, H., ed. (1976) *Love, Therapy and Politics: Issues in Radical Therapy – The First Year* (New York: Grove Press).

Young, R.M. (1994) *Mental Space* (London: Process Press).

Young, R.M. (1996) *The Culture of British Psychoanalysis and Related Essays on Character and Morality and on the Psychodynamics of Psychoanalytic Organisations* (unpublished; available on the Internet at http://www.shef.ac.uk/uni/academic/N-Q/psysc/staff/rmyoung/paper53.html).

Young-Eisendrath, P. and Wiedemann, F. (1987) *Female Authority: Empowering Women Through Psychotherapy* (London: Guildford Press).

Index